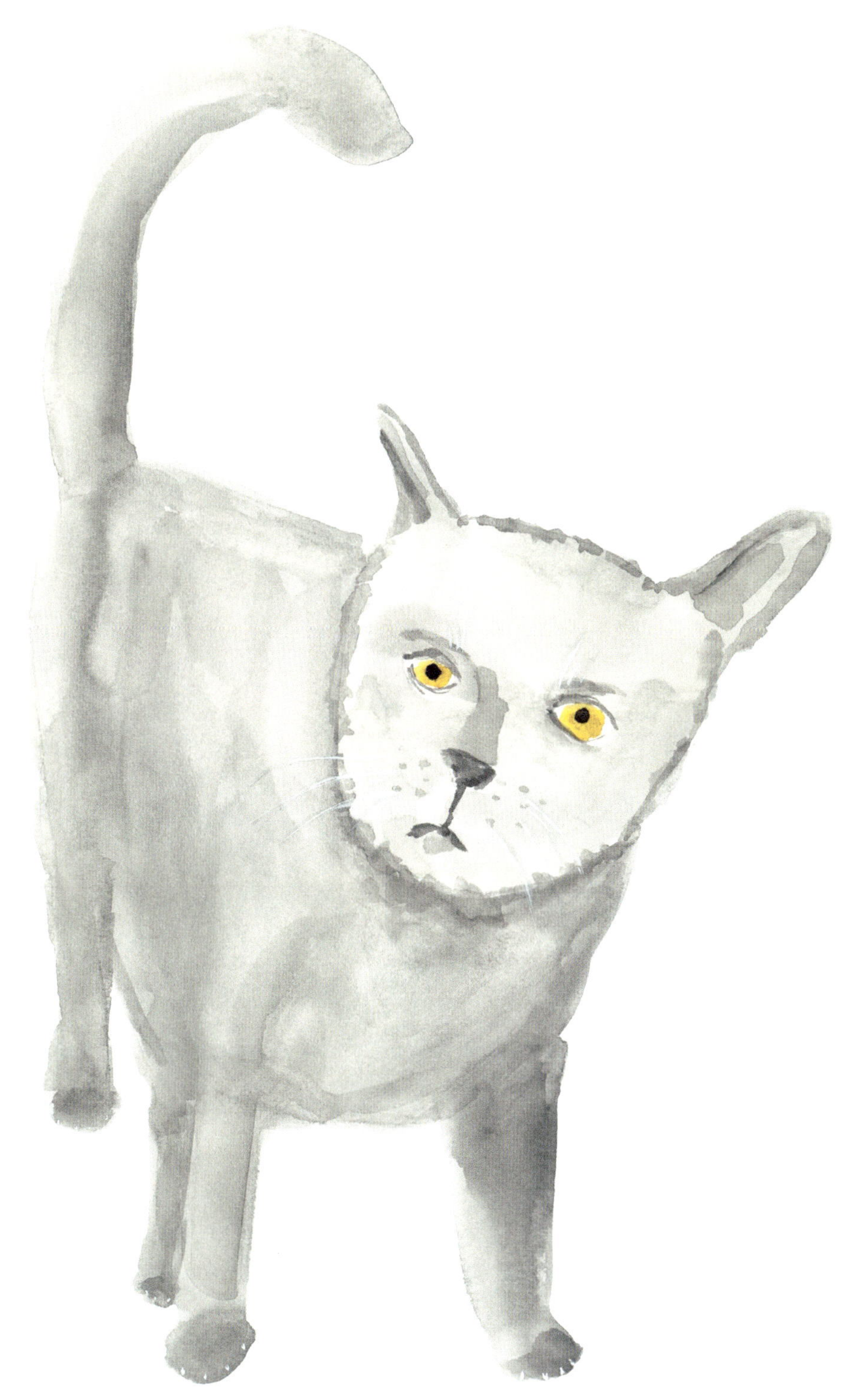

THE ICE PLANT LOS ANGELES 2022

JON HUCK

AT THE DROP OF A HAT

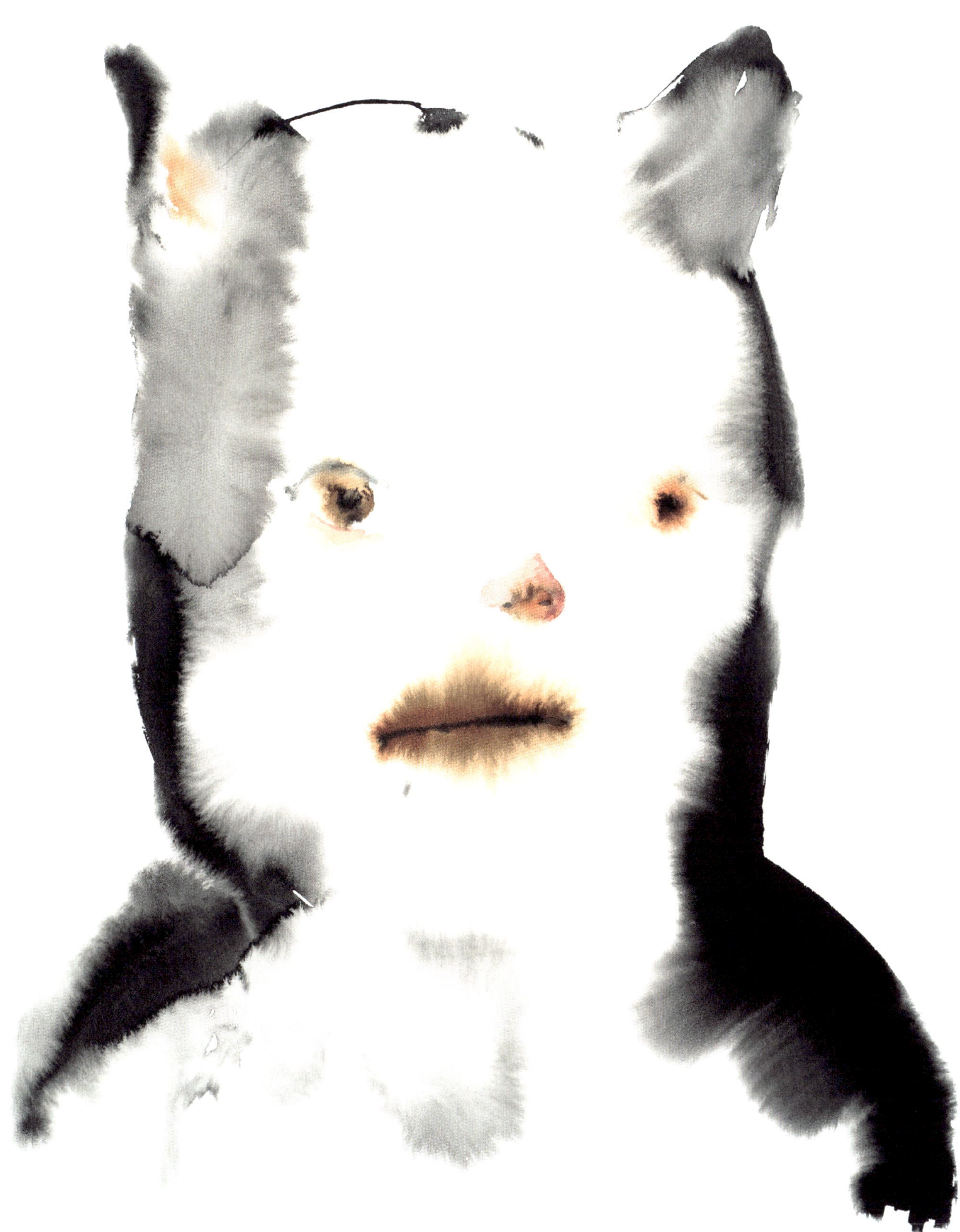

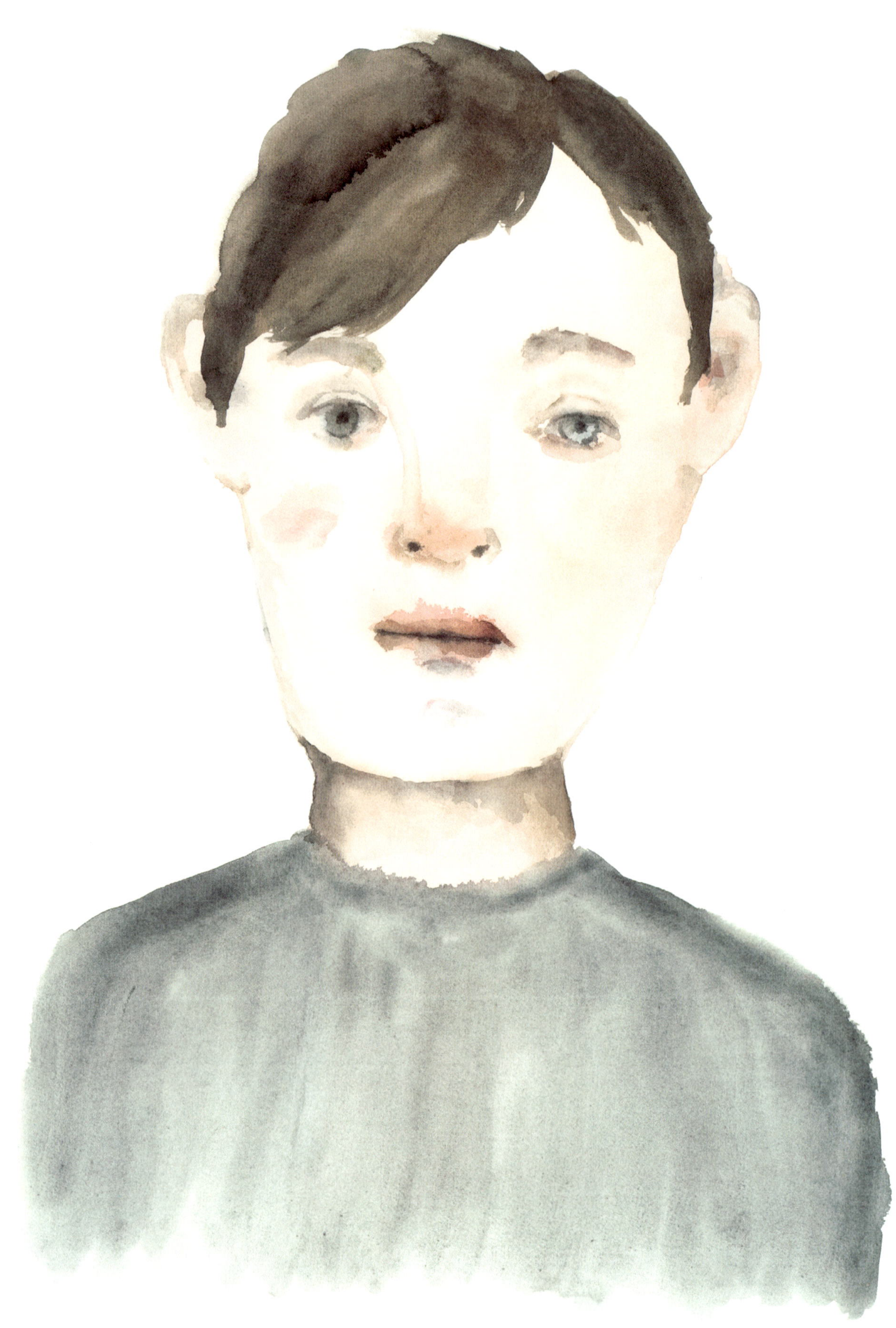

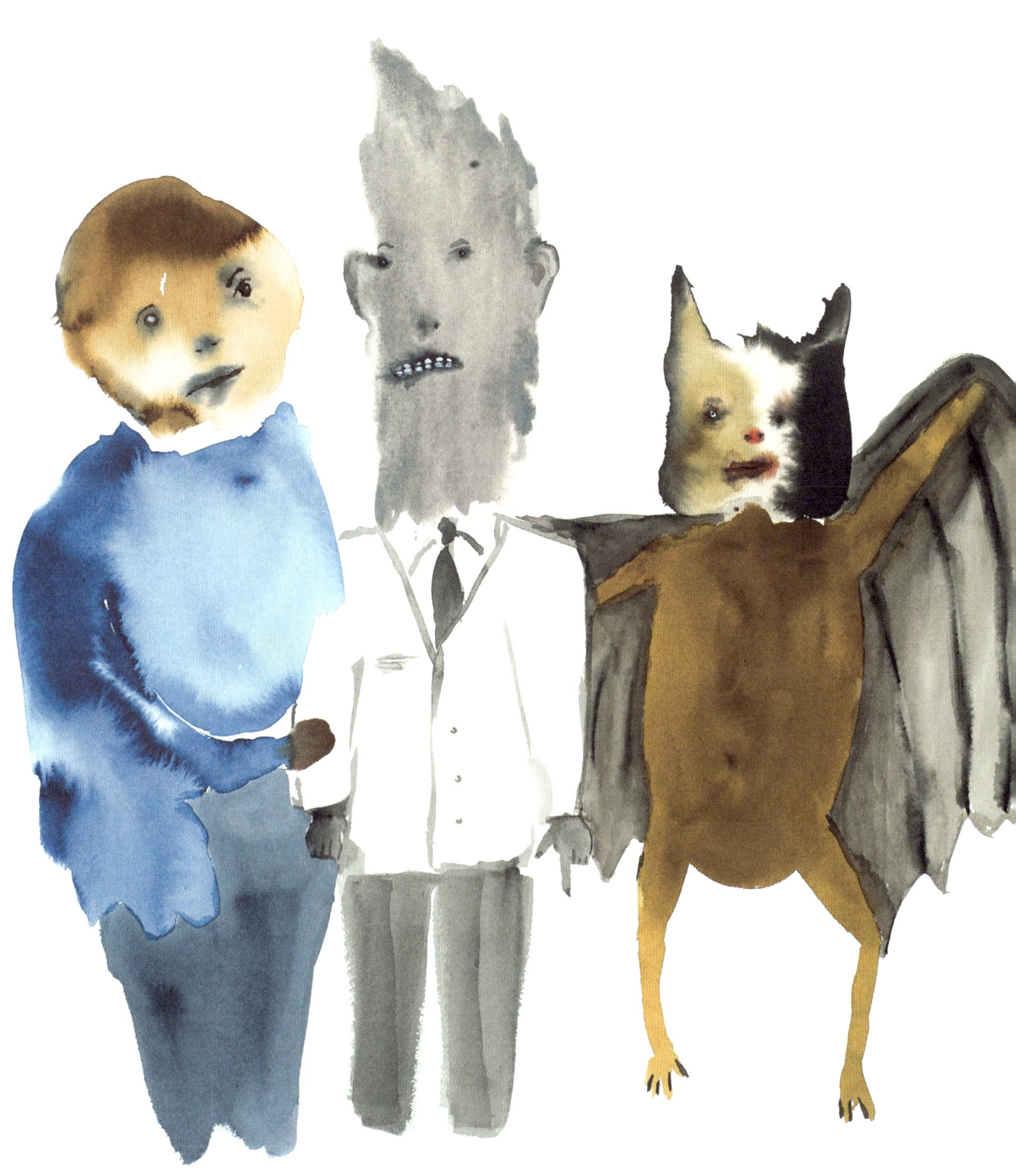

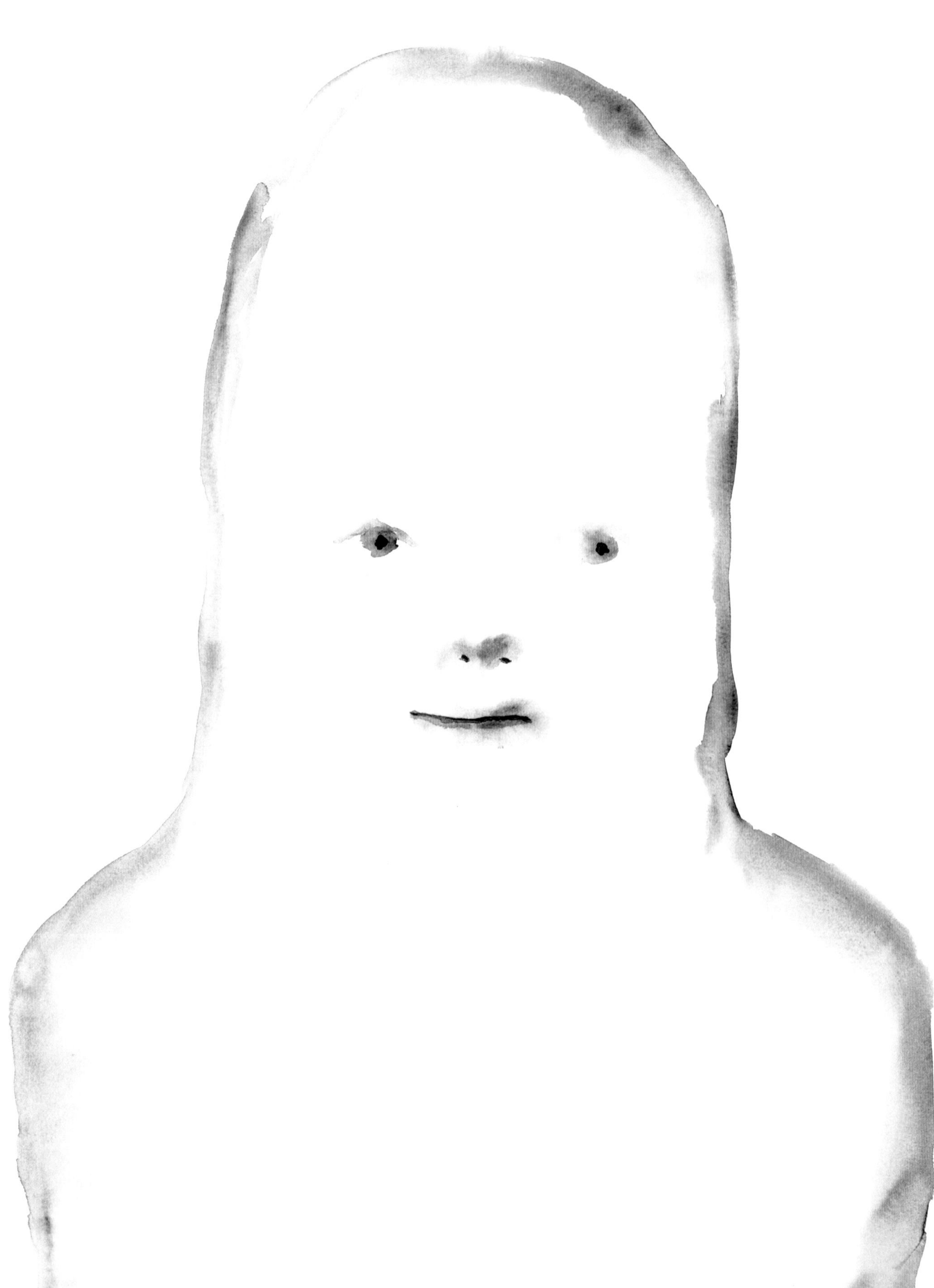

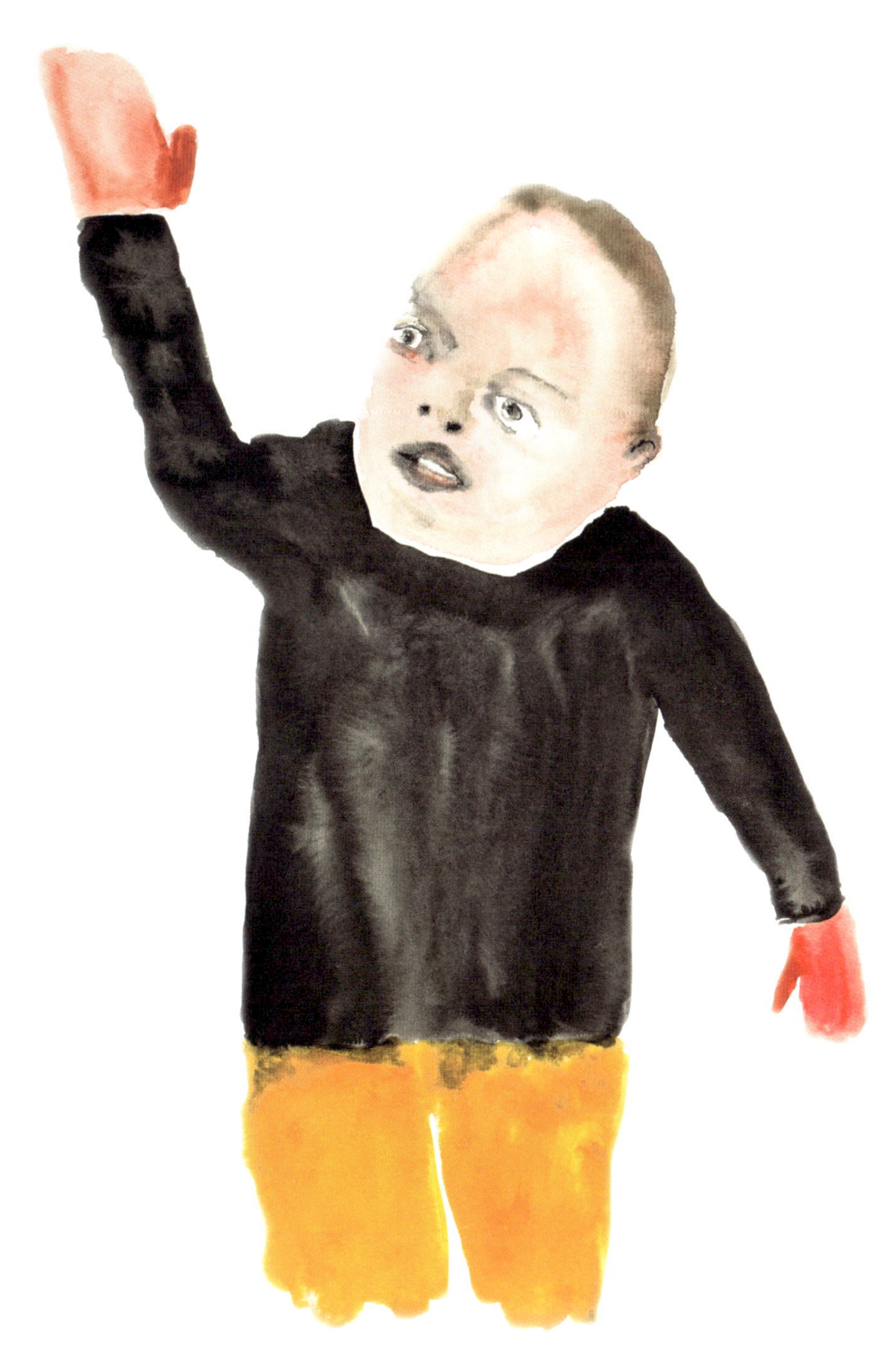

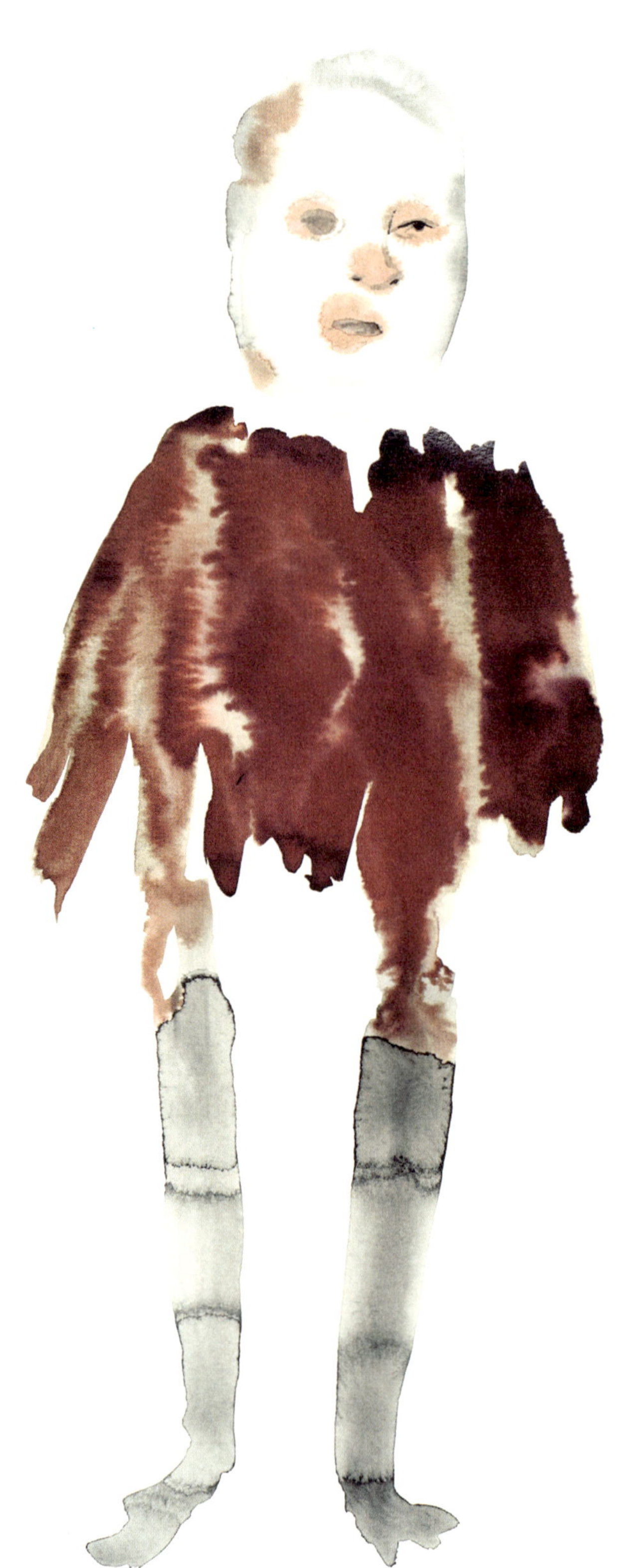

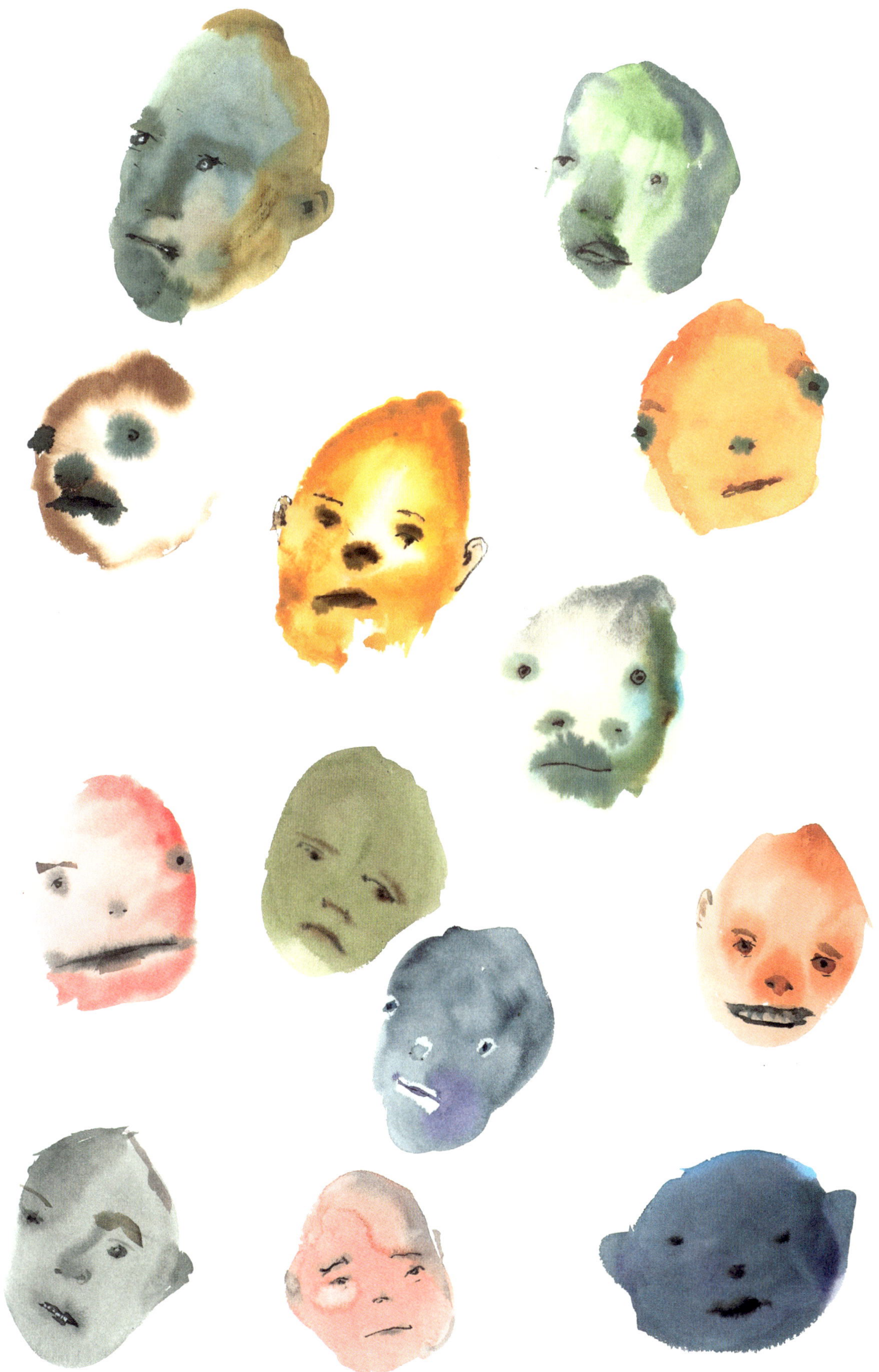

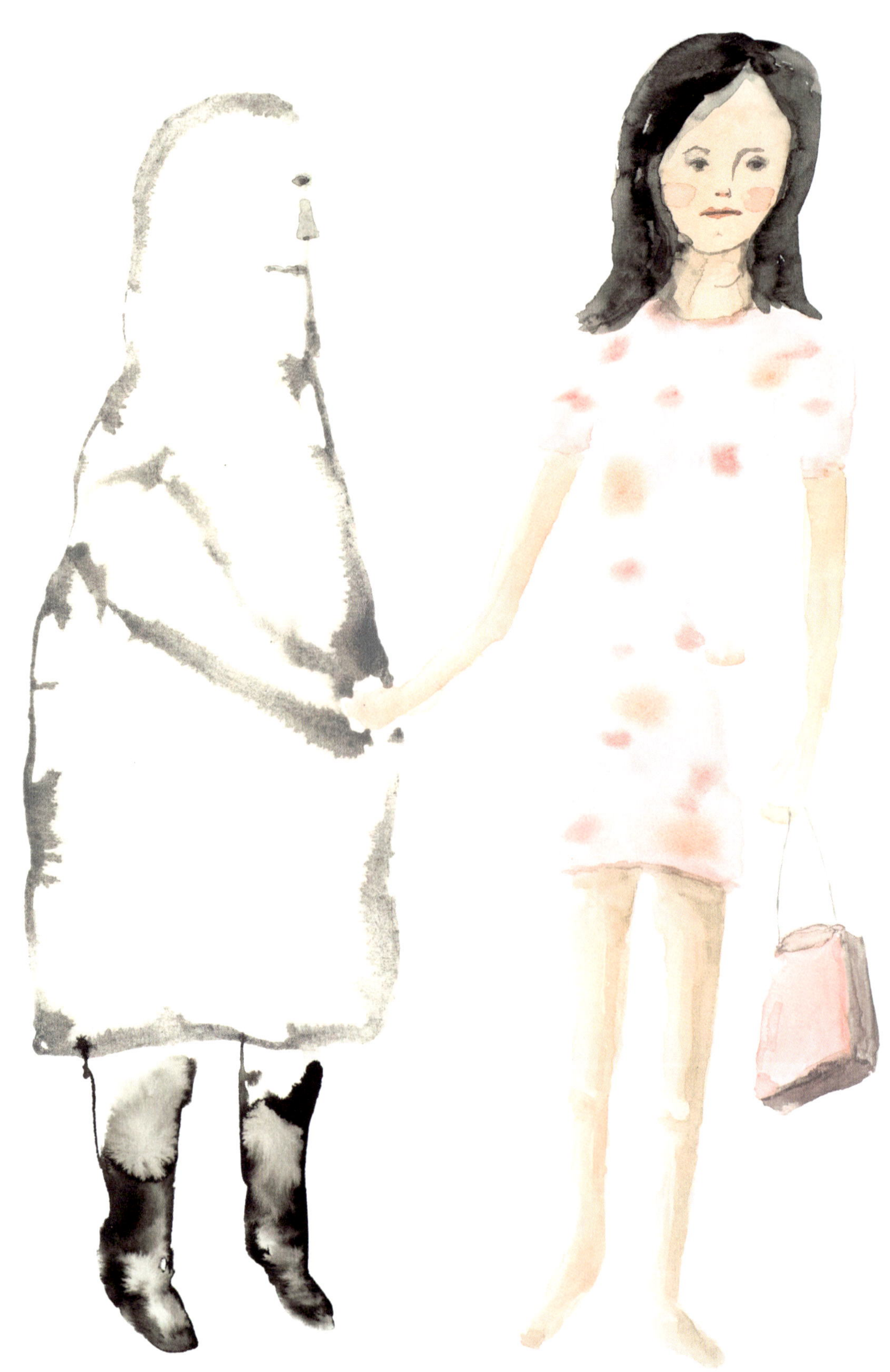

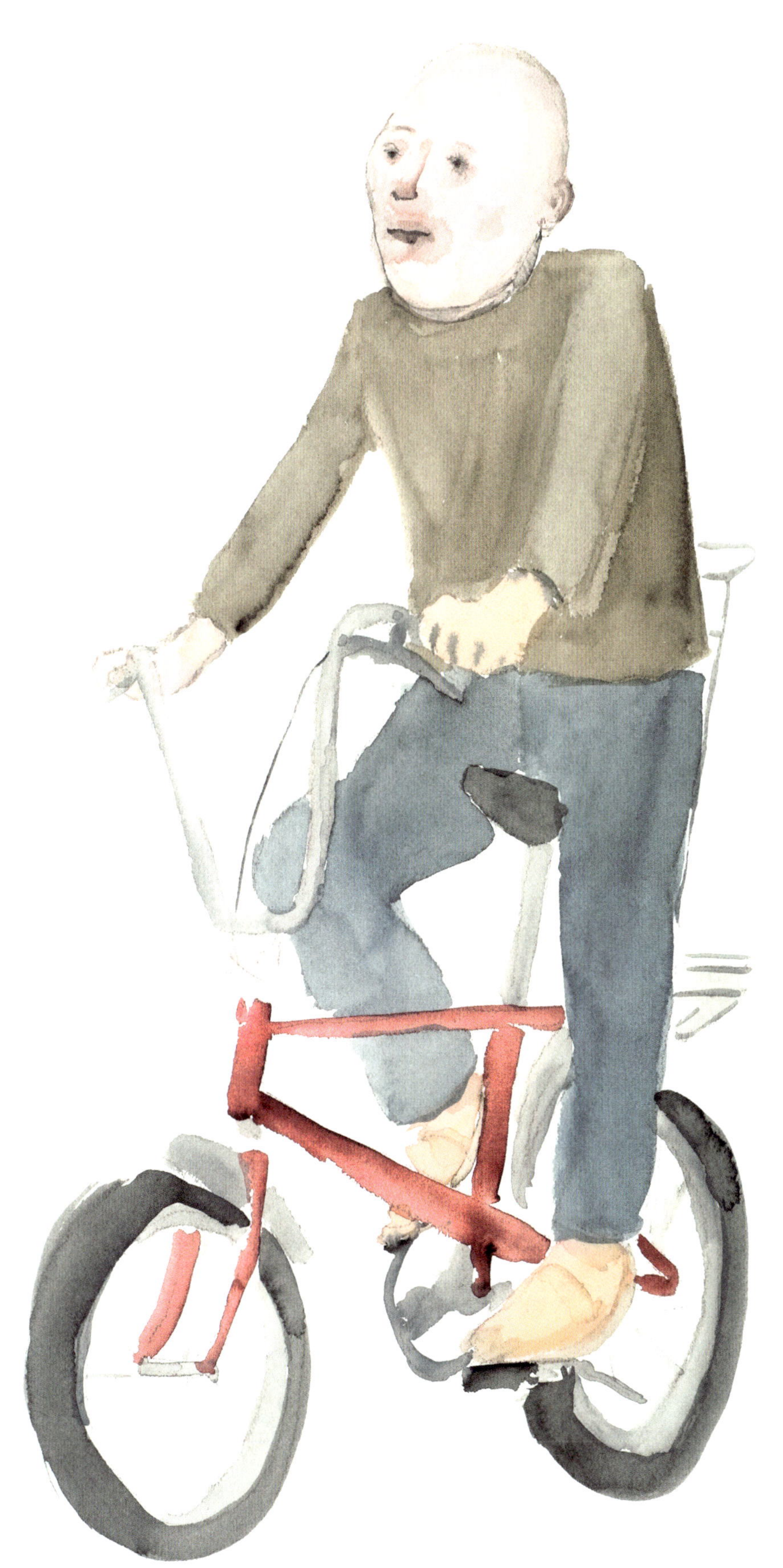

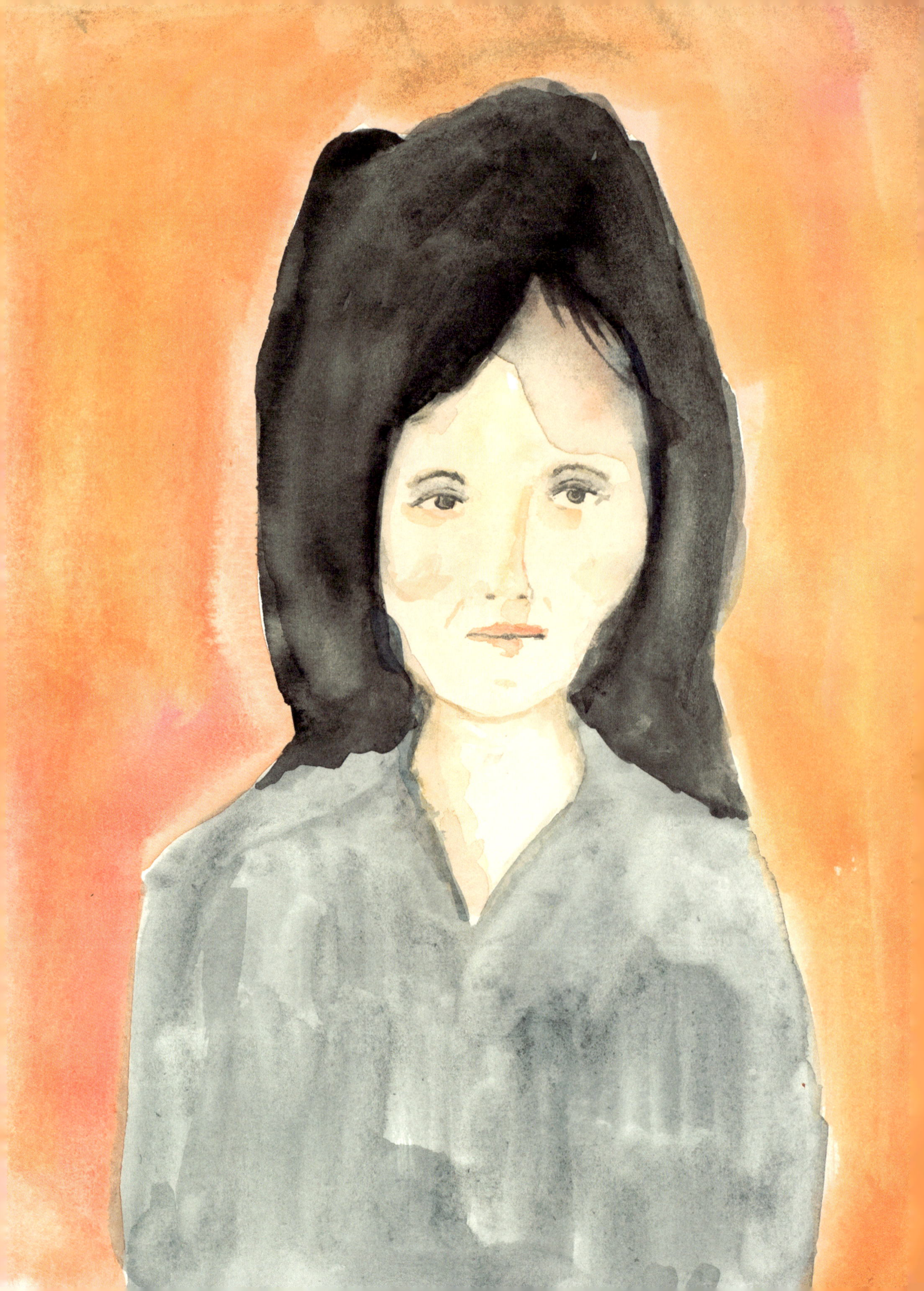

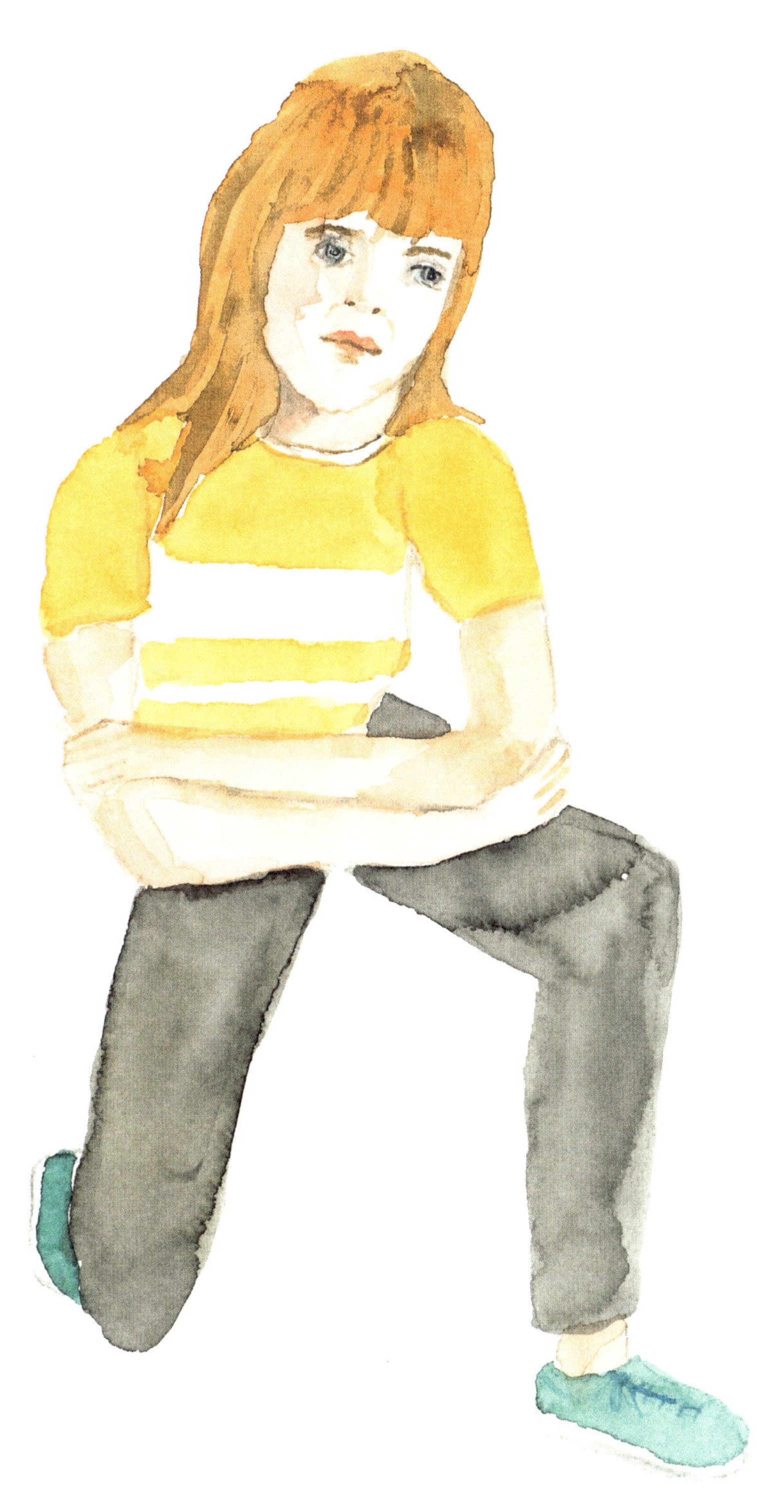

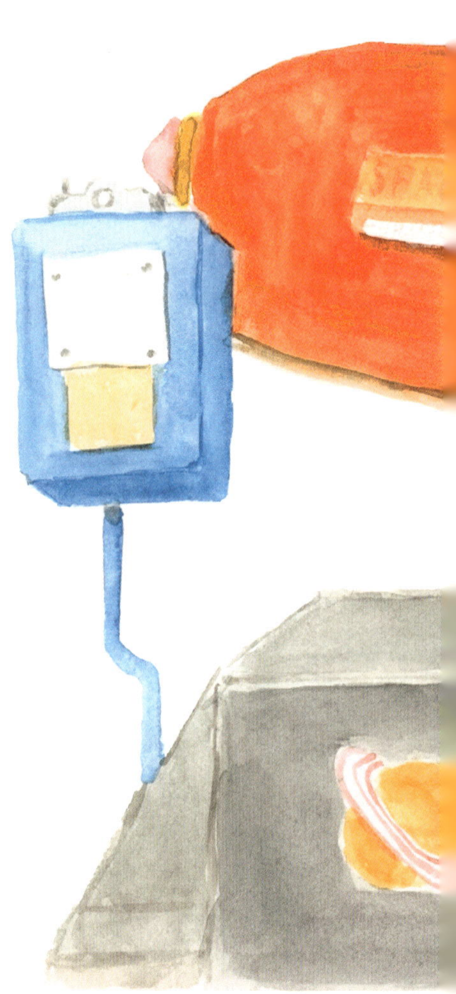

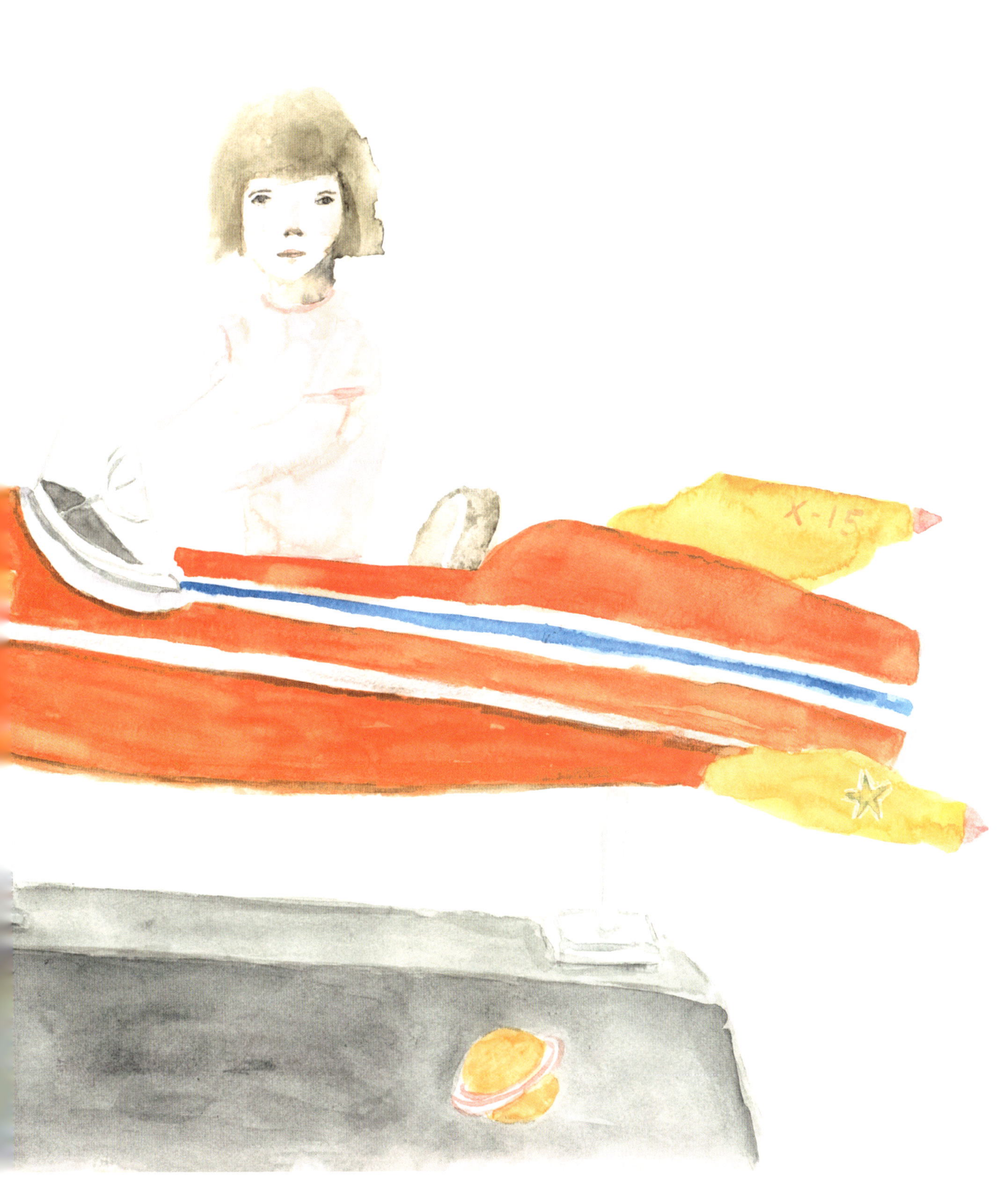
X-15

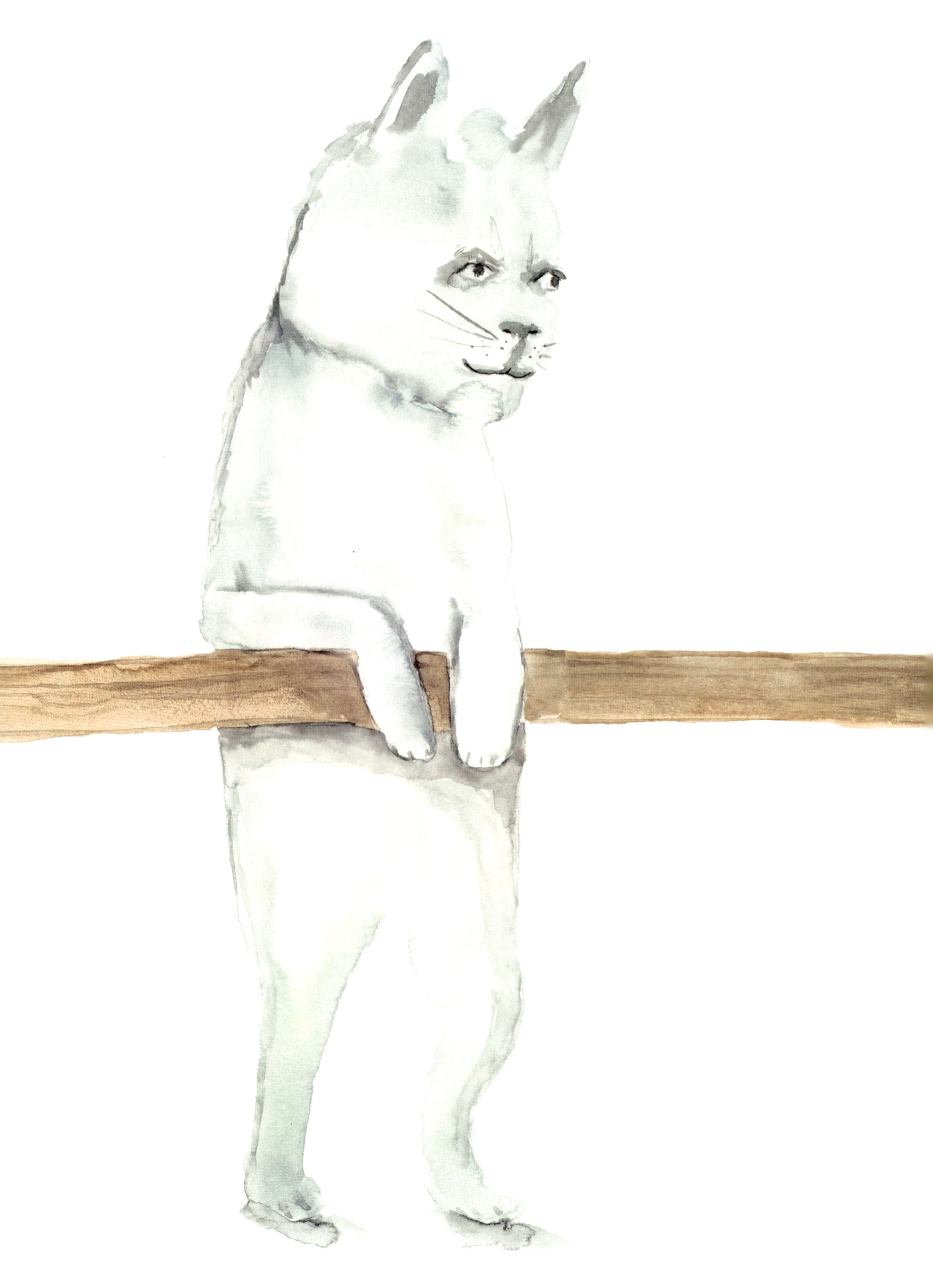

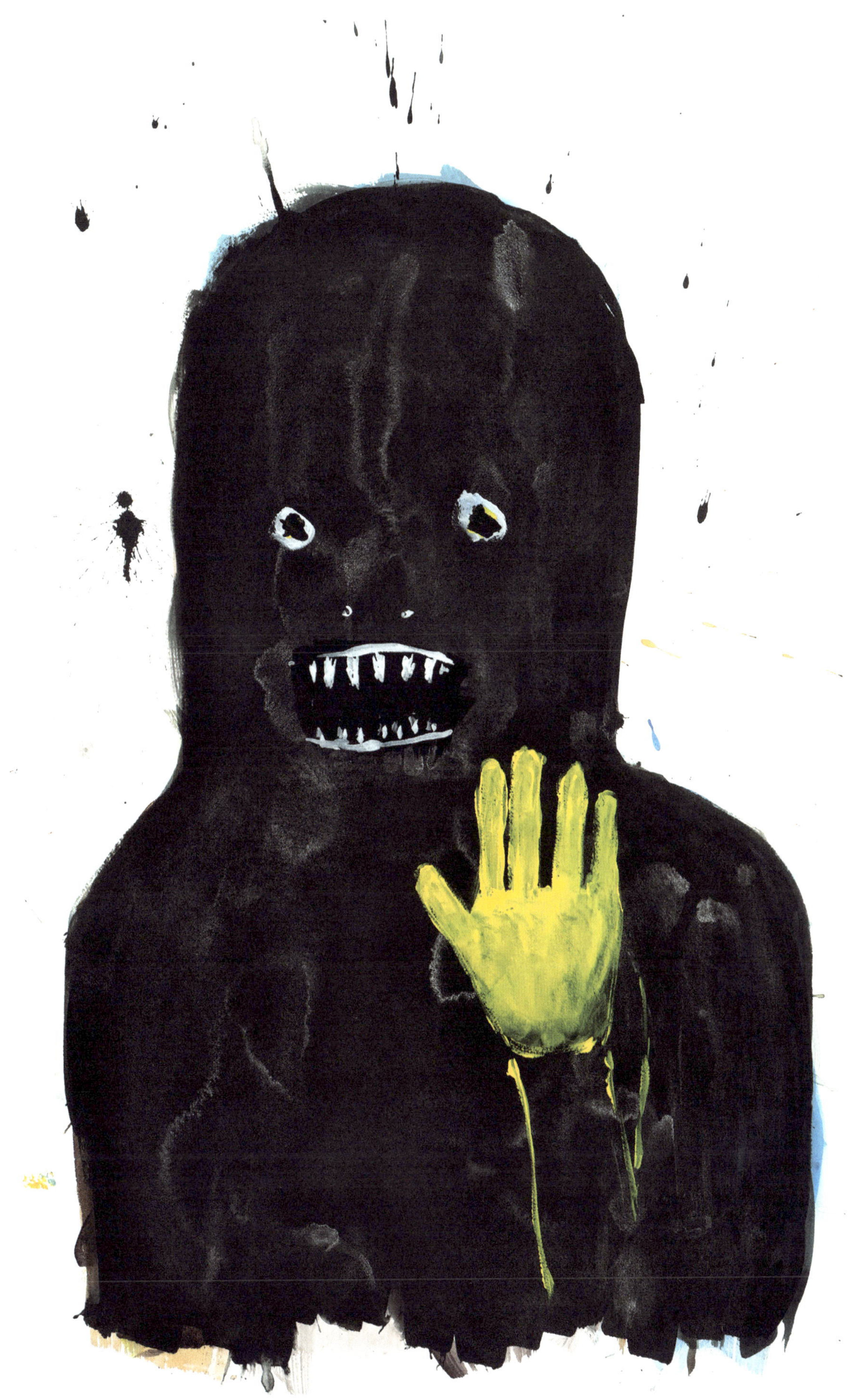

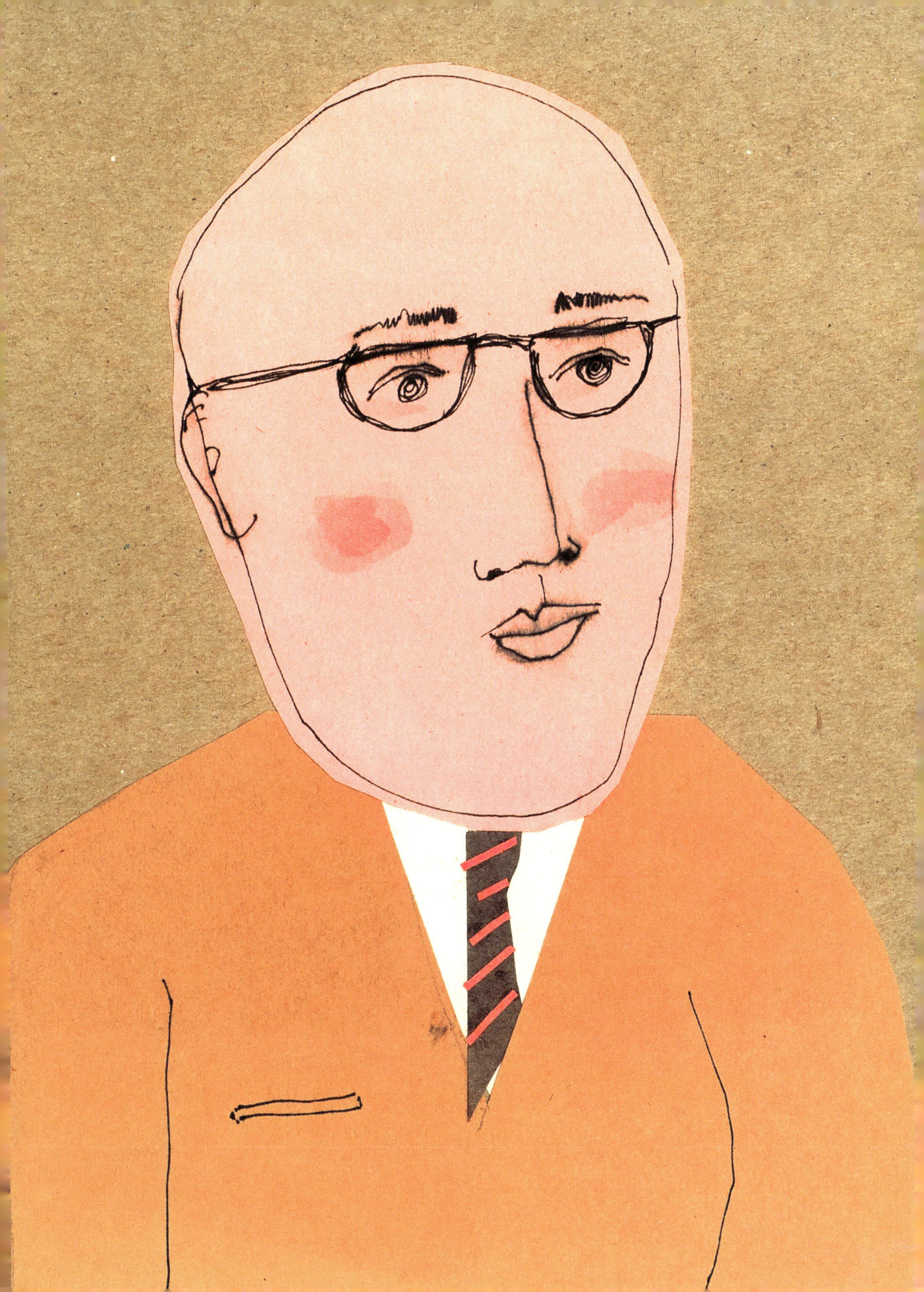

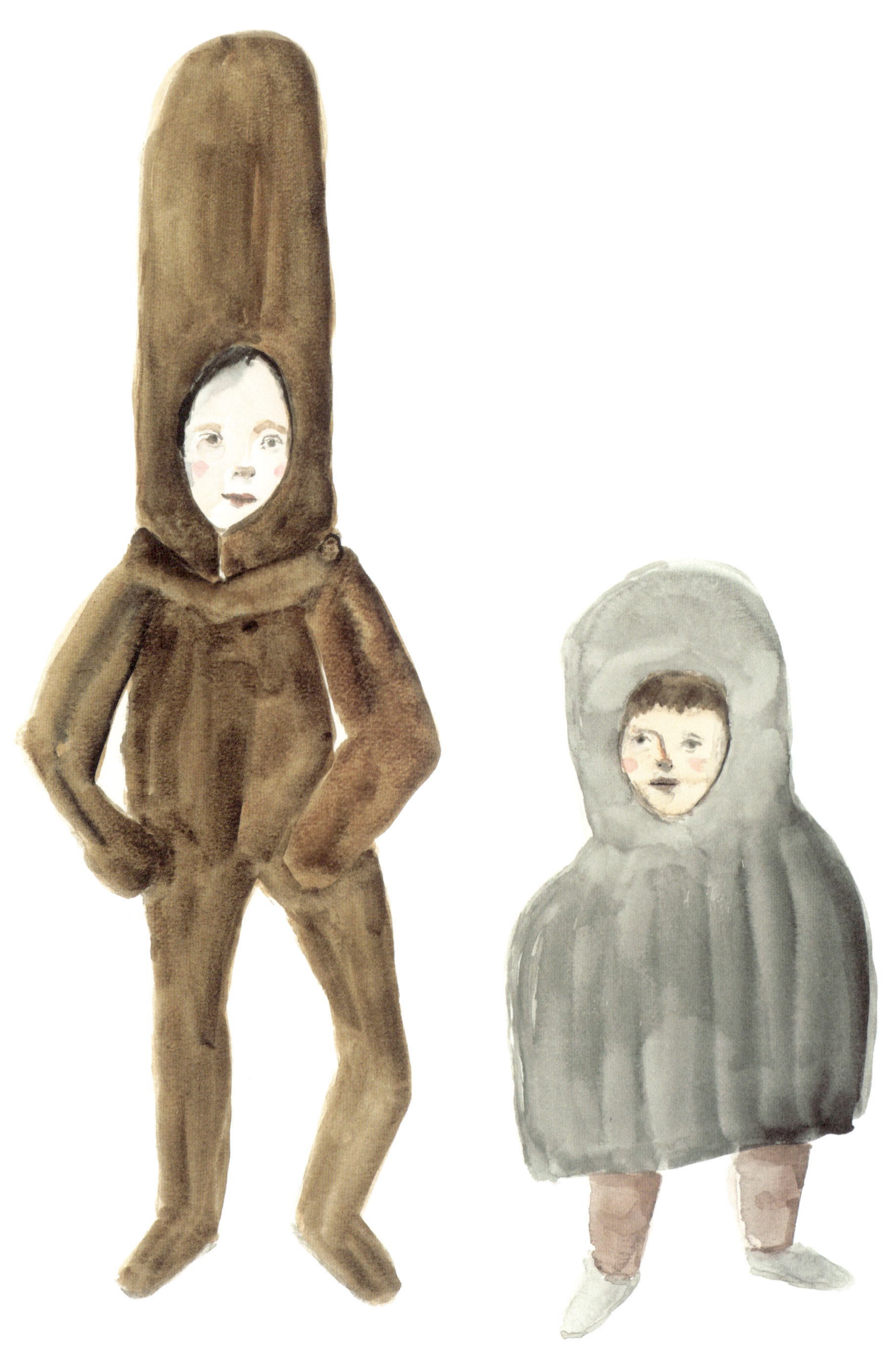

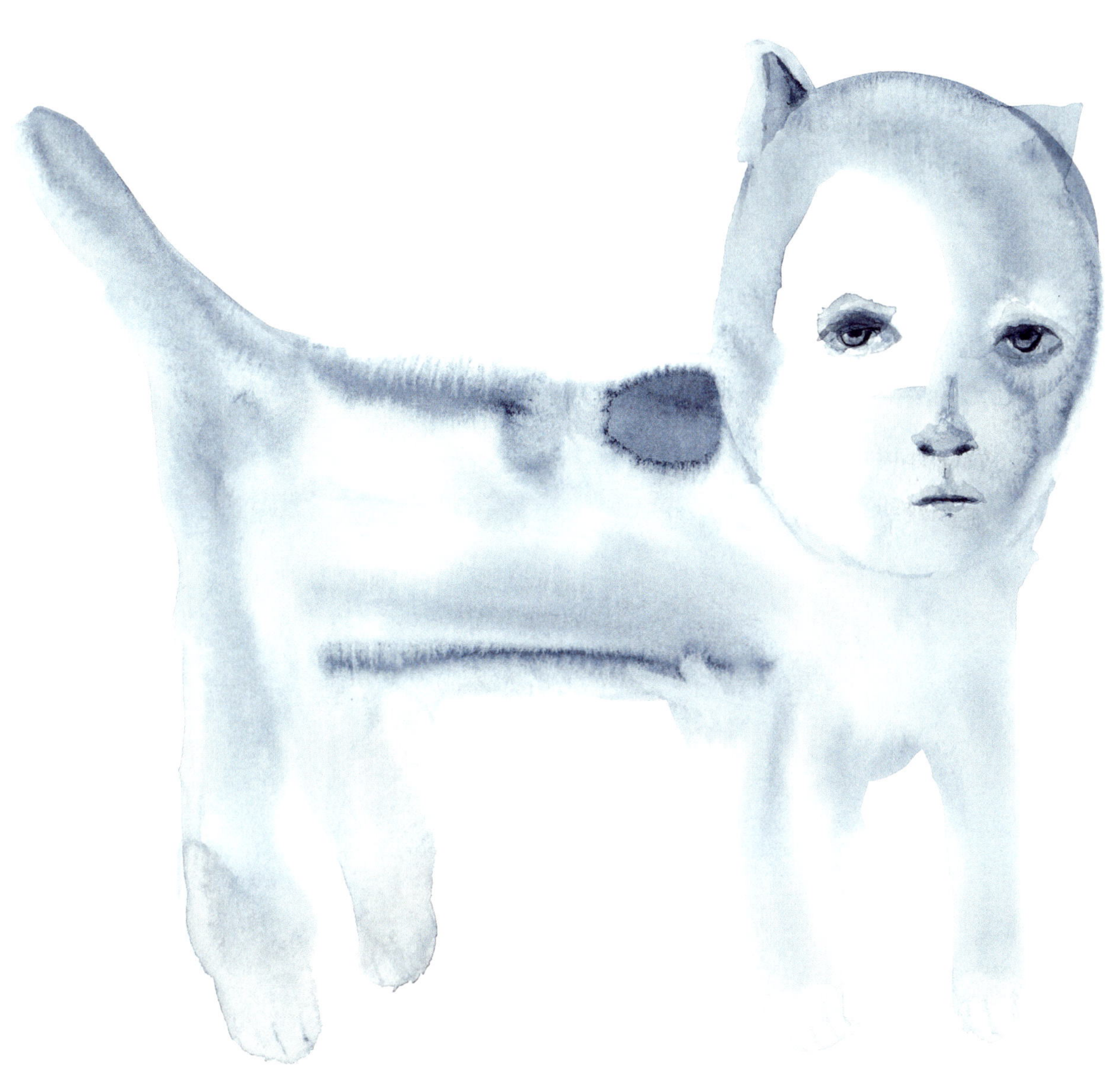

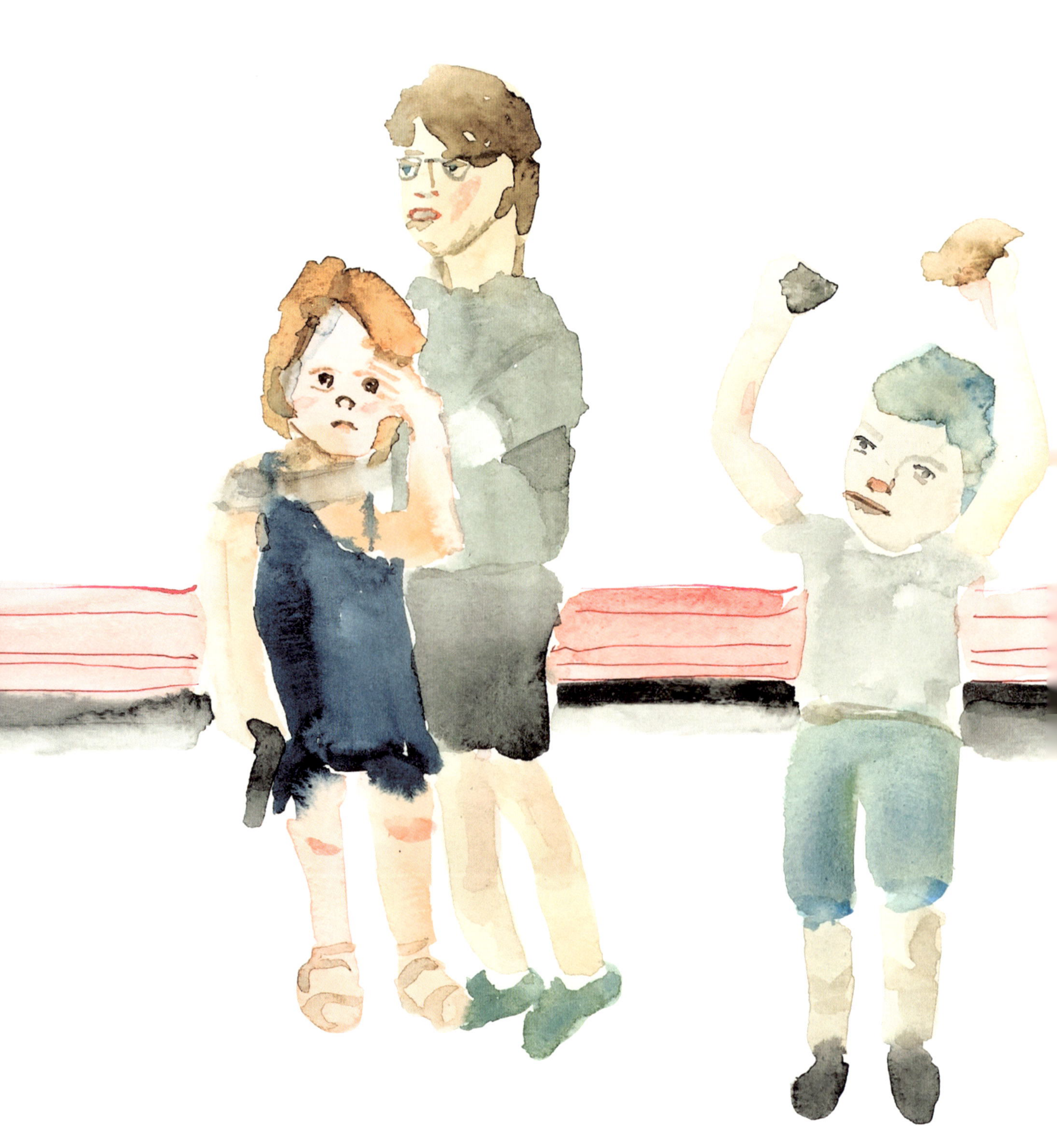

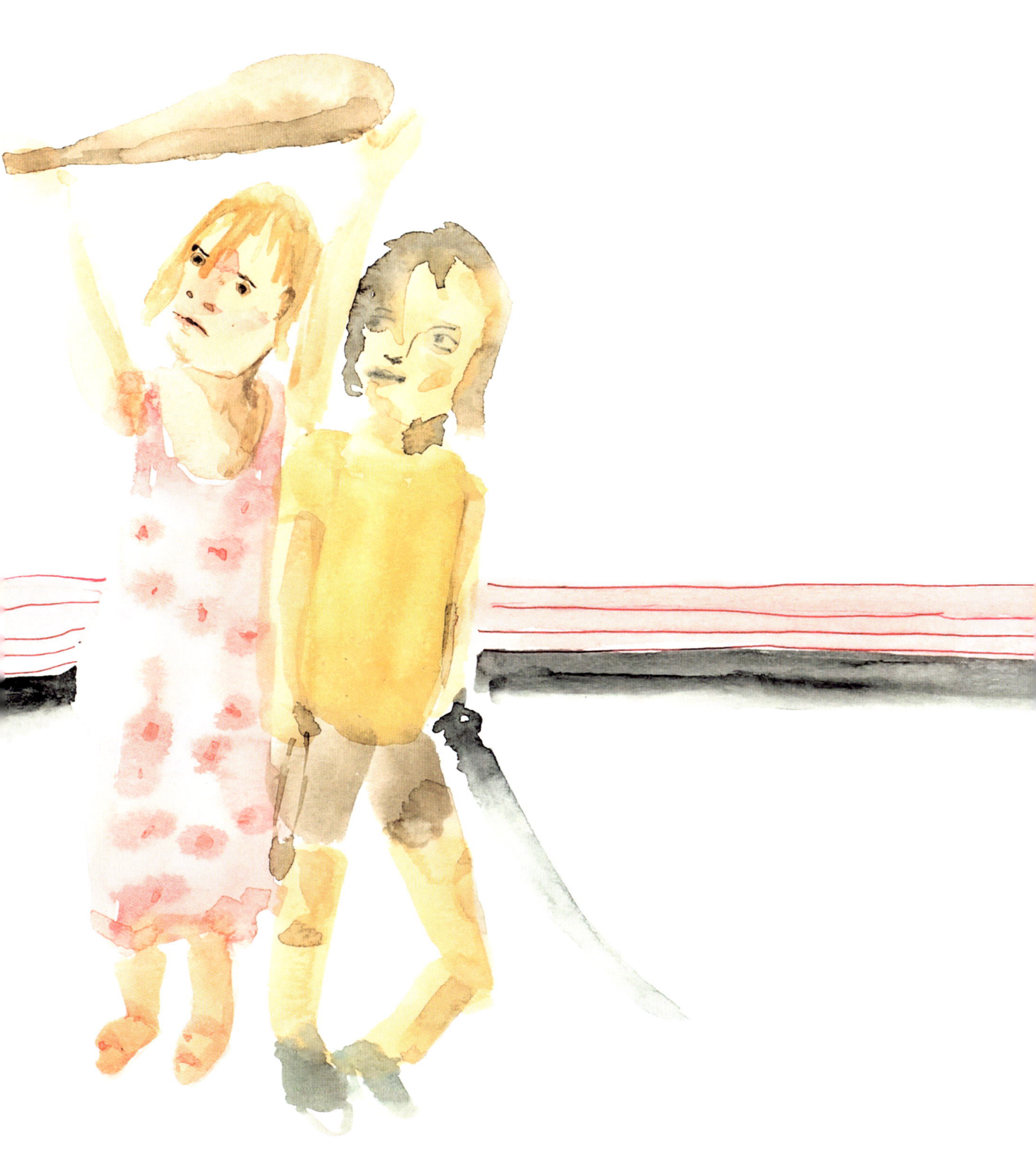

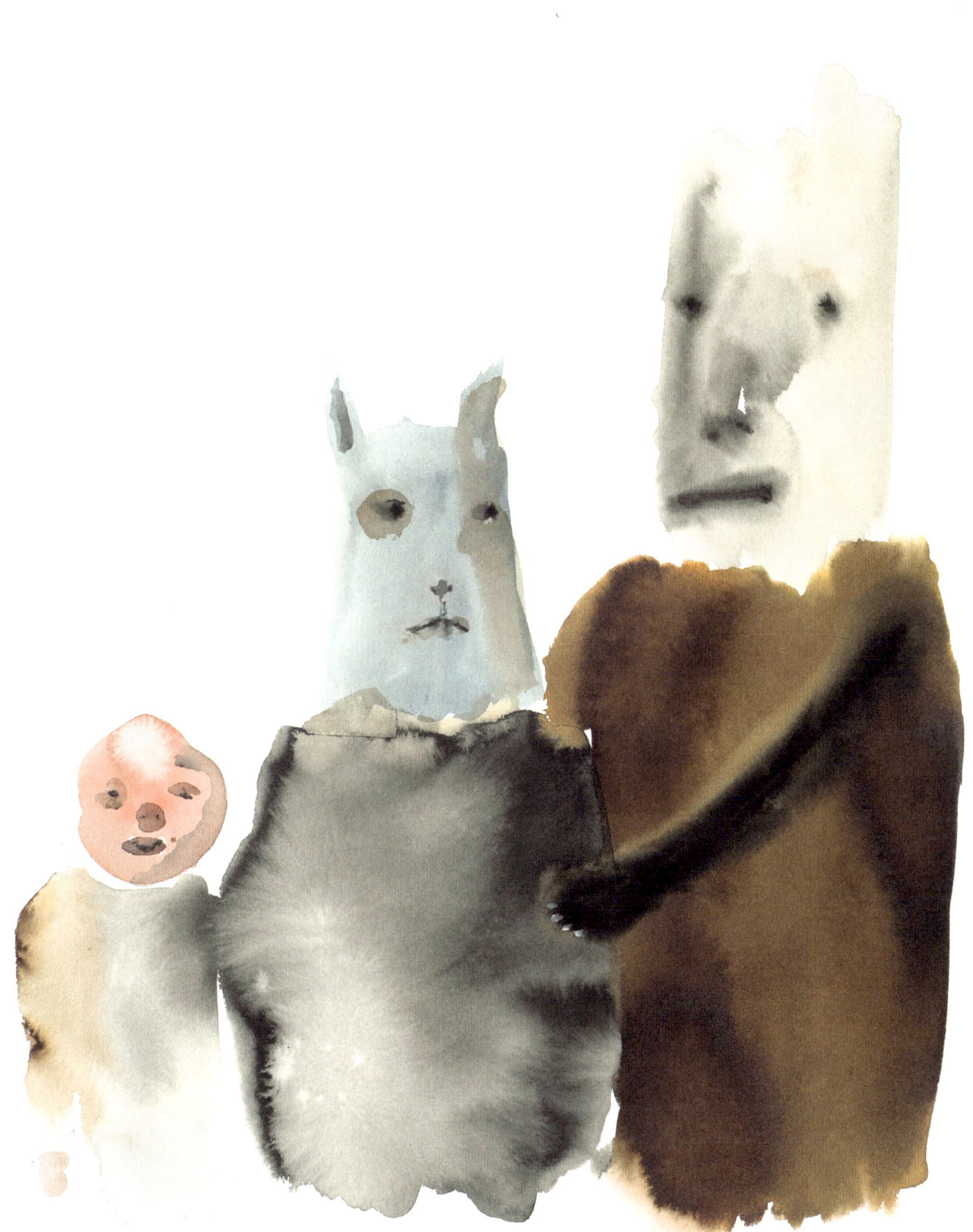

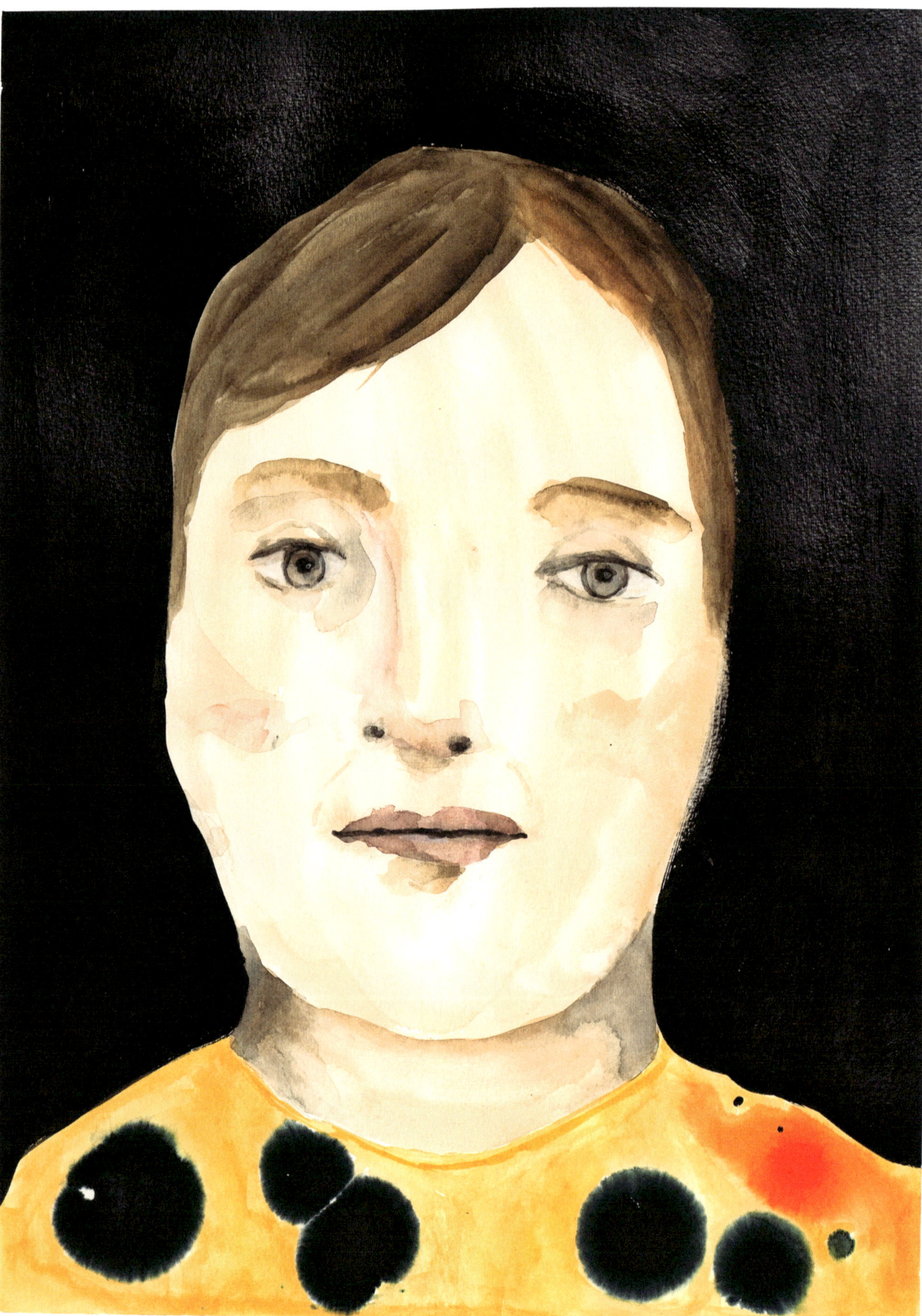

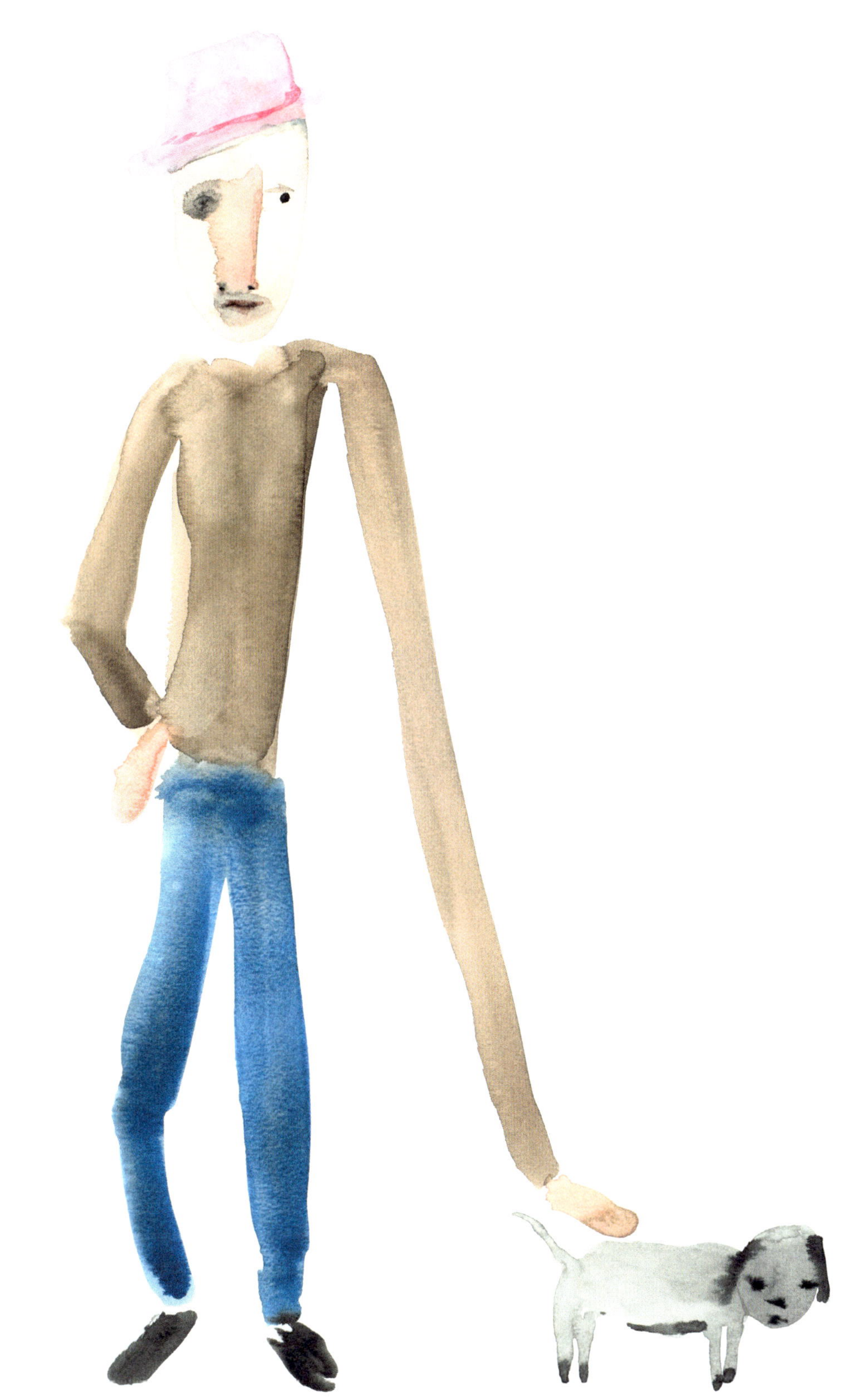

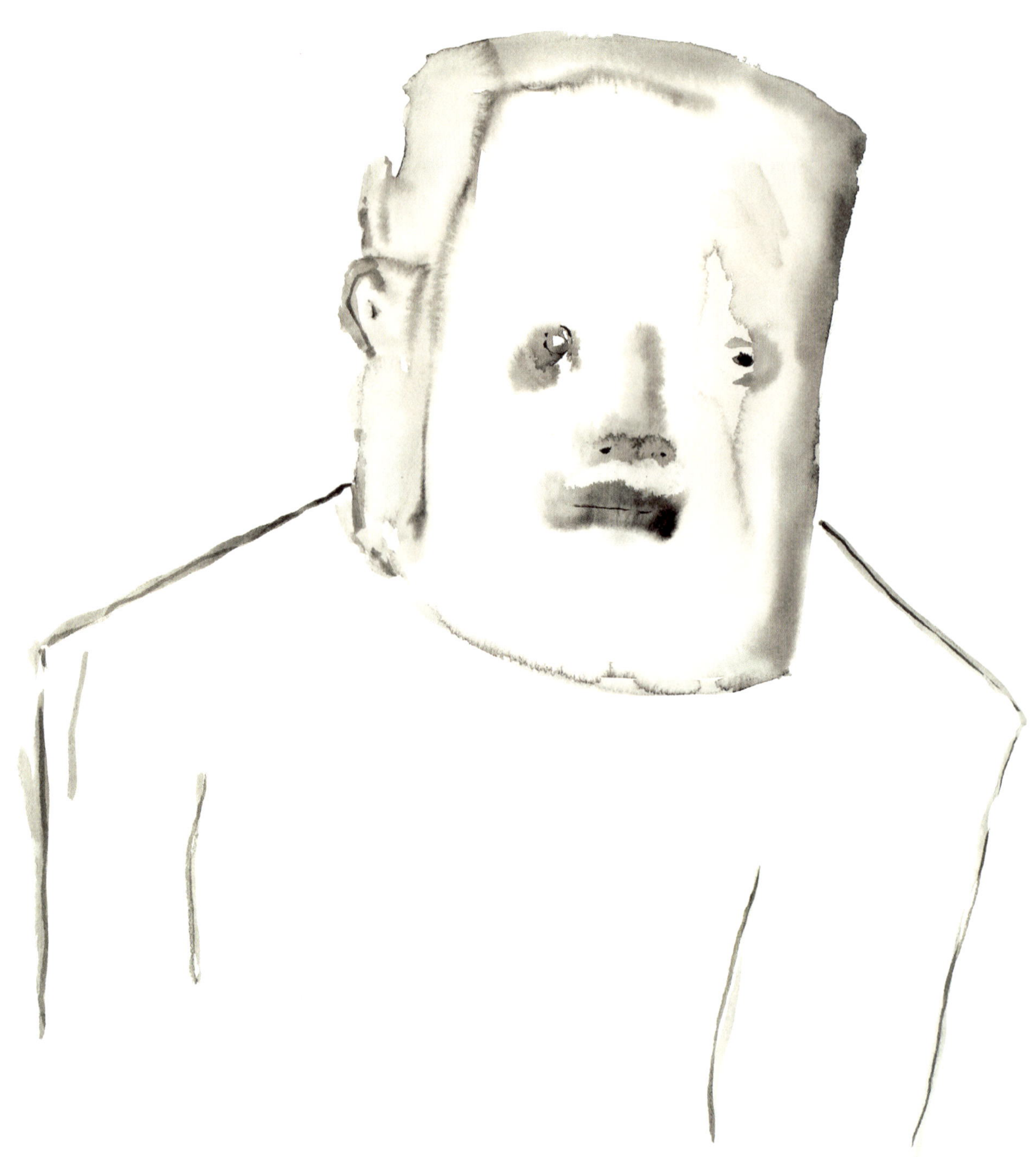

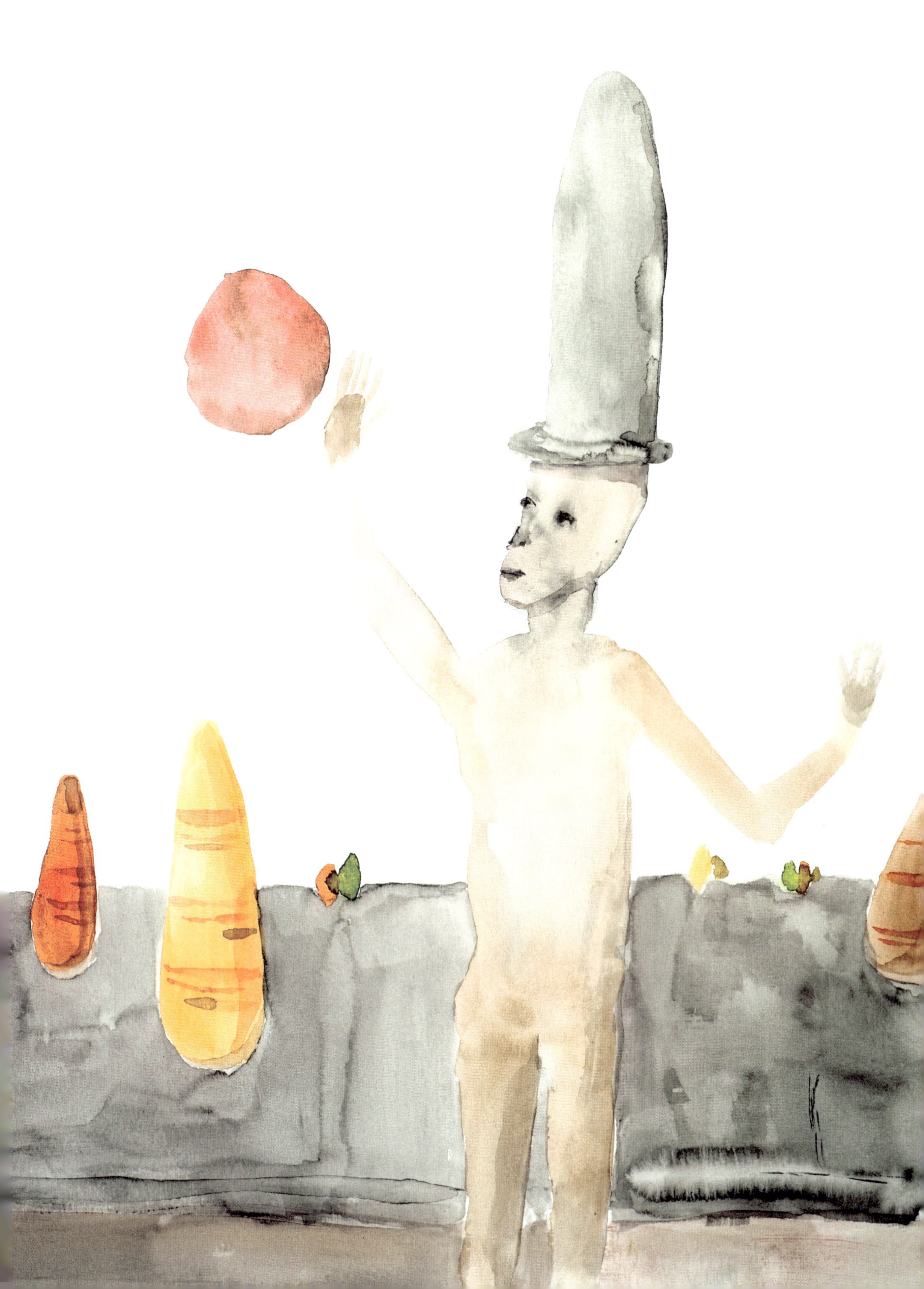

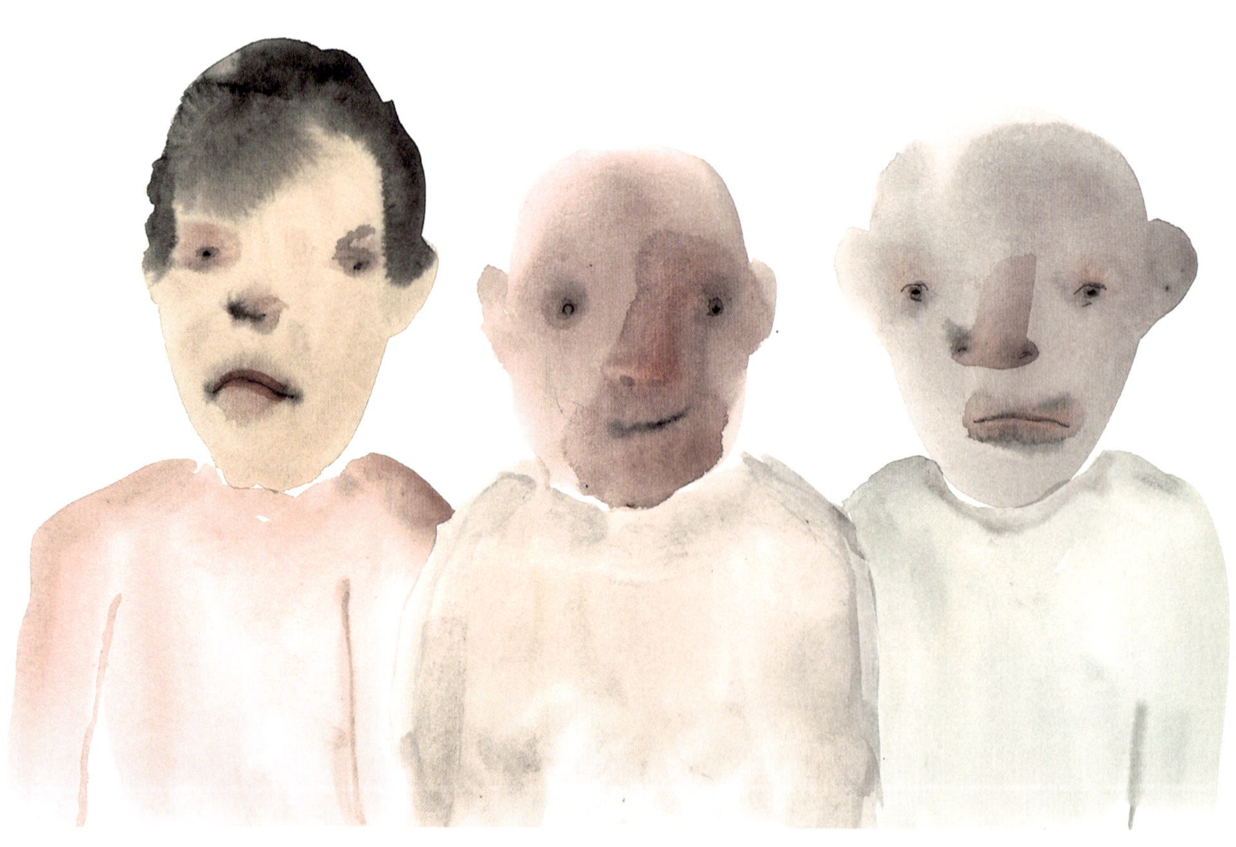

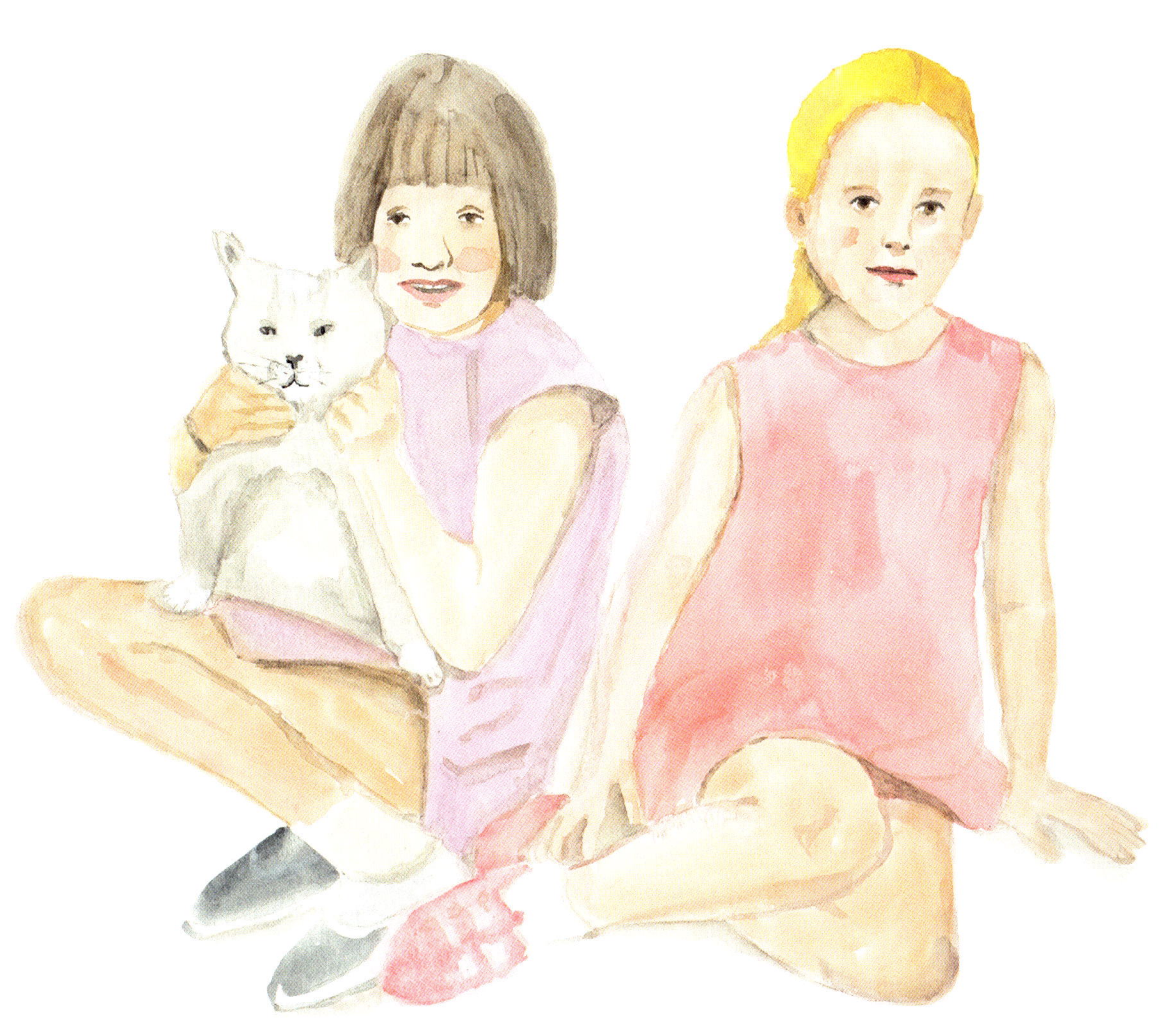

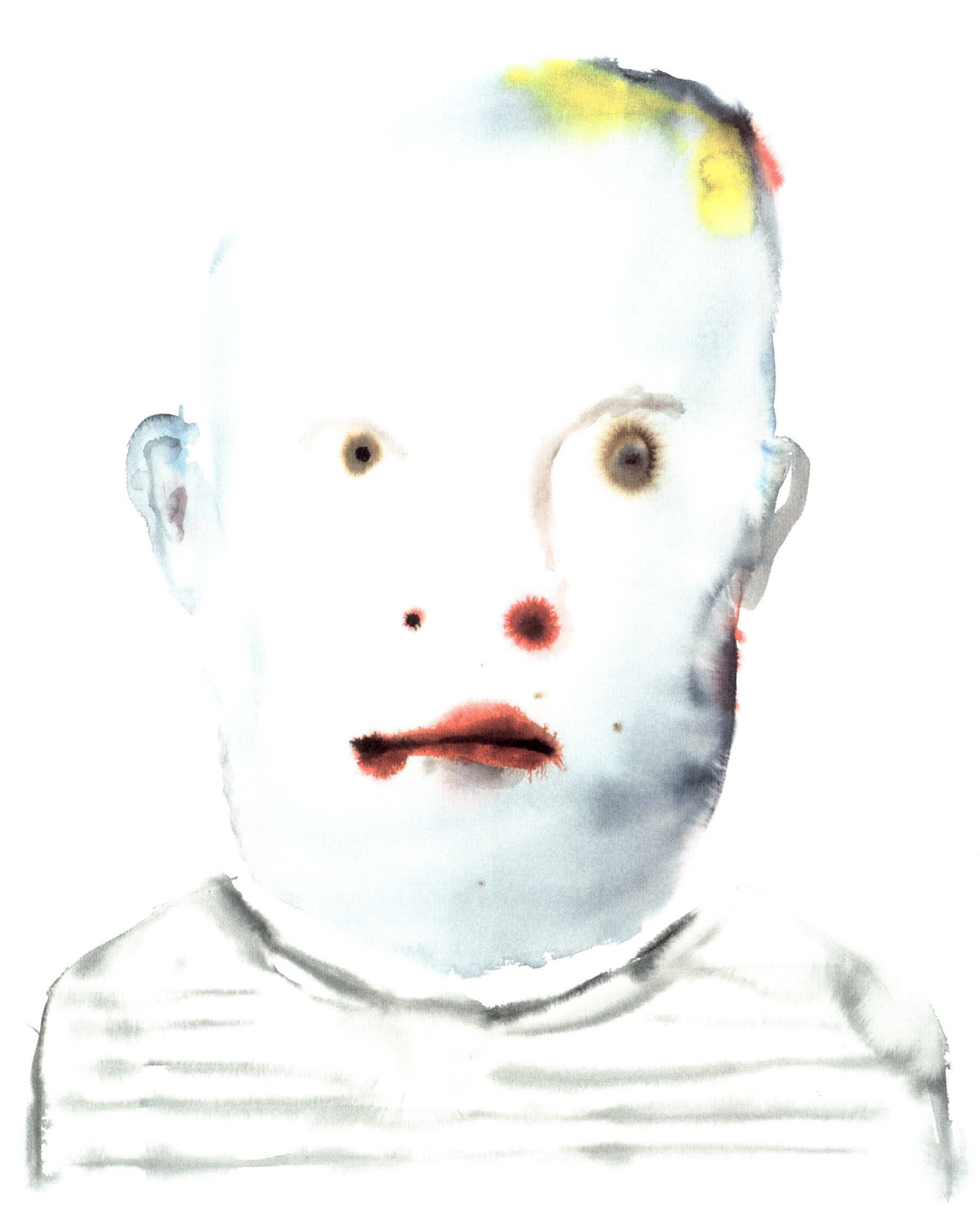

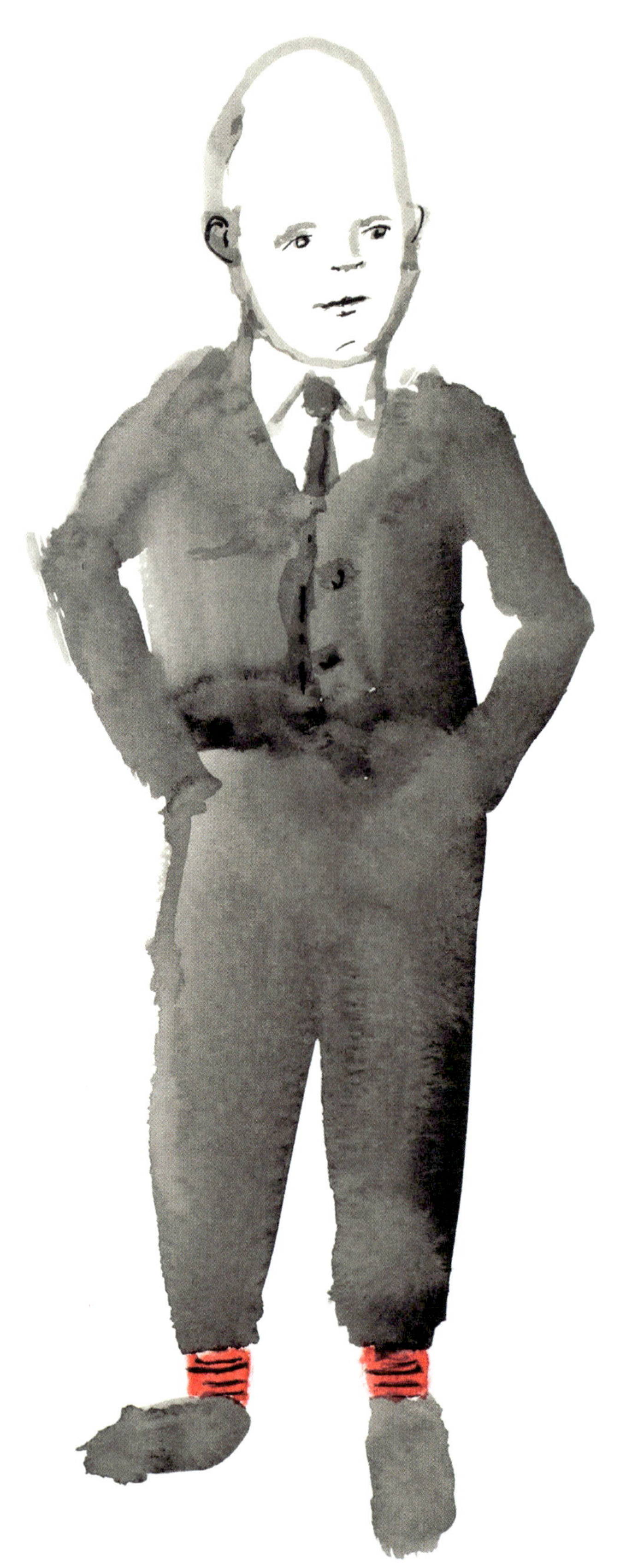

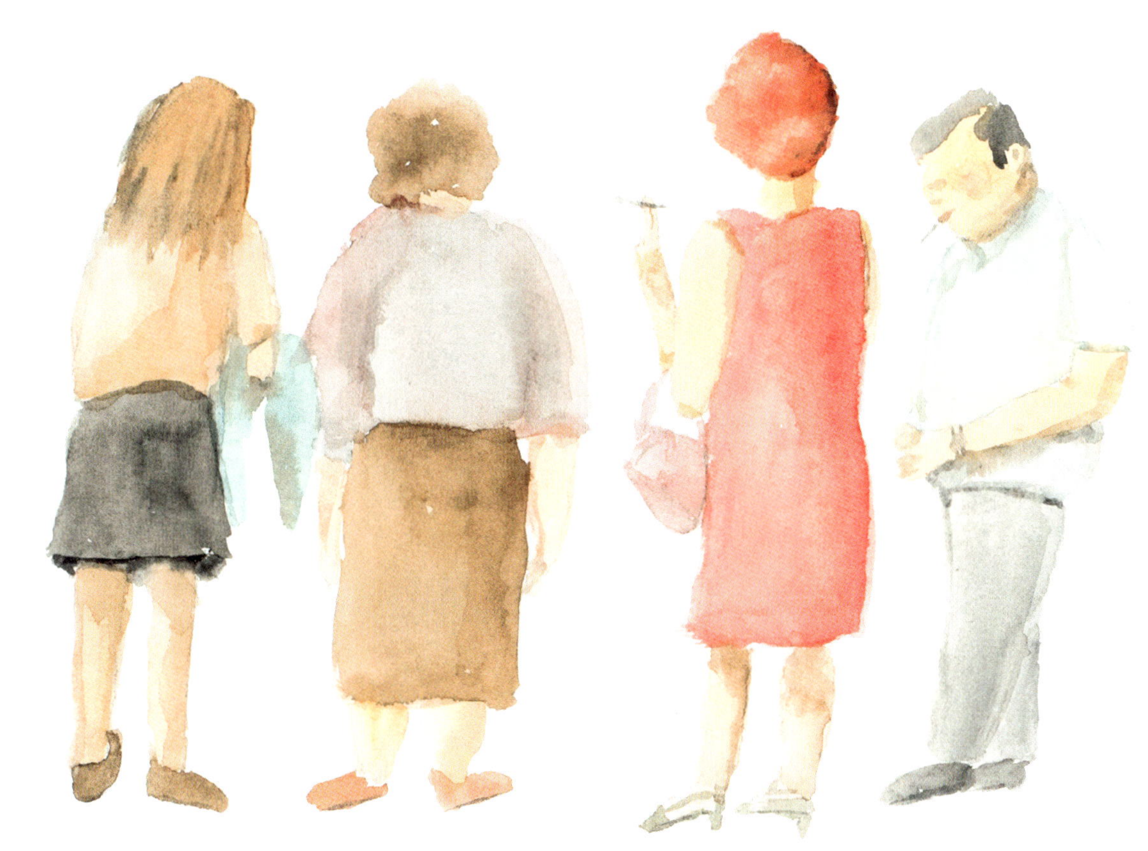

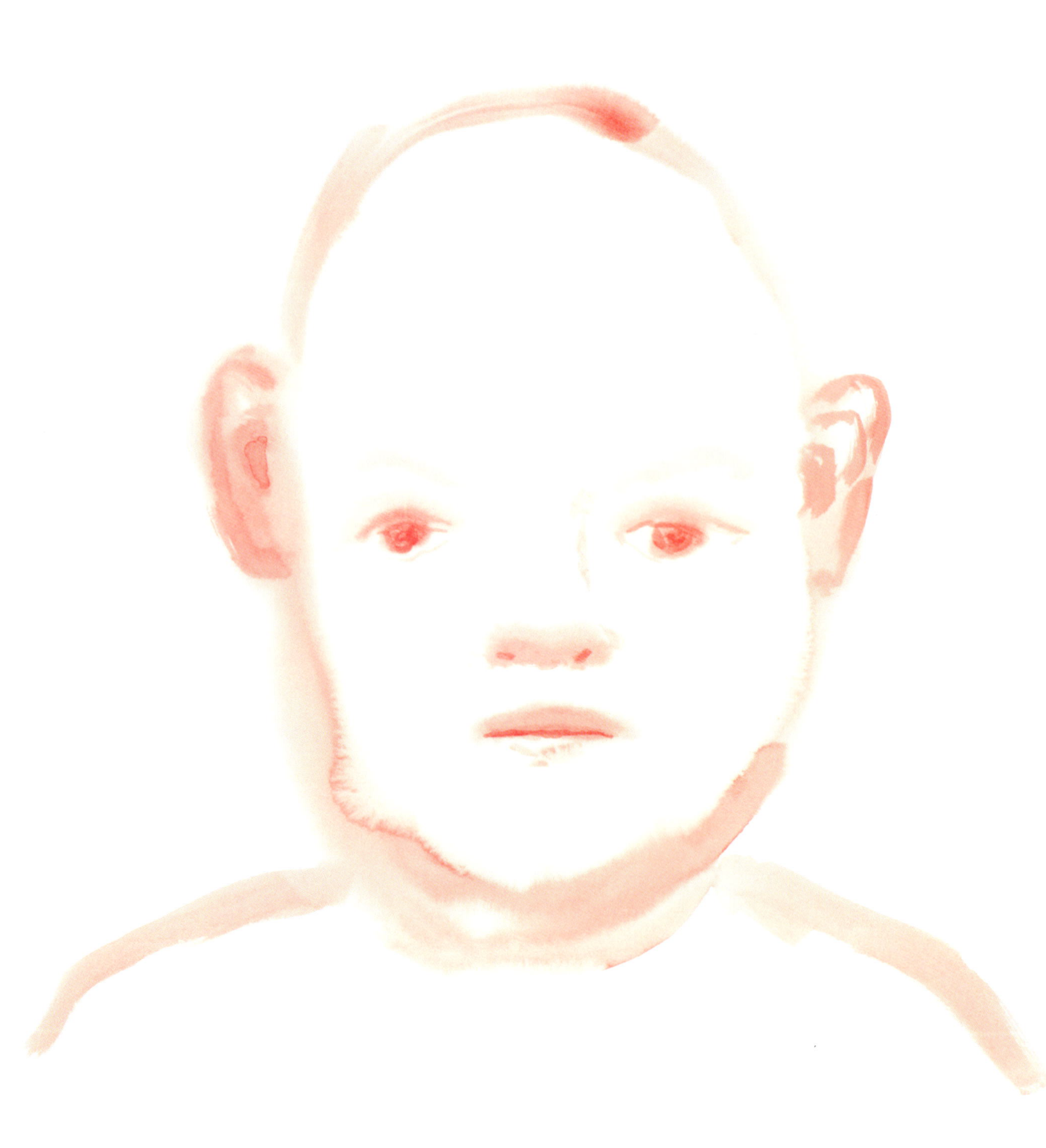

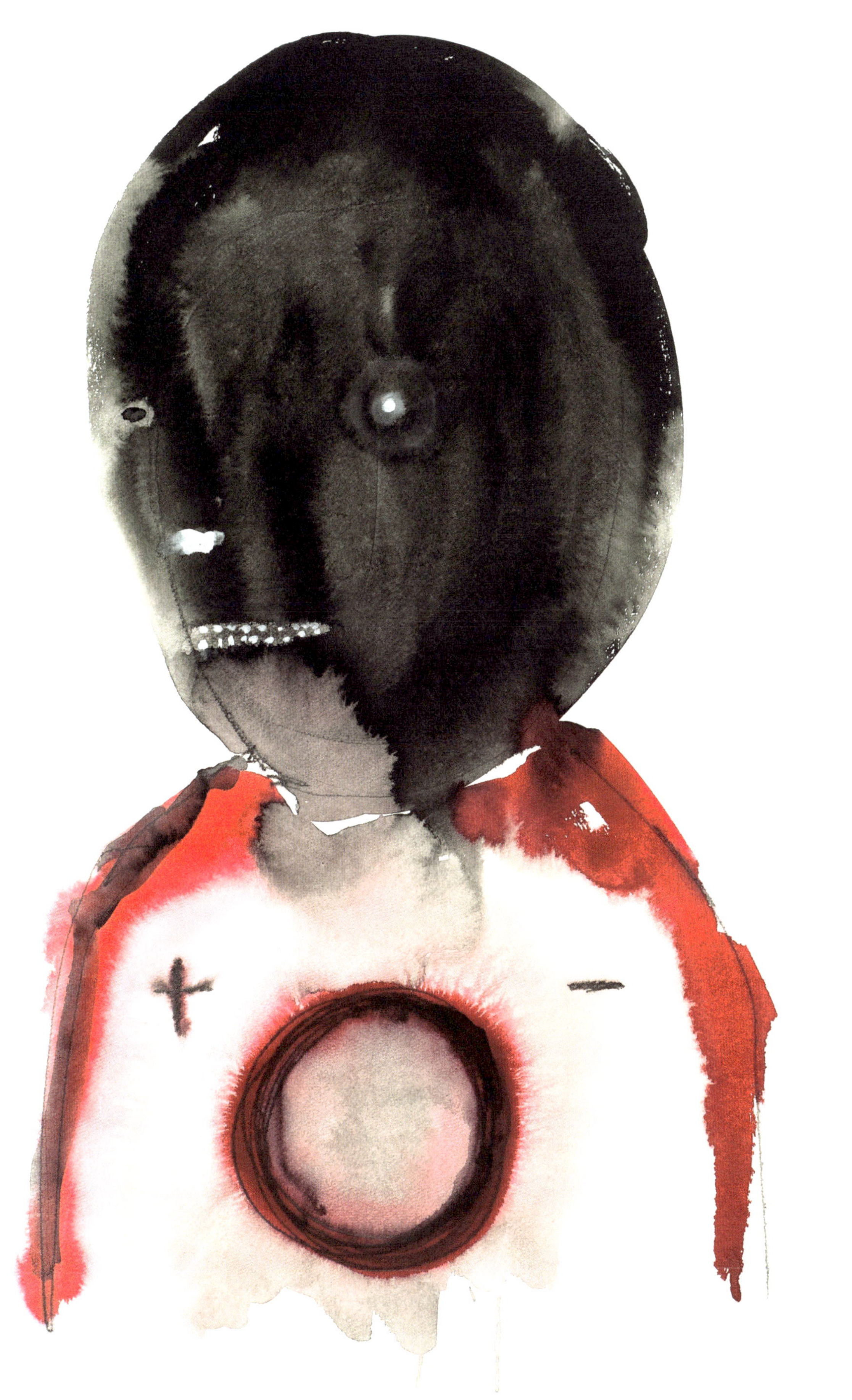

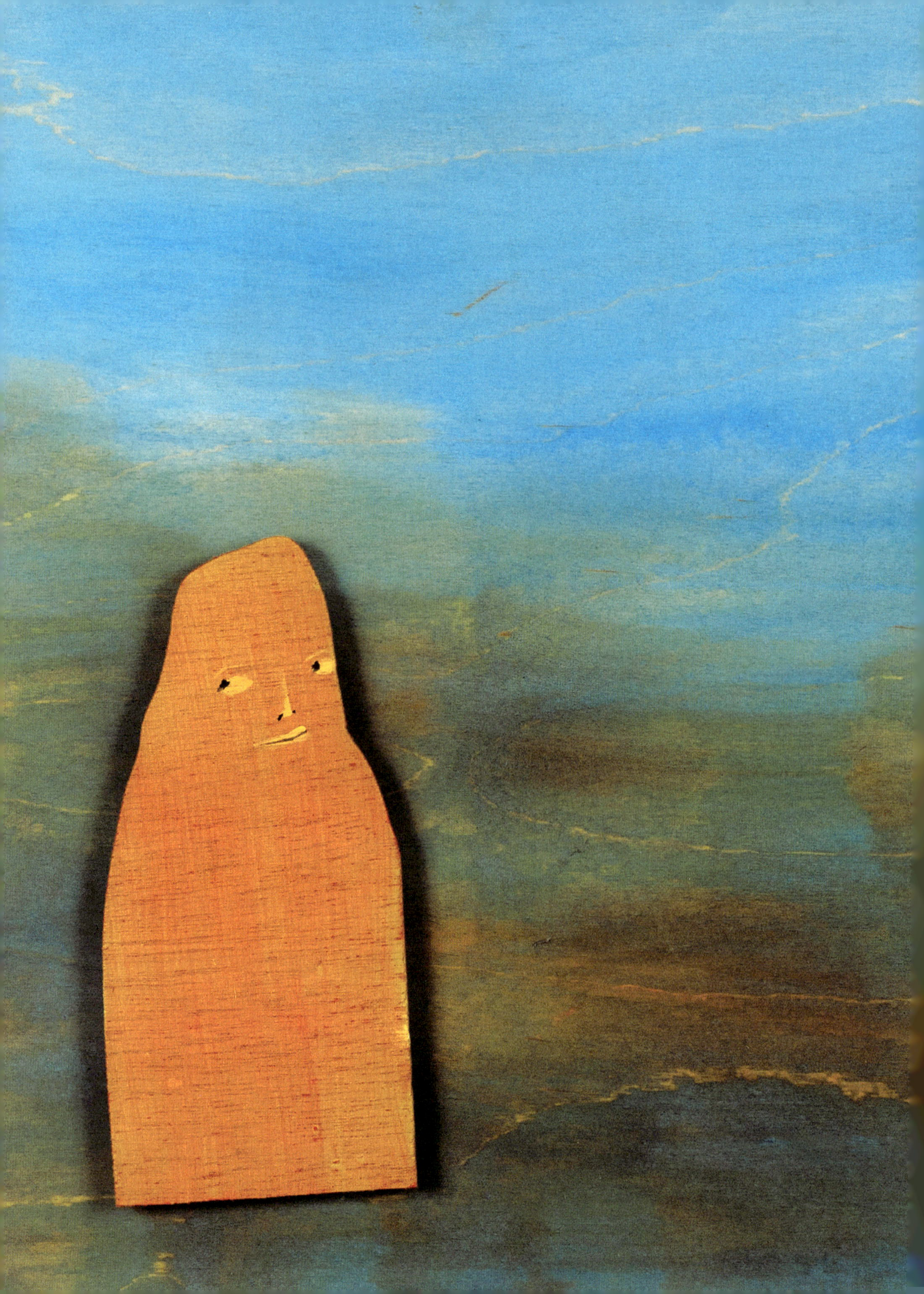

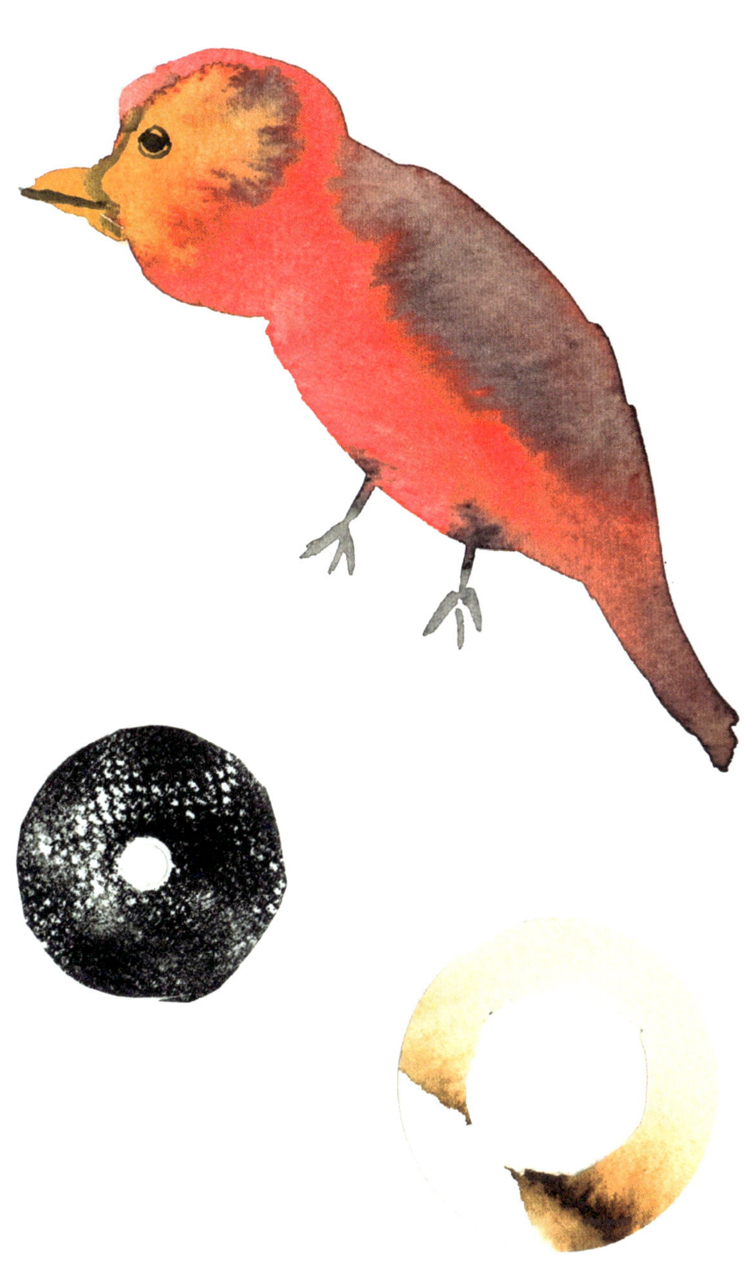

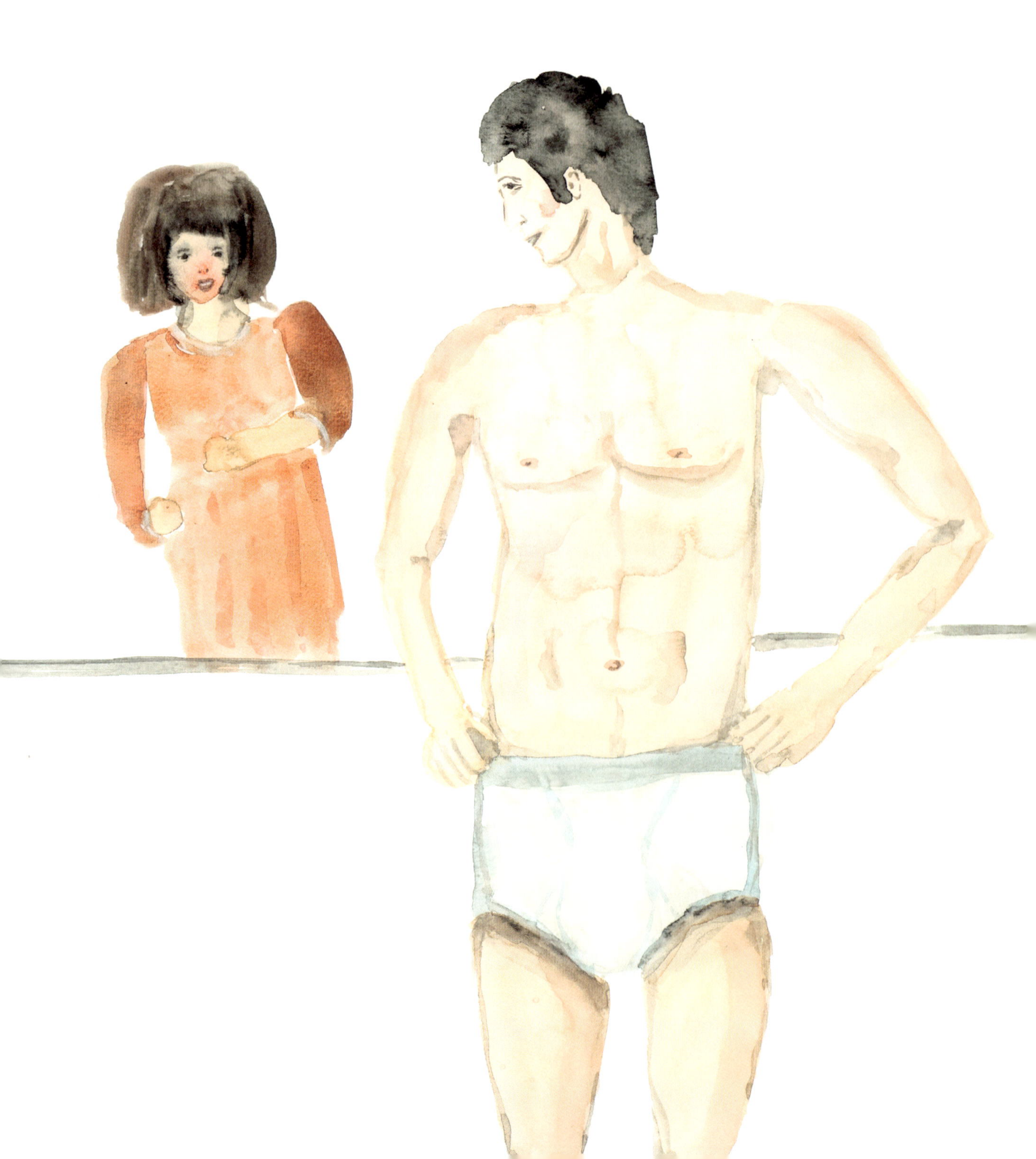

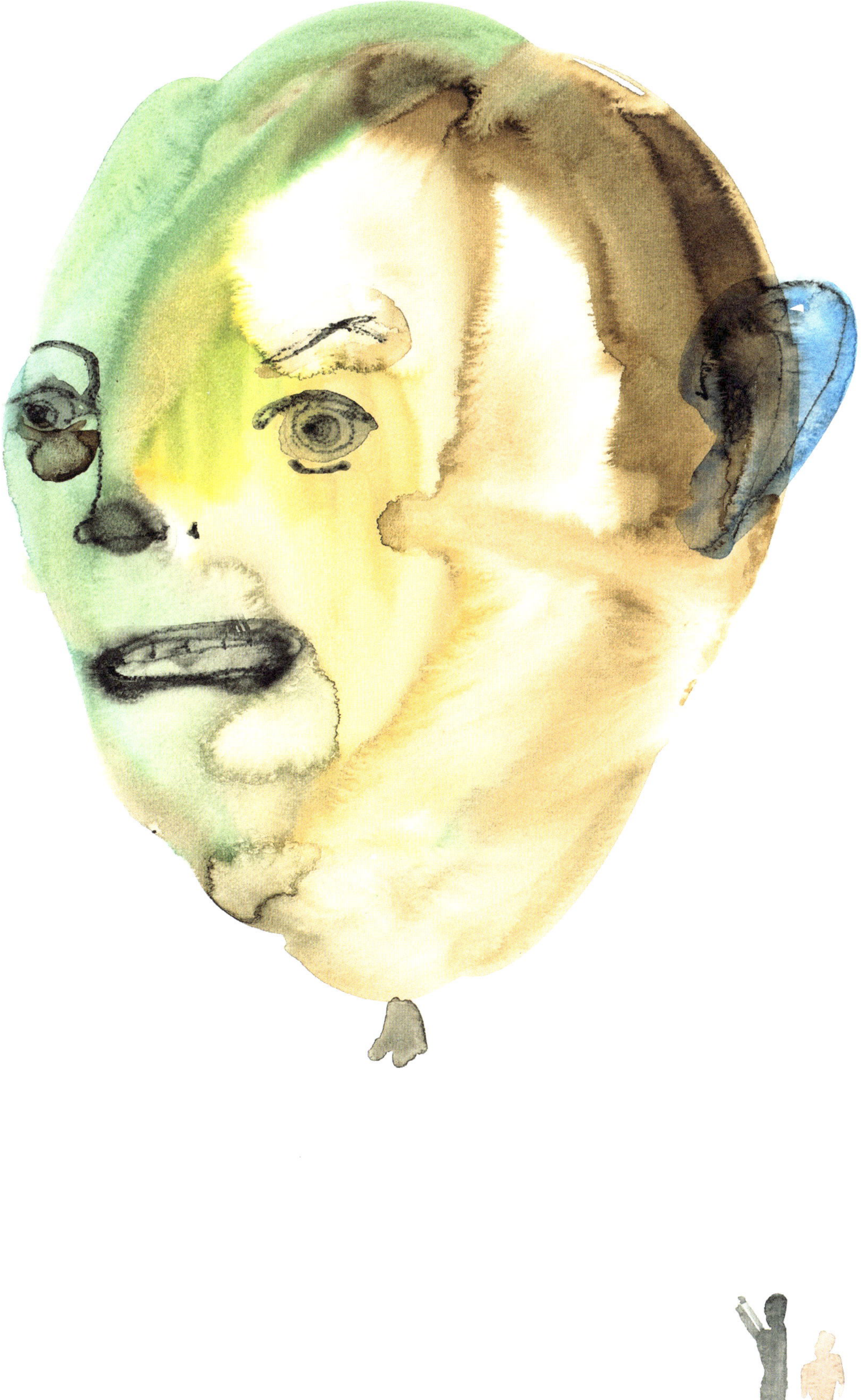

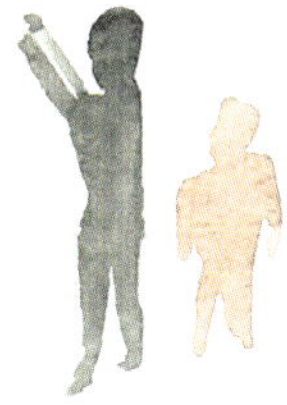

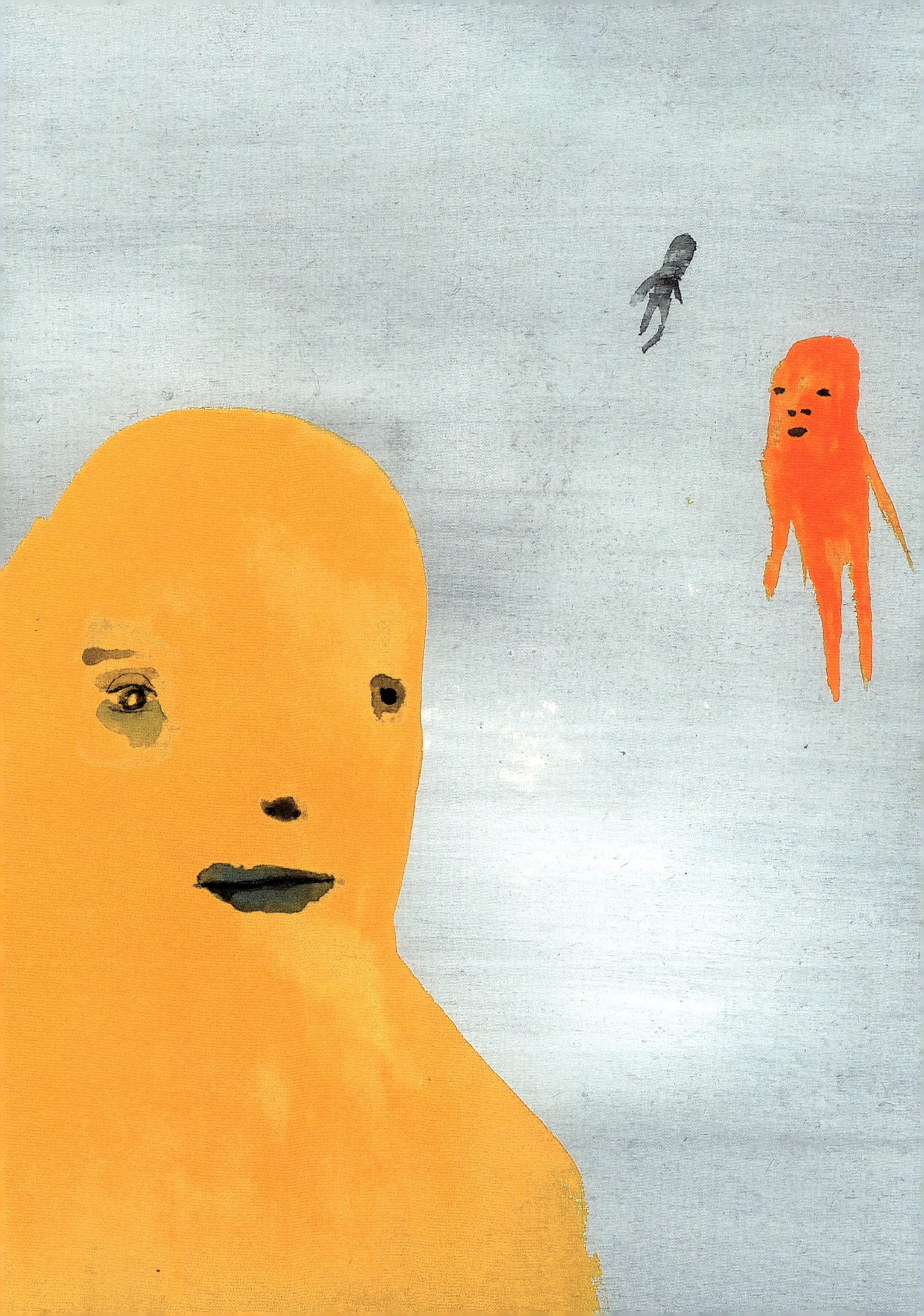

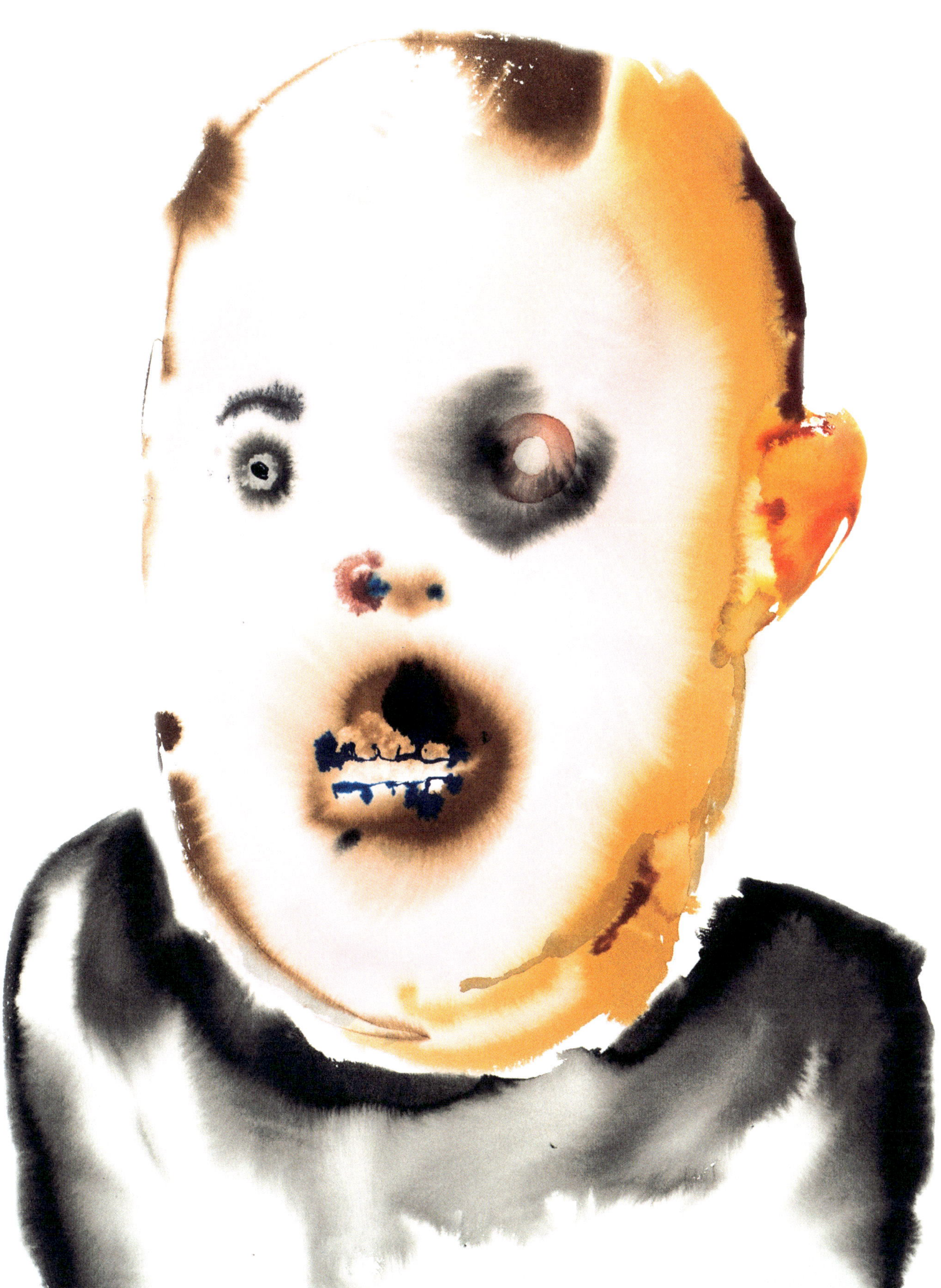

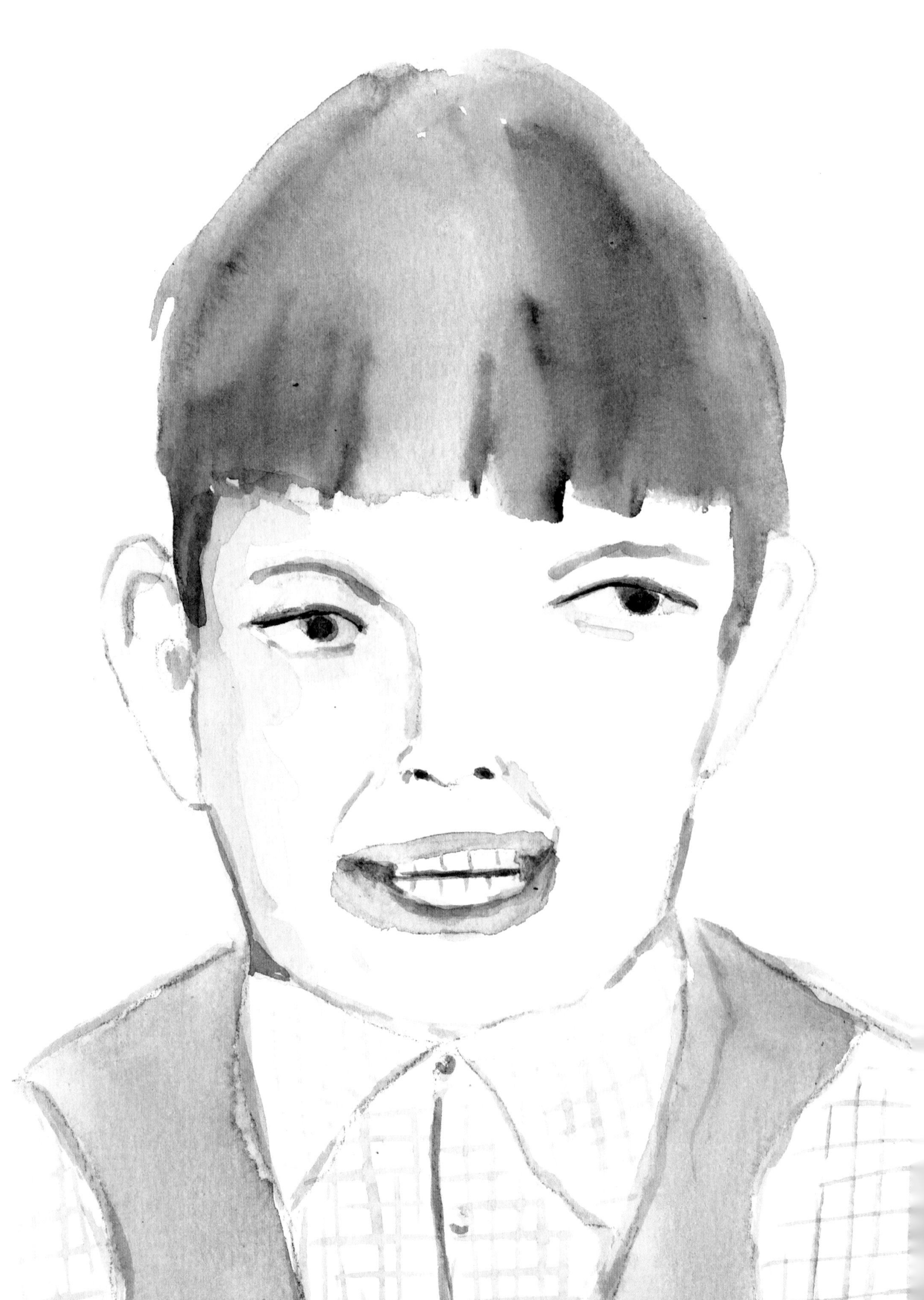

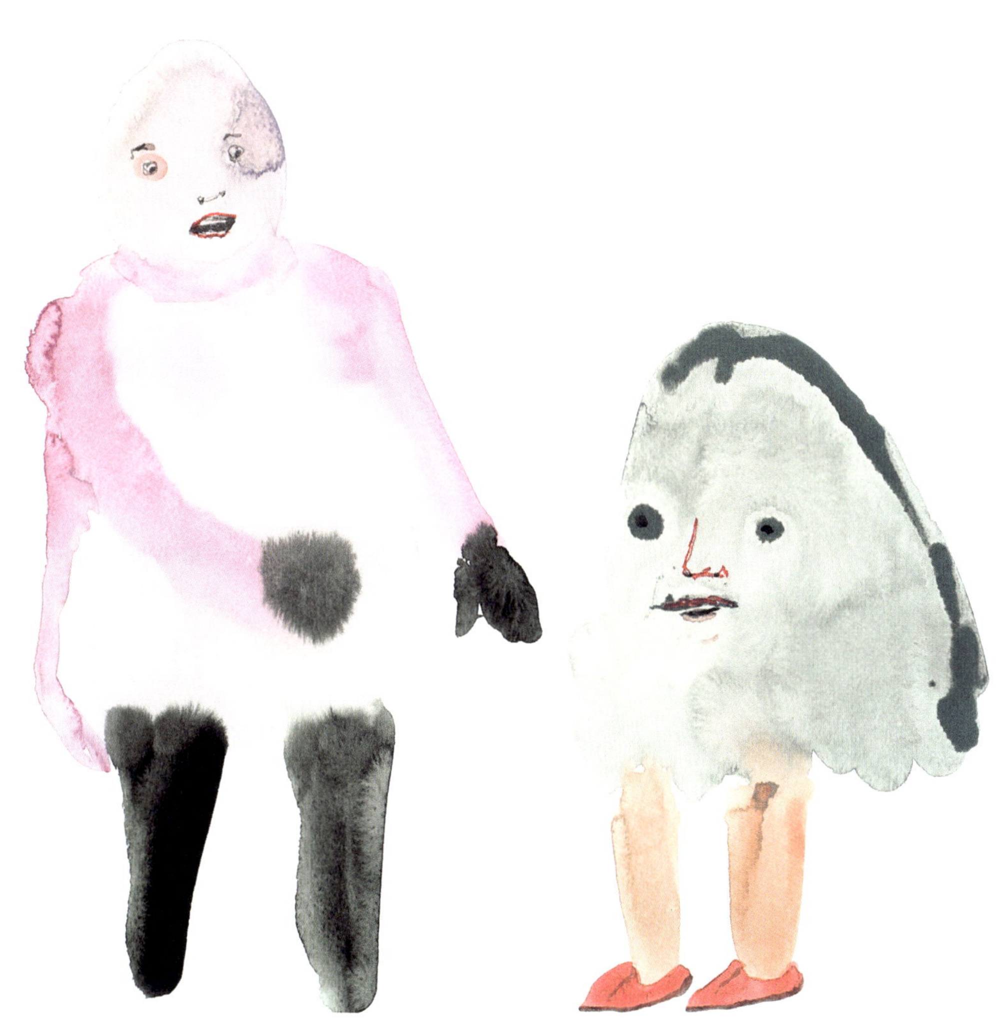

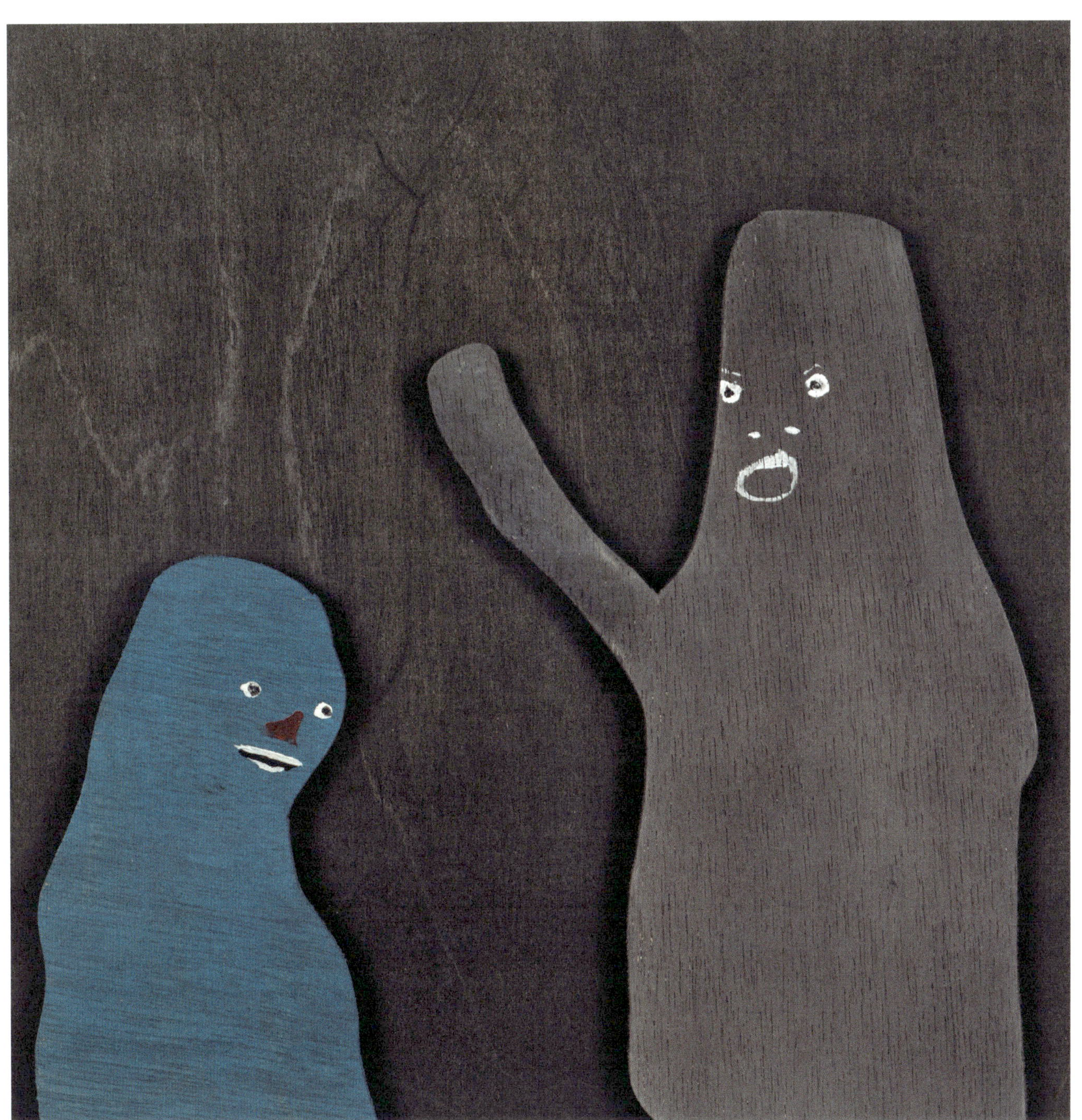

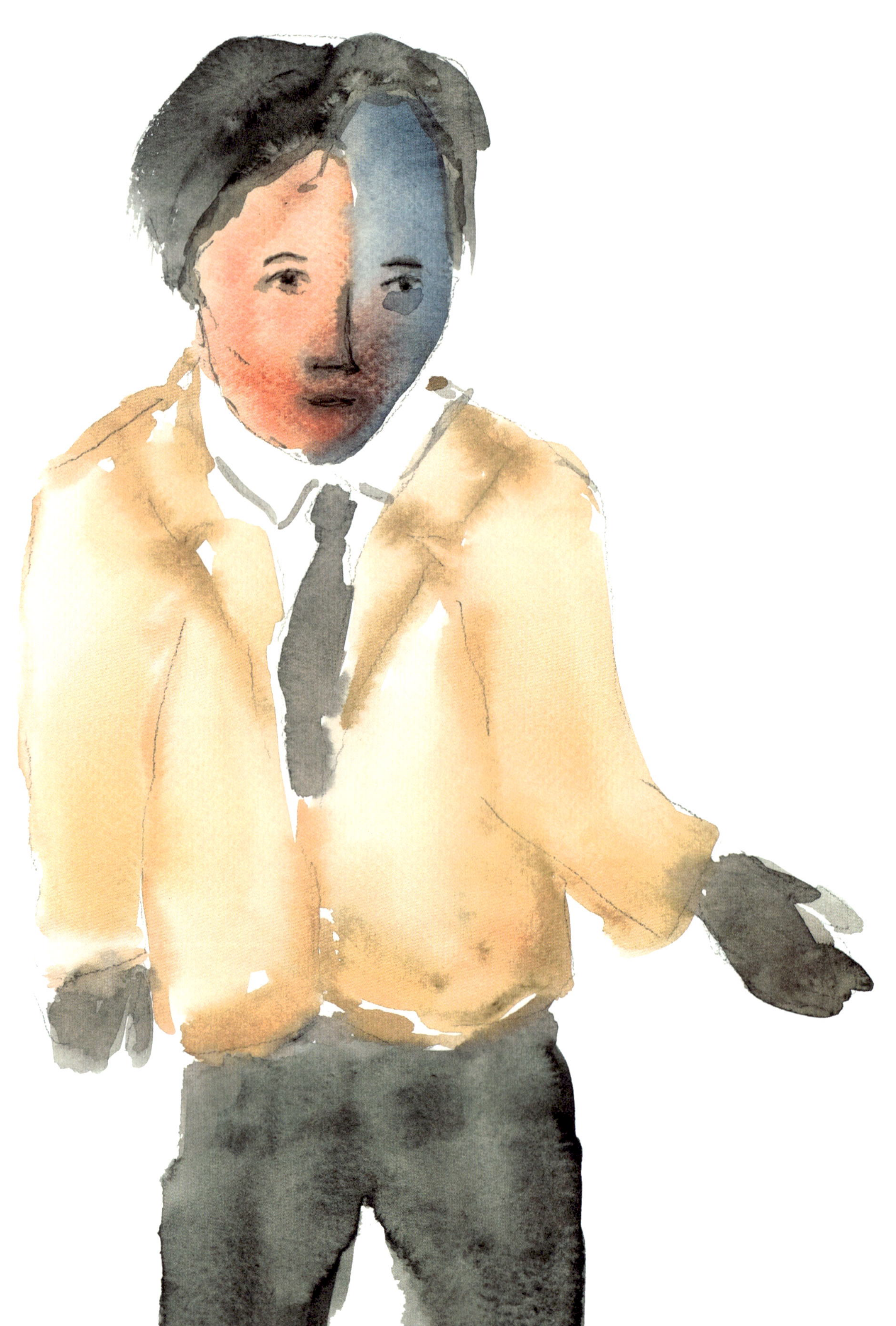

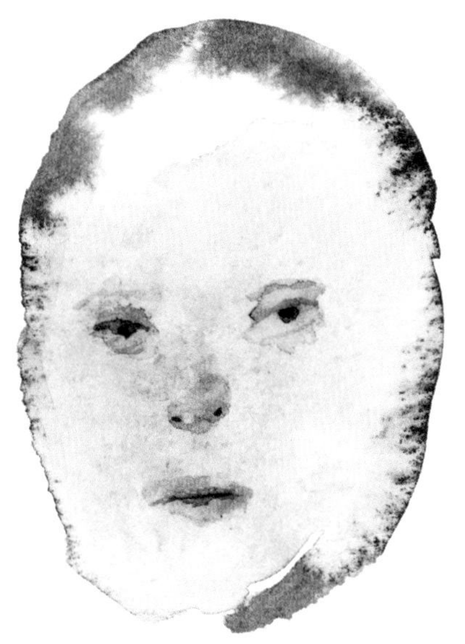

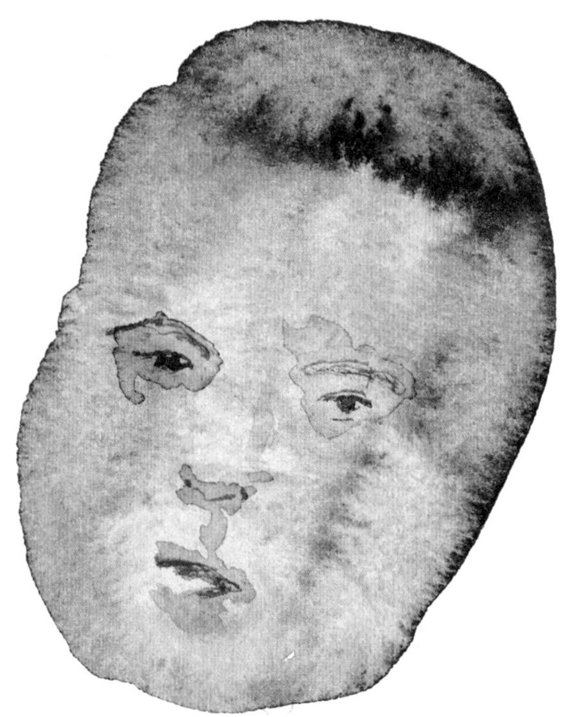

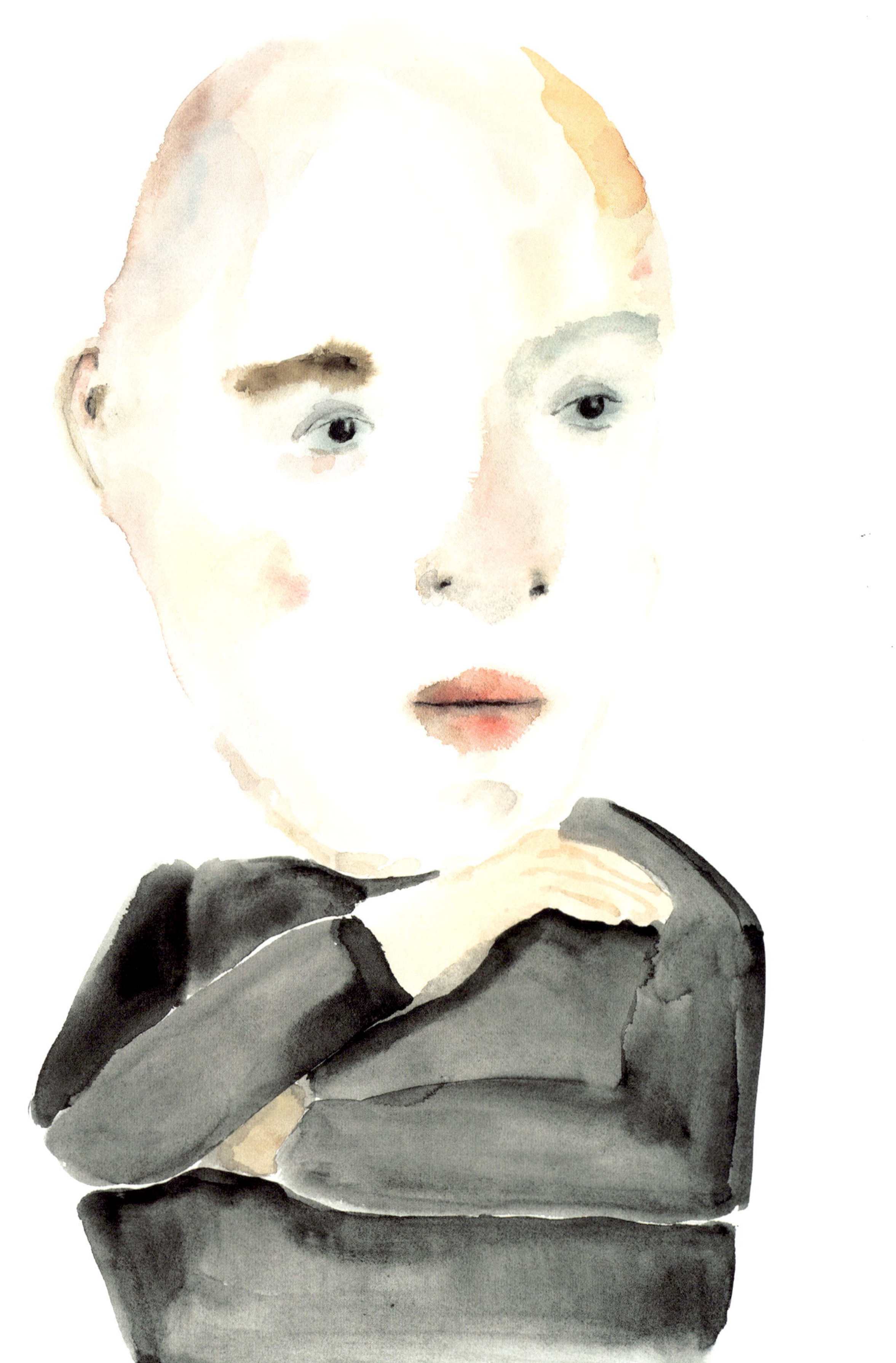

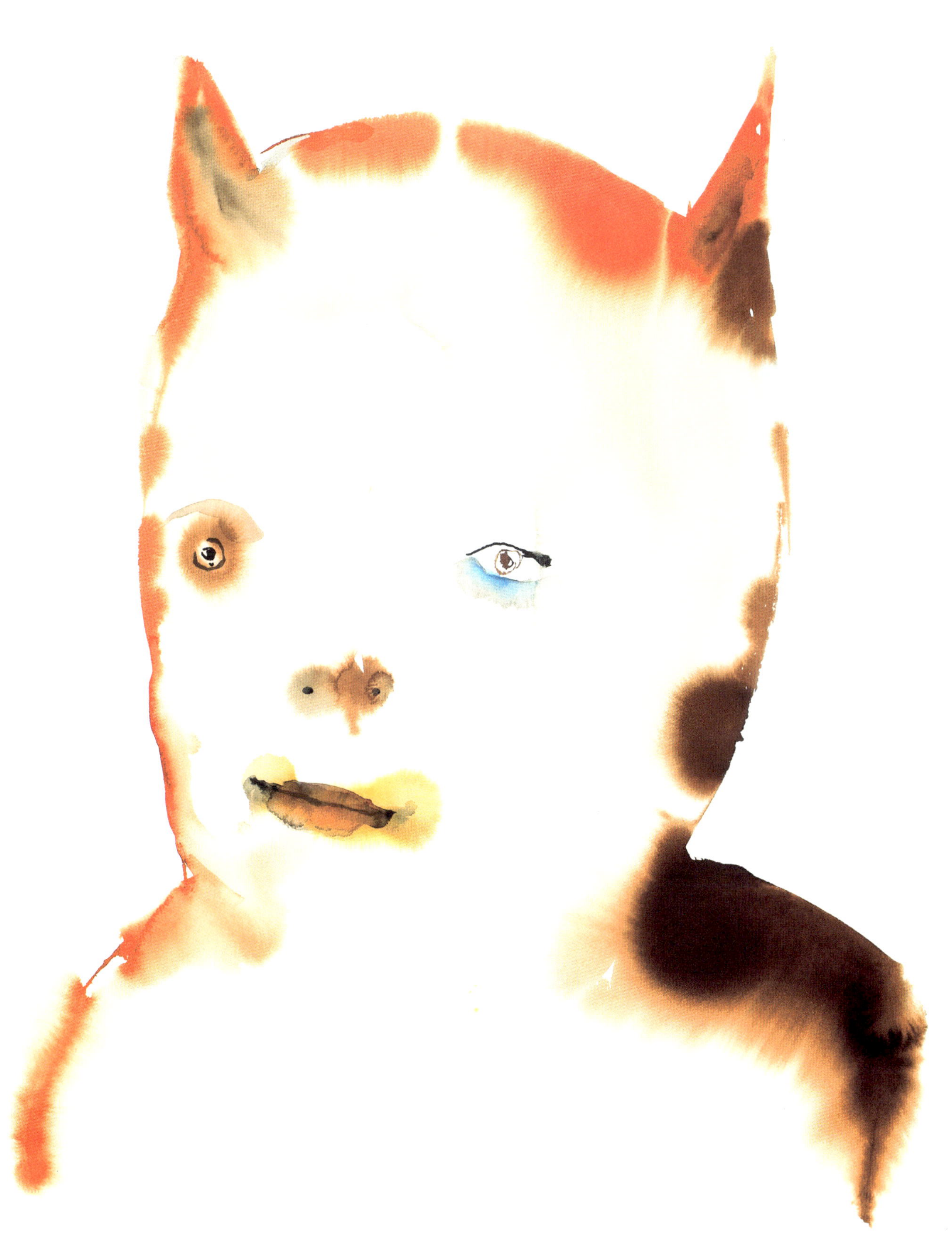

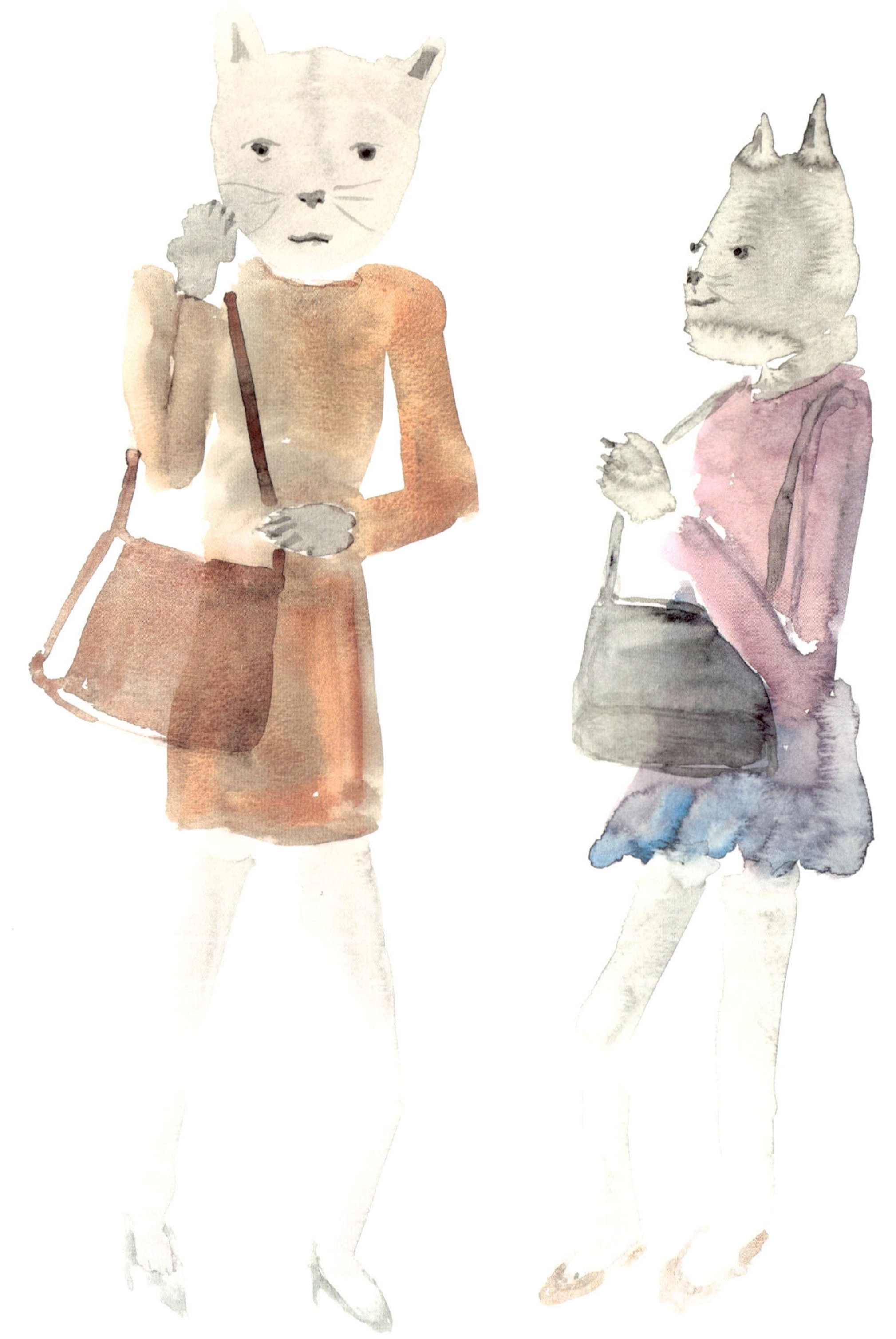

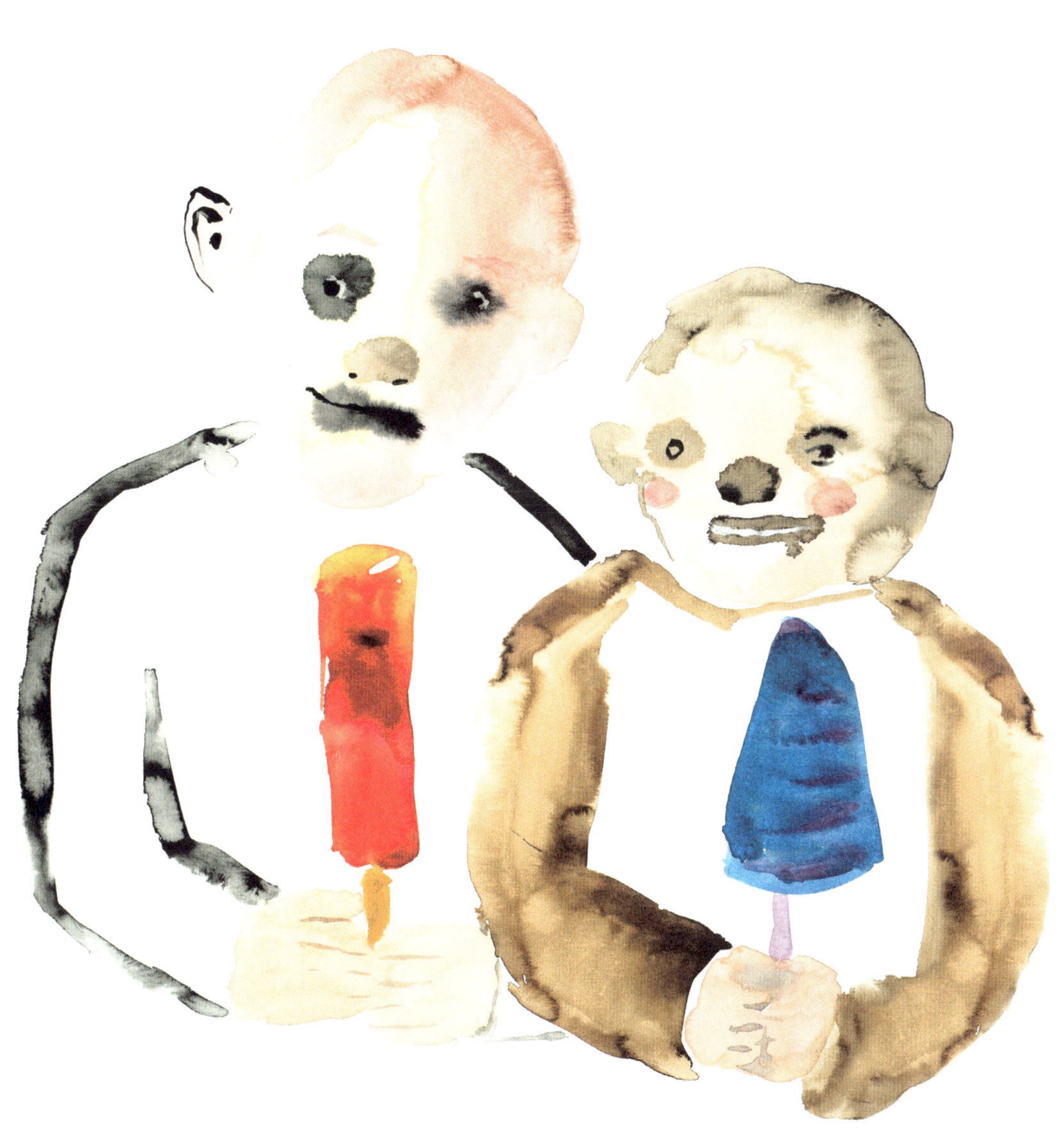

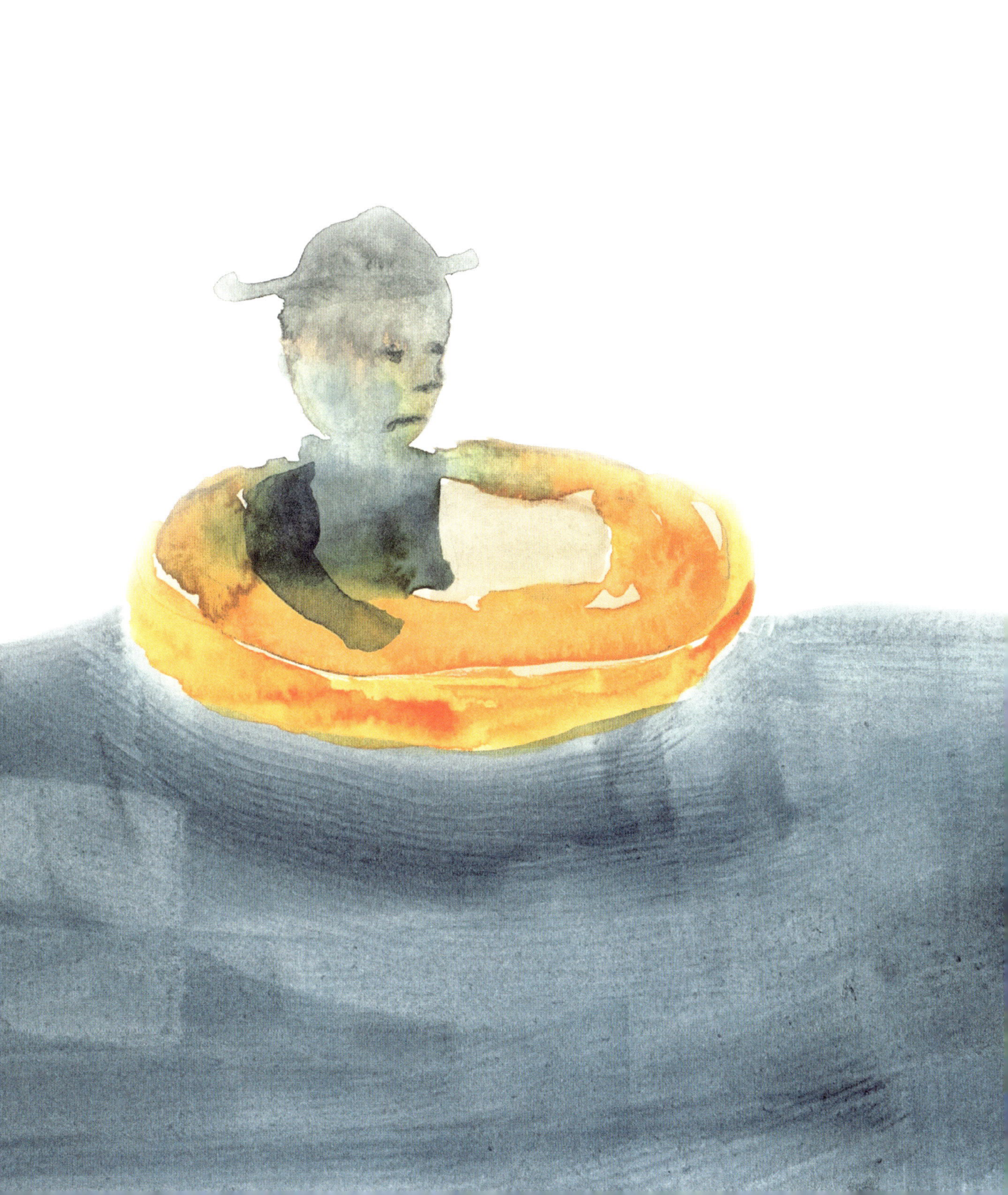

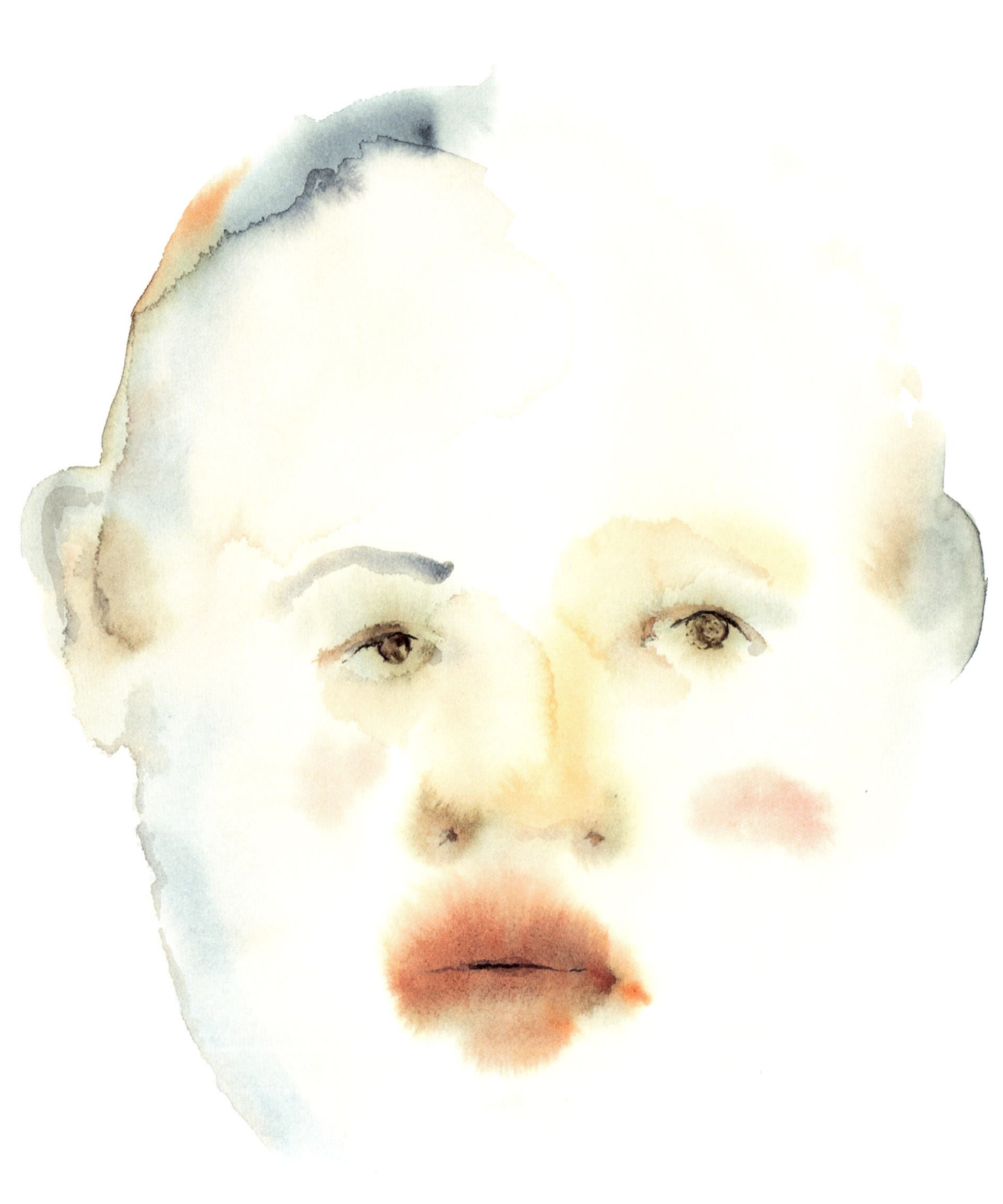

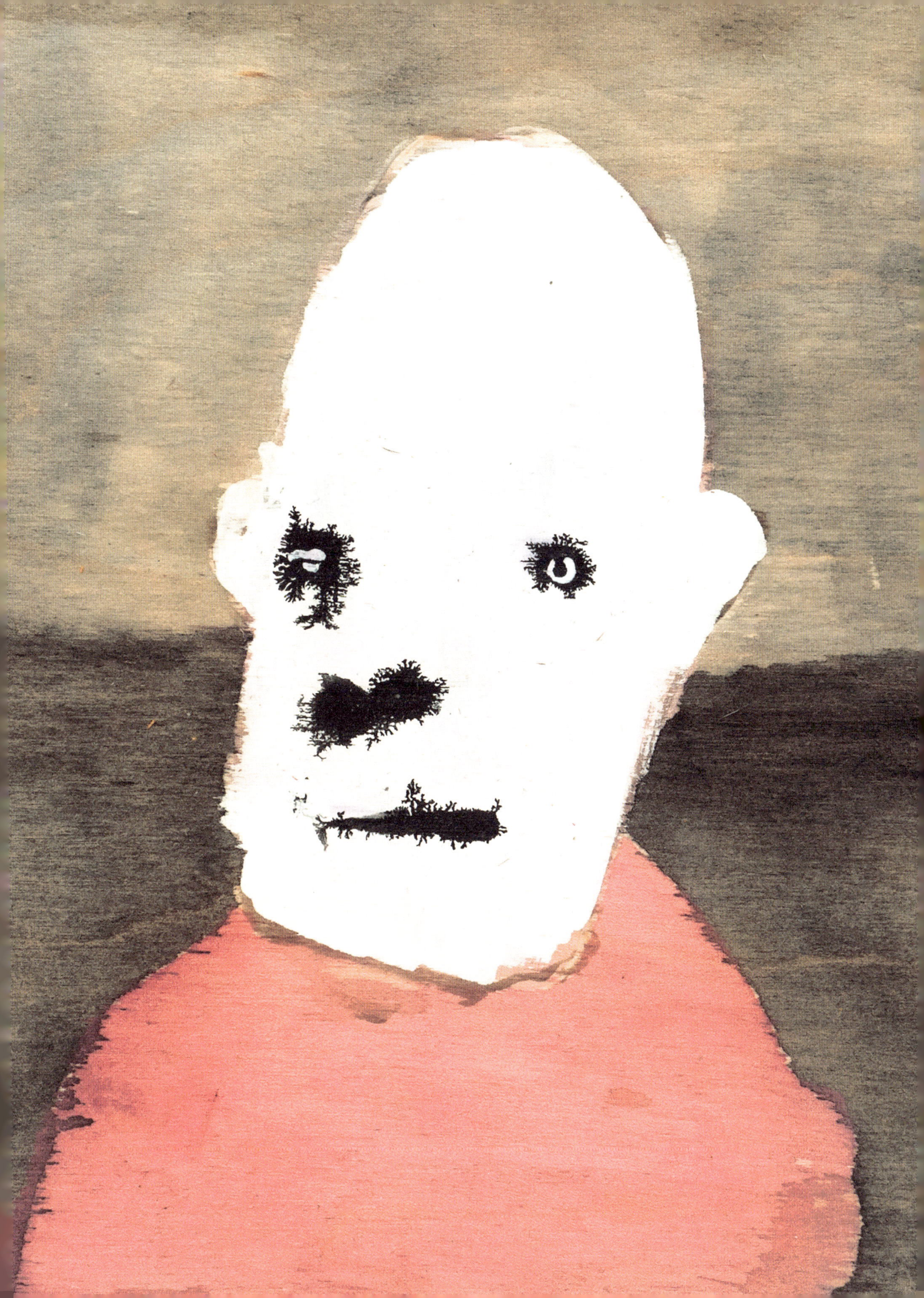

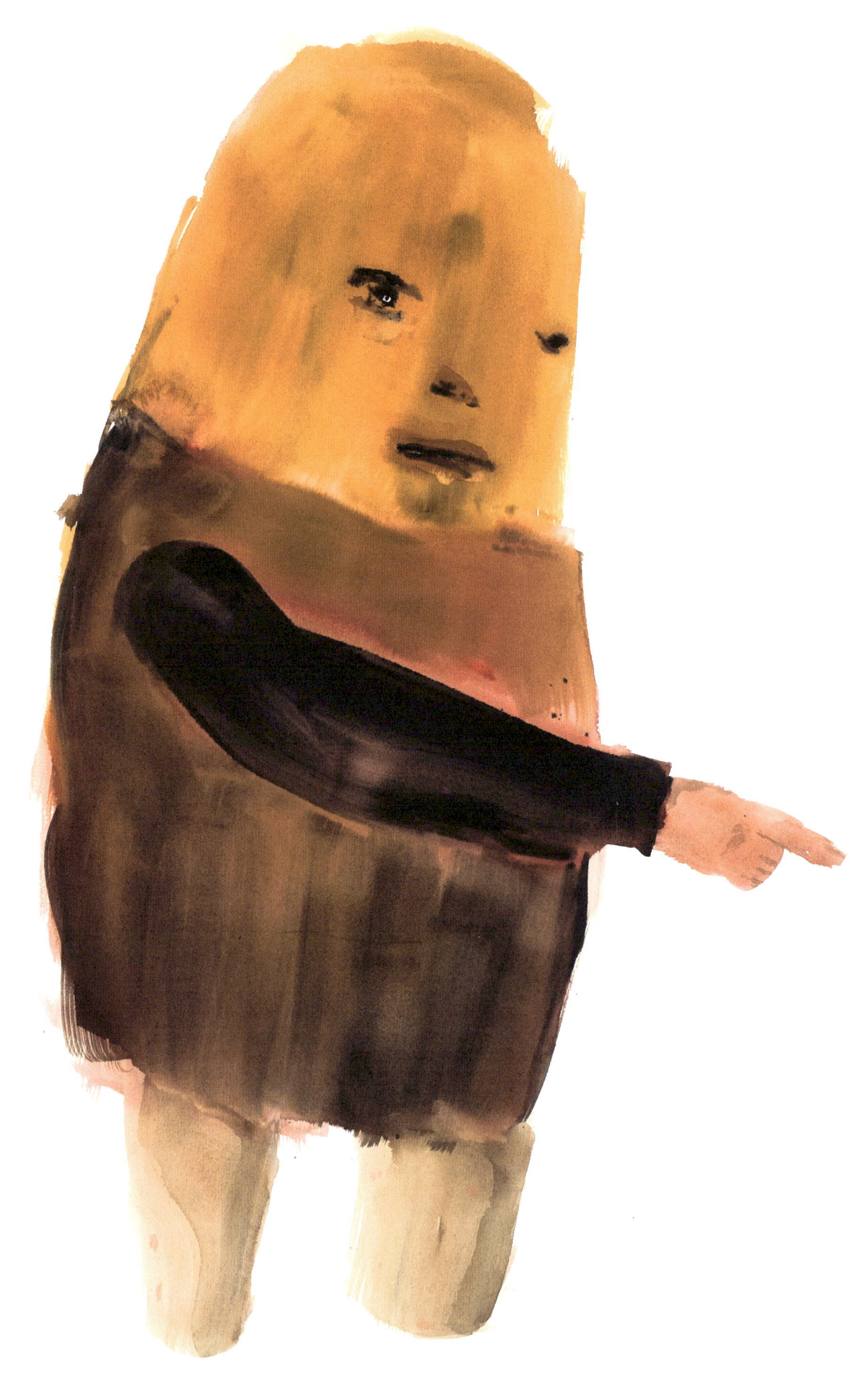

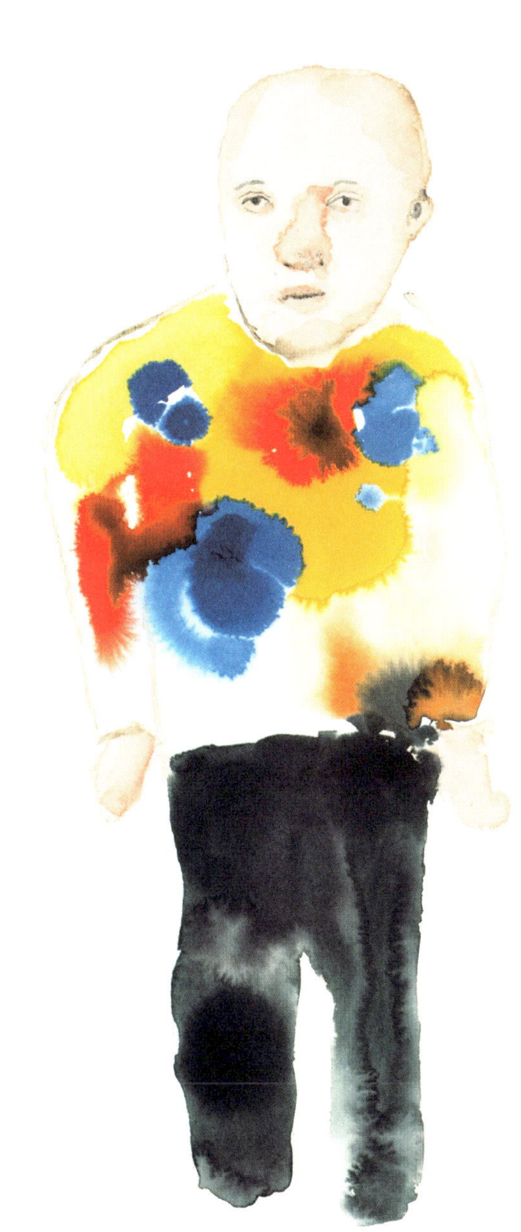

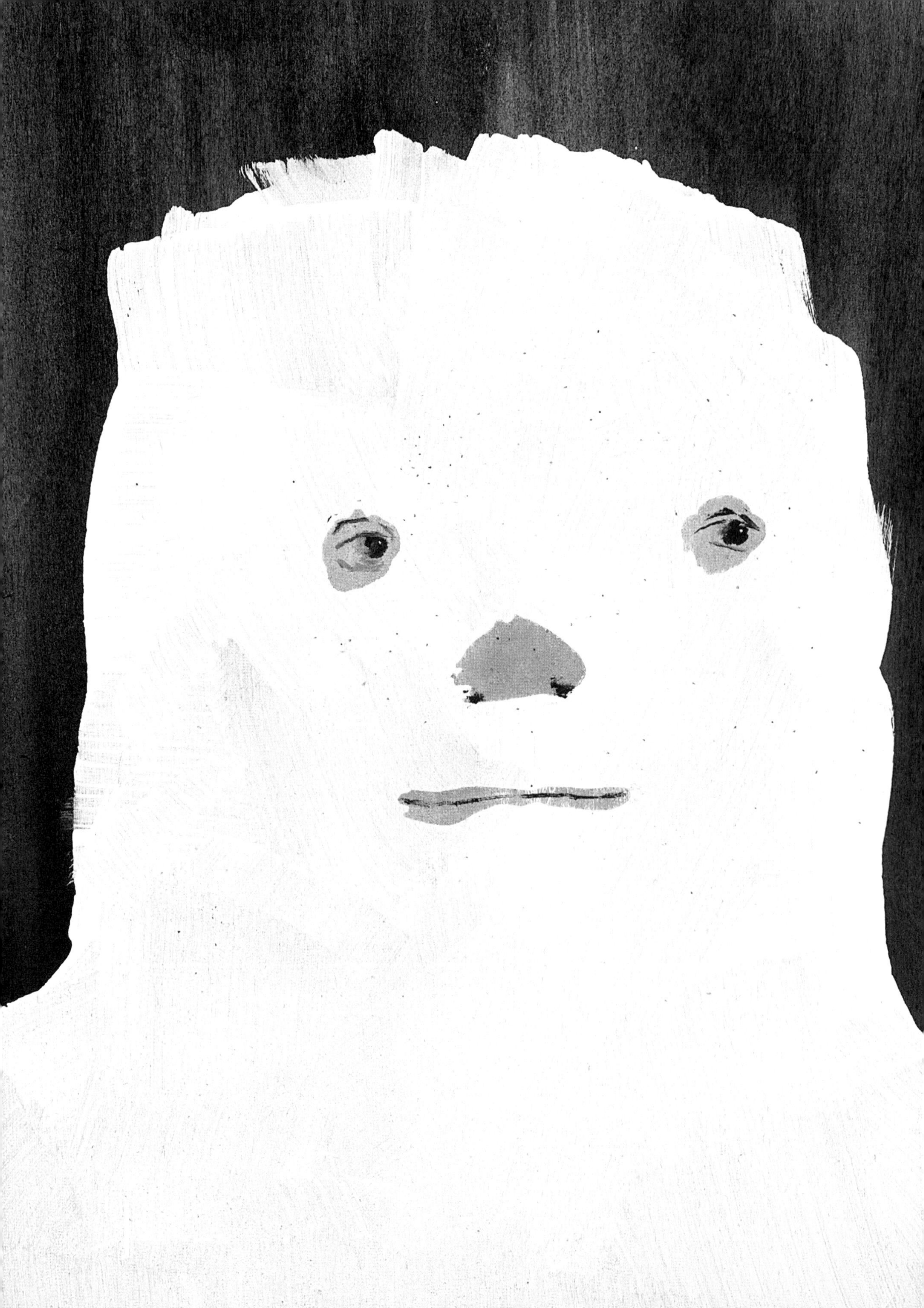

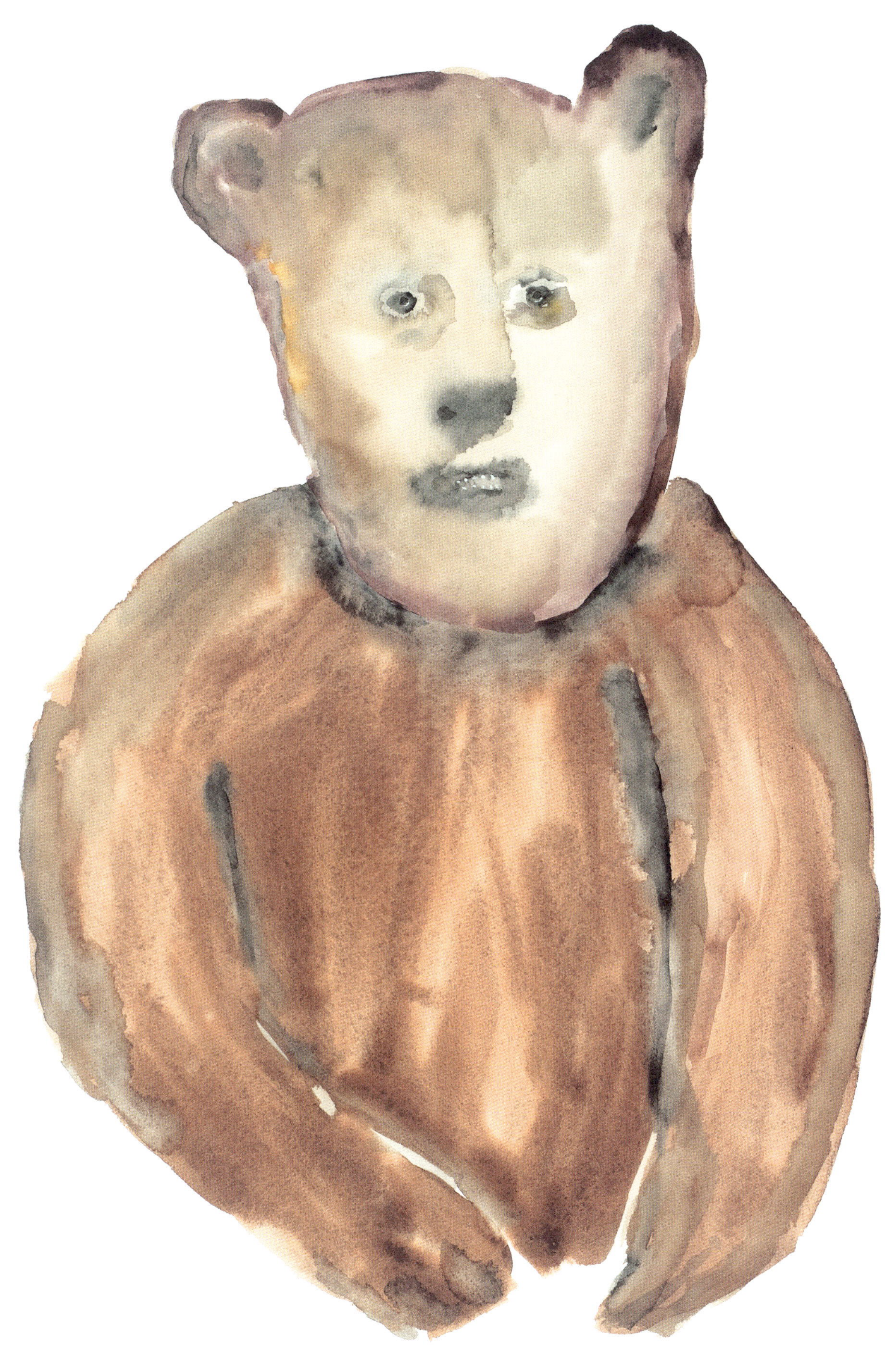

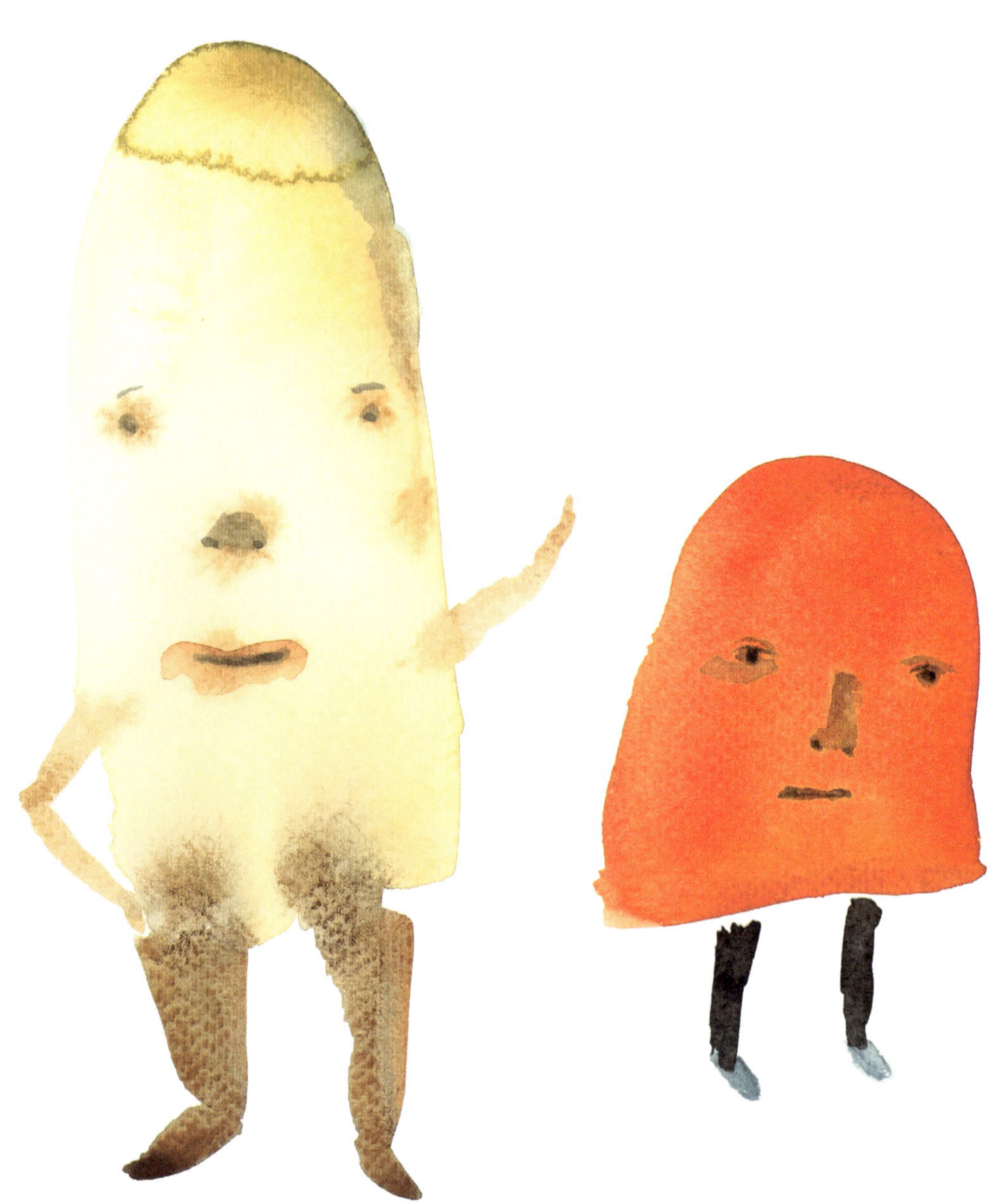

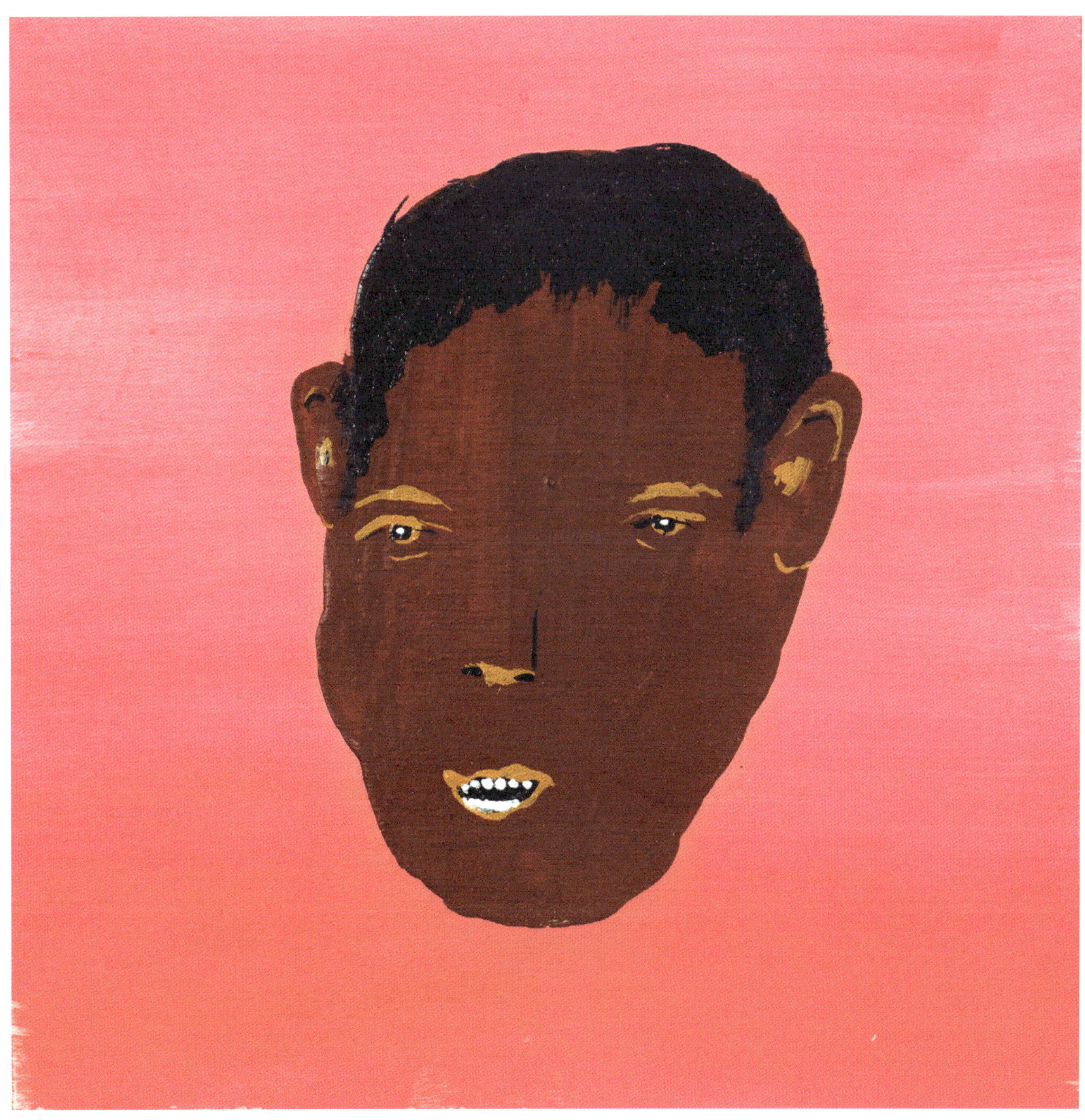

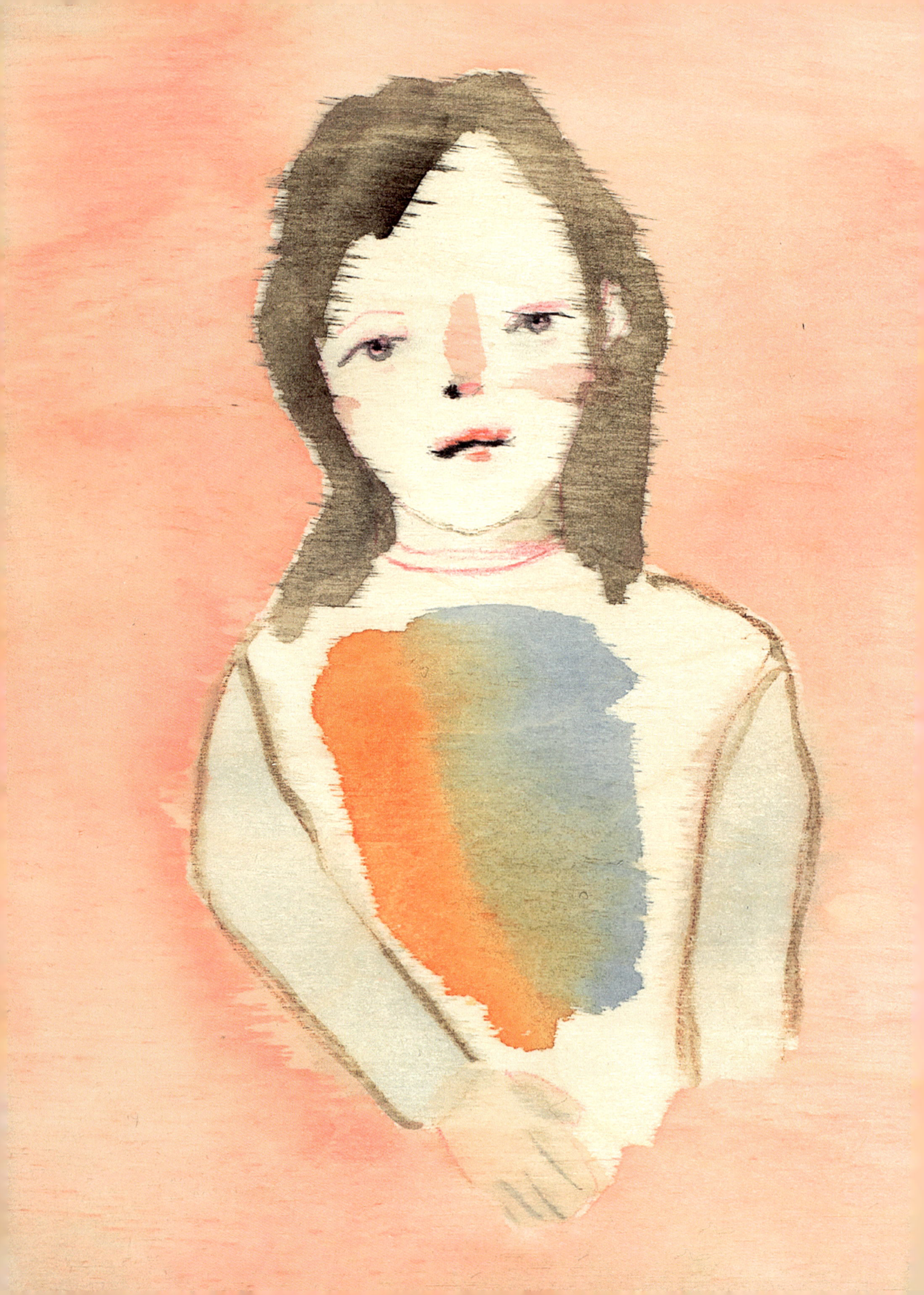

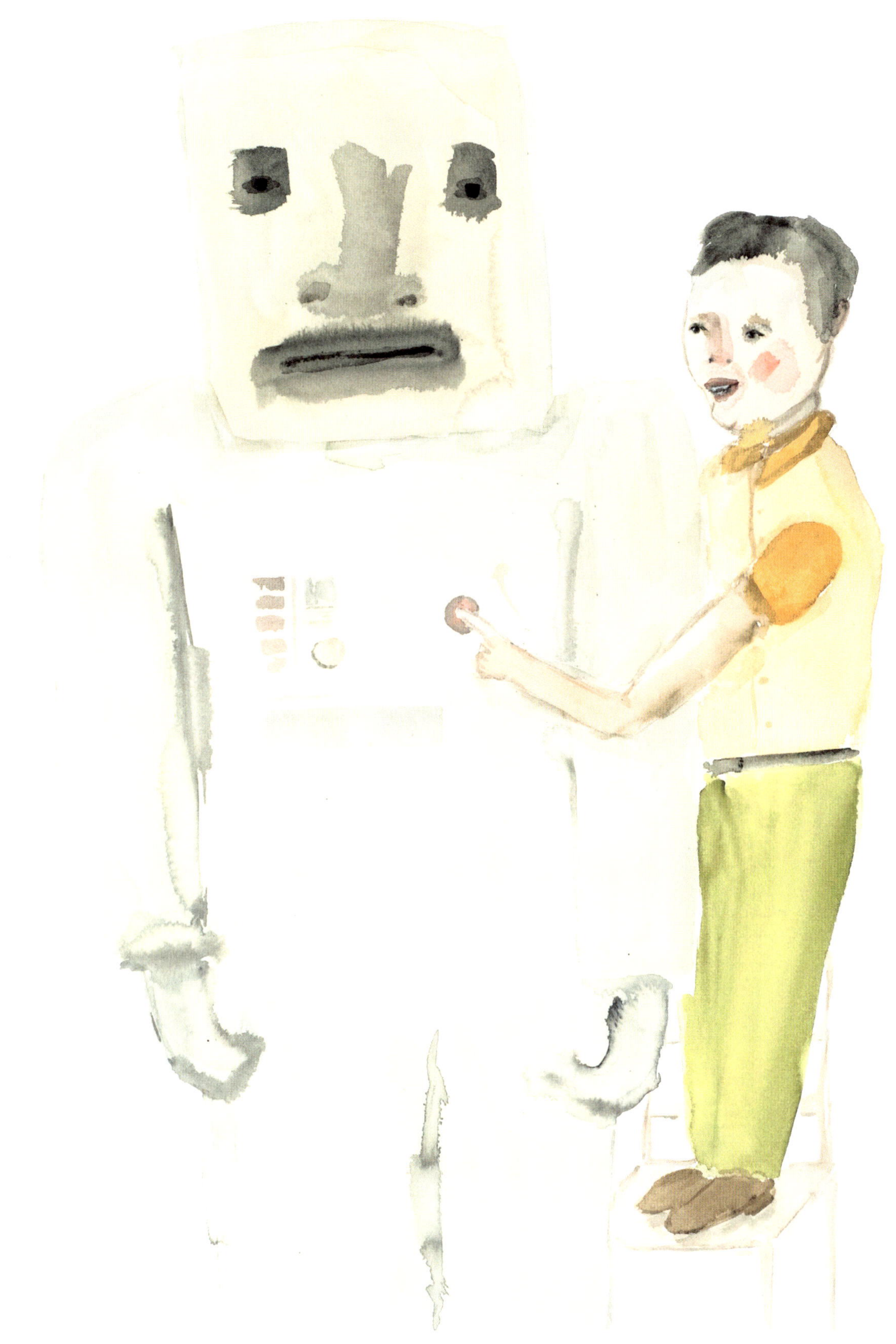

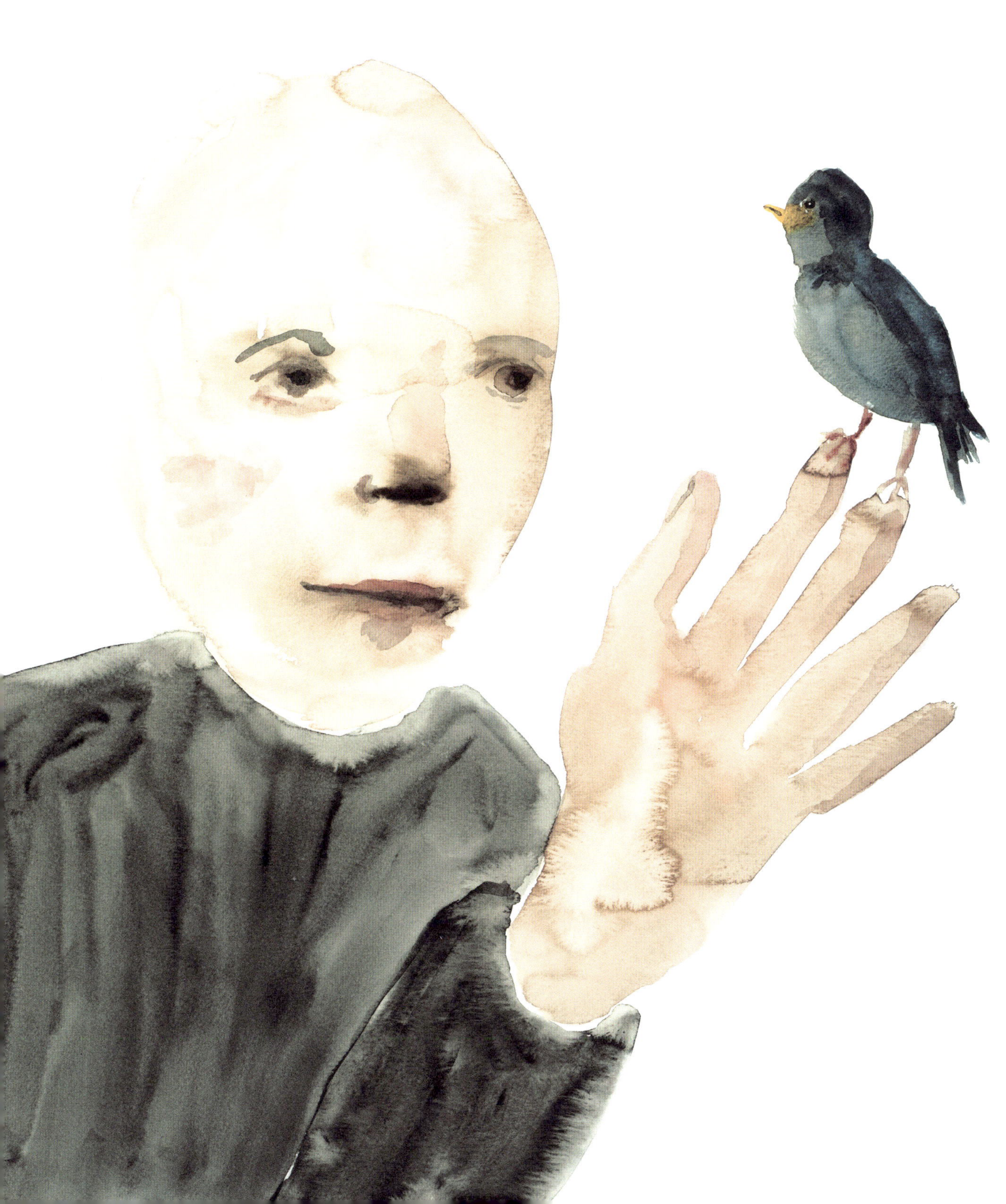

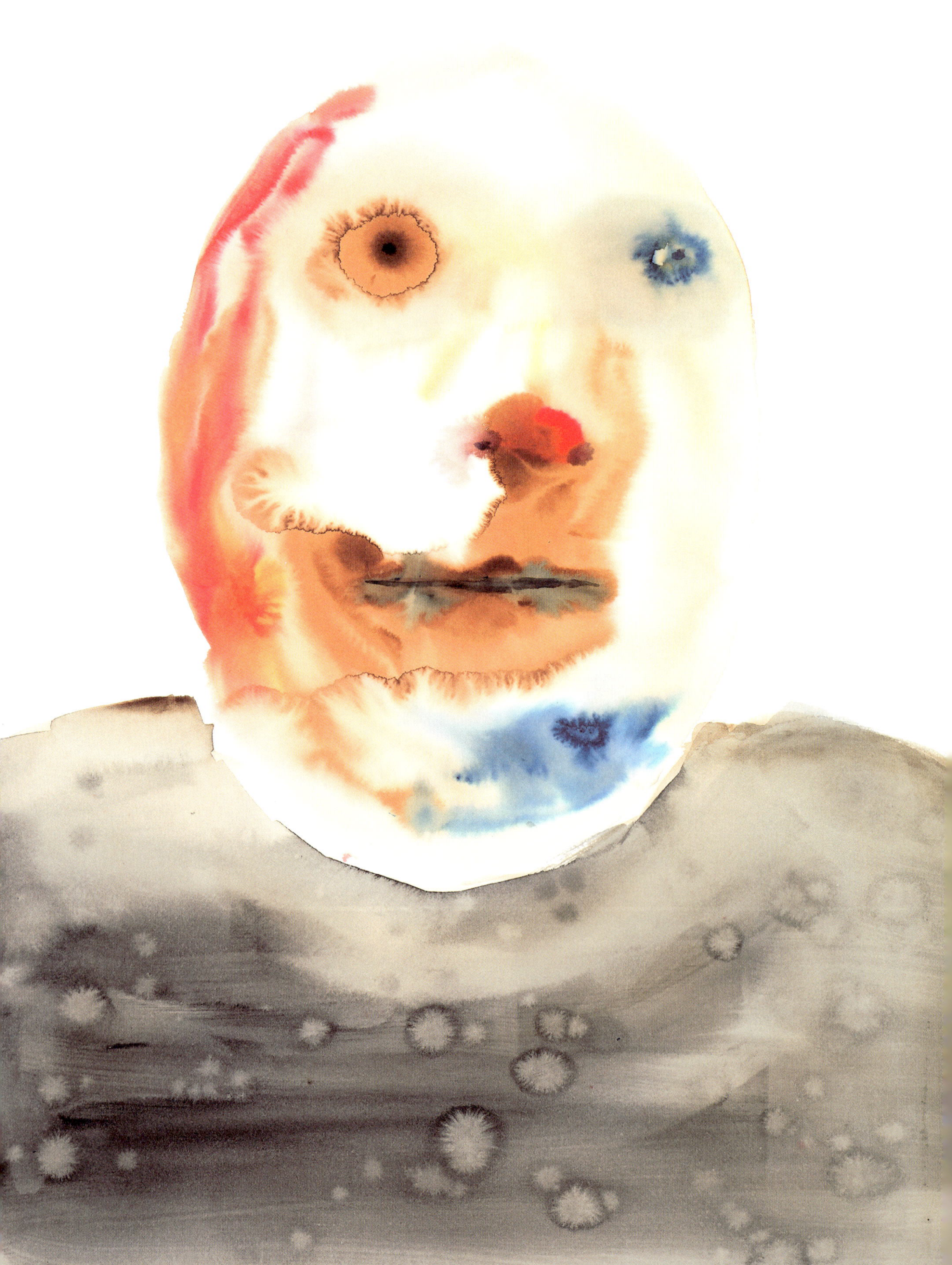

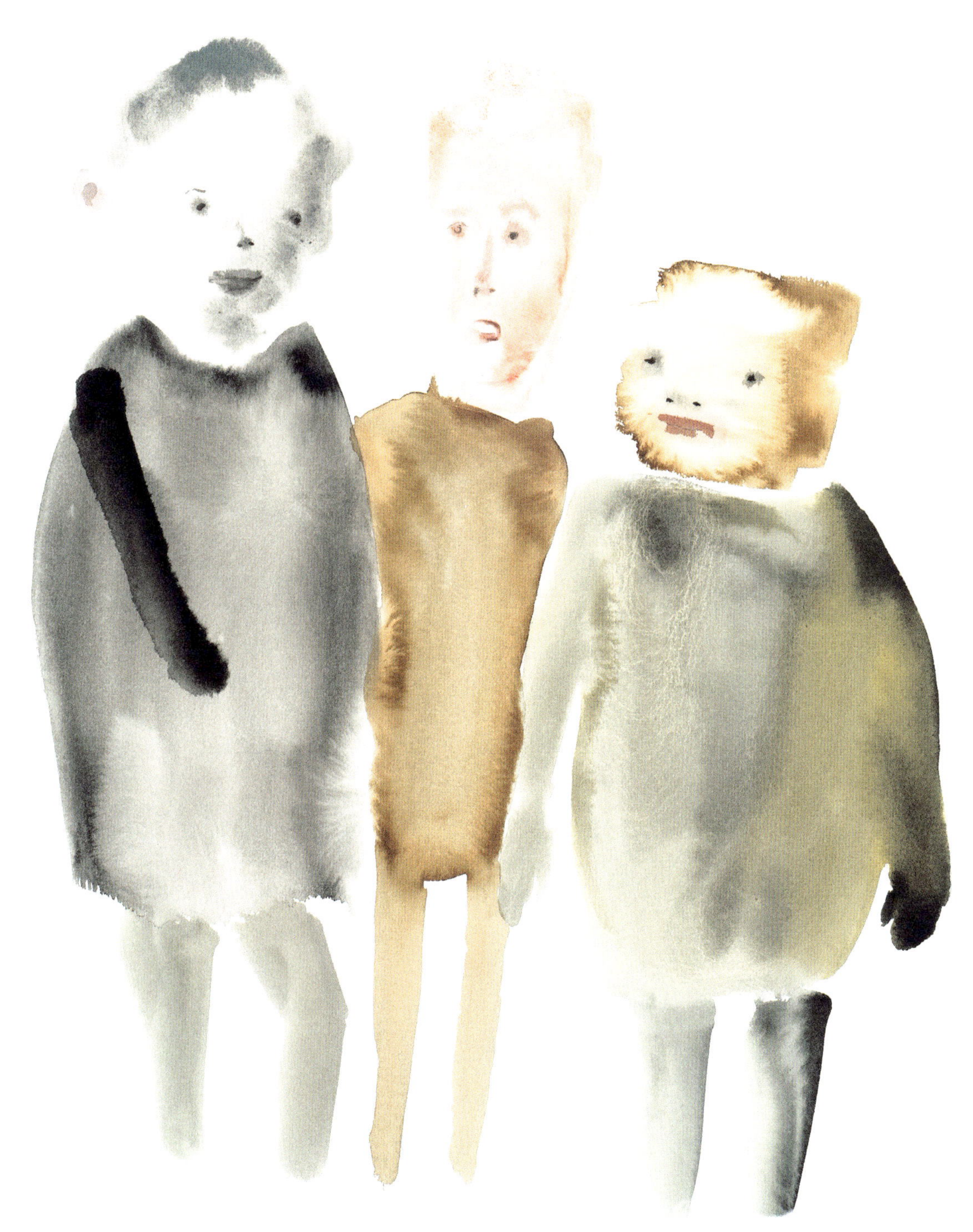

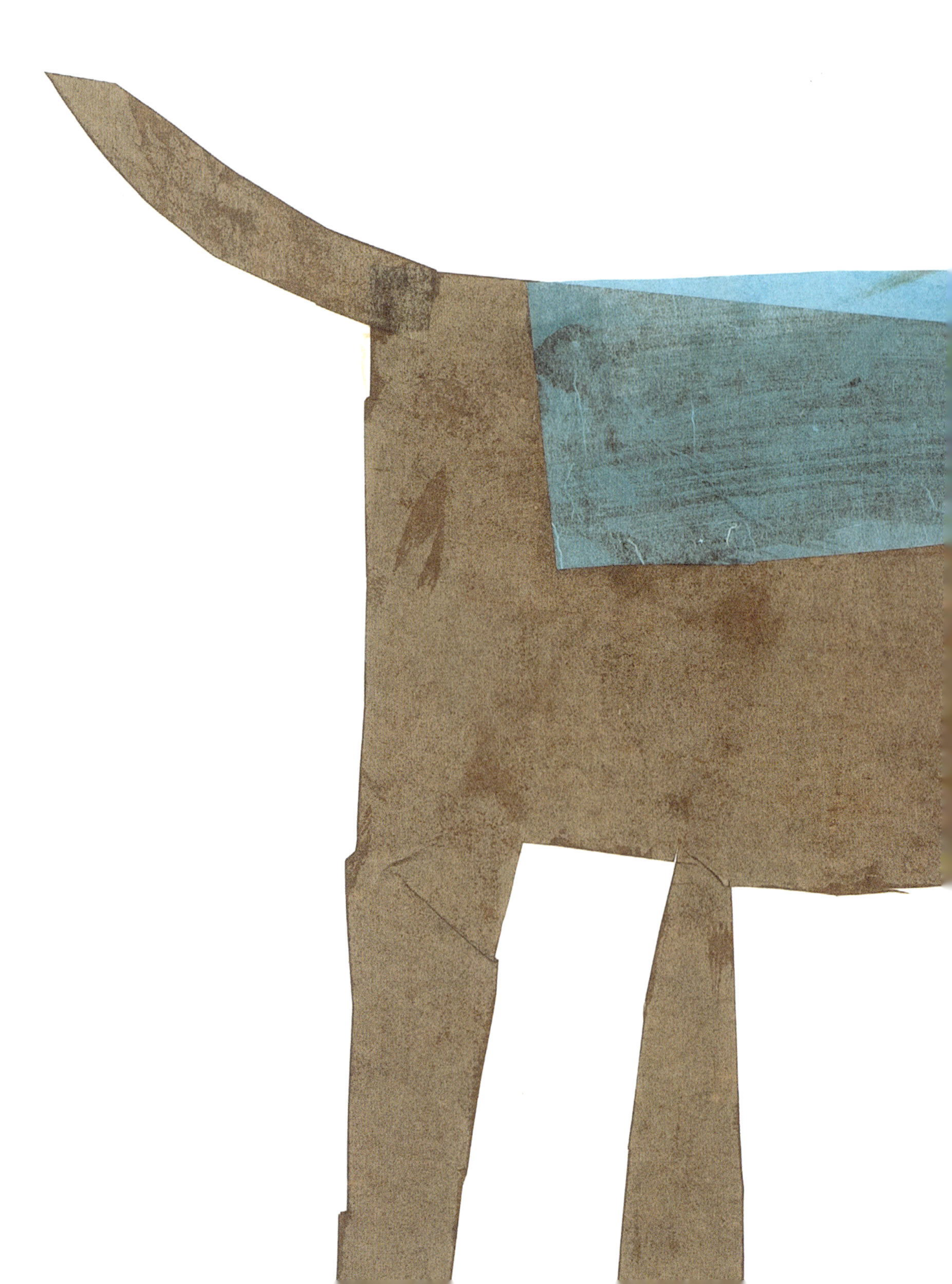

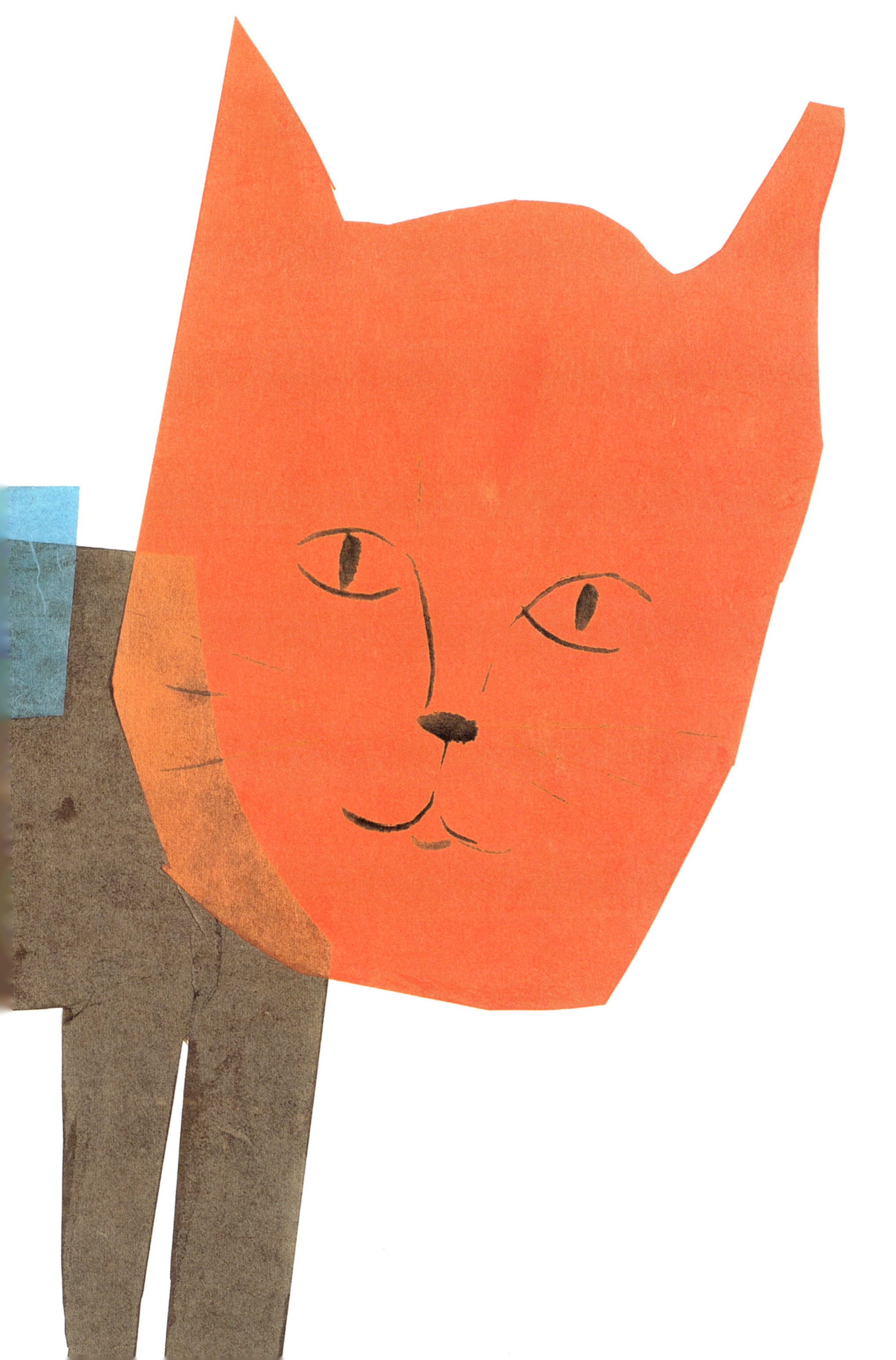

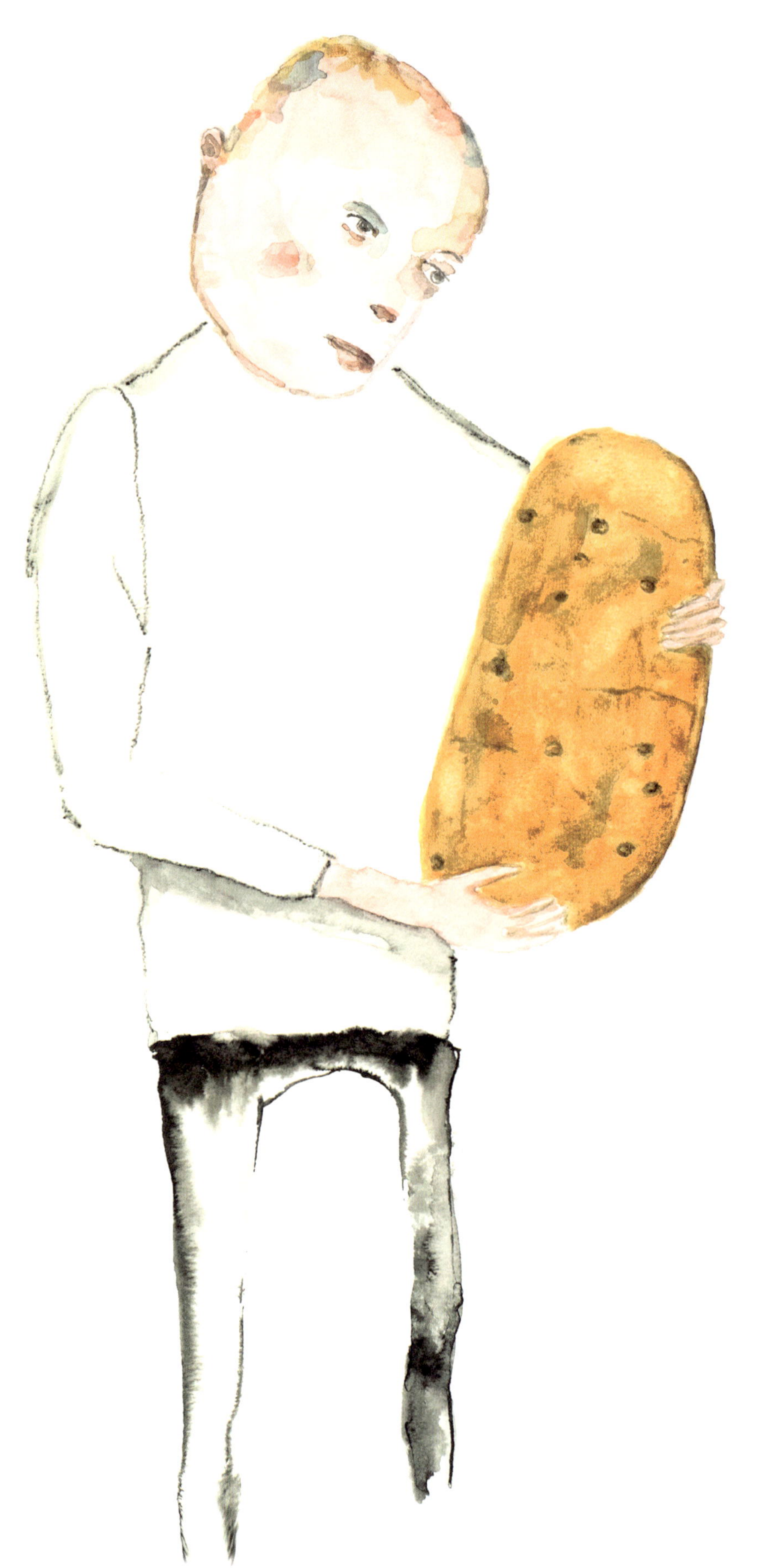

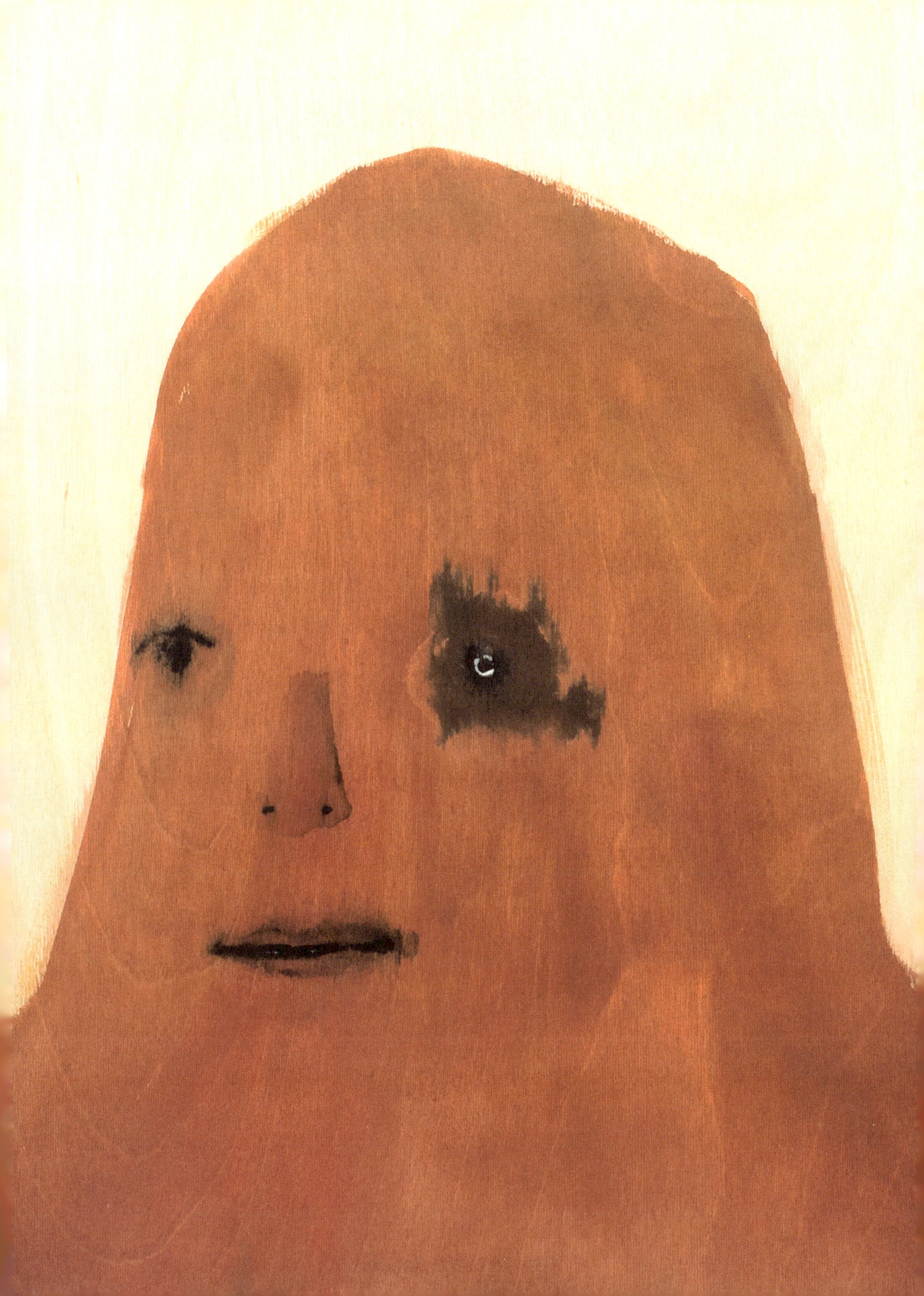

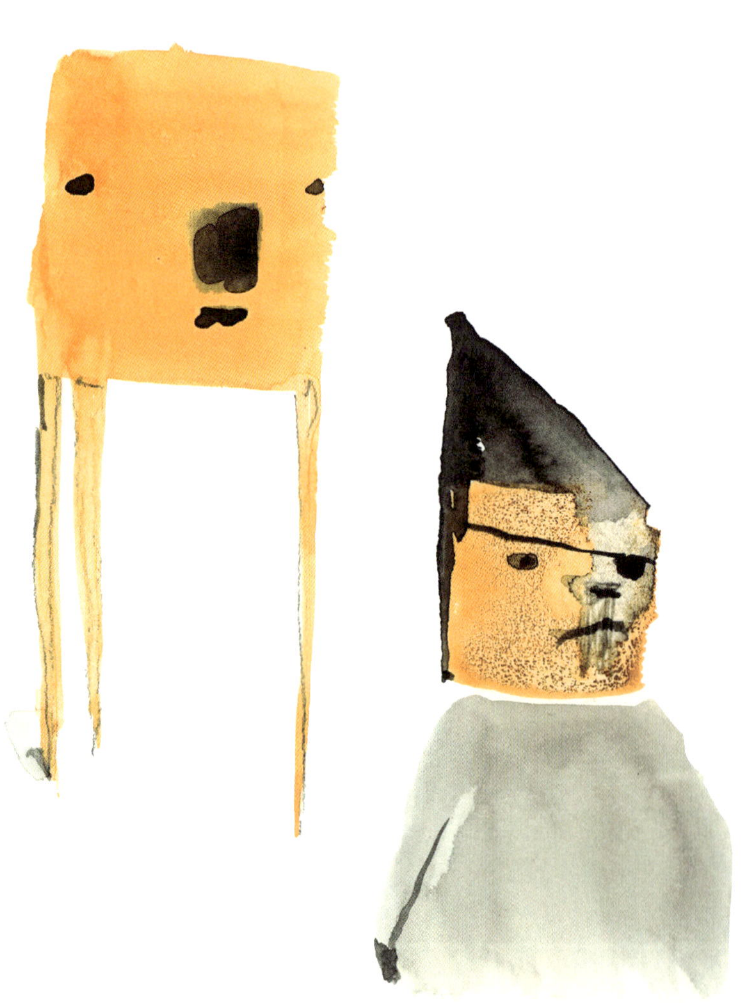

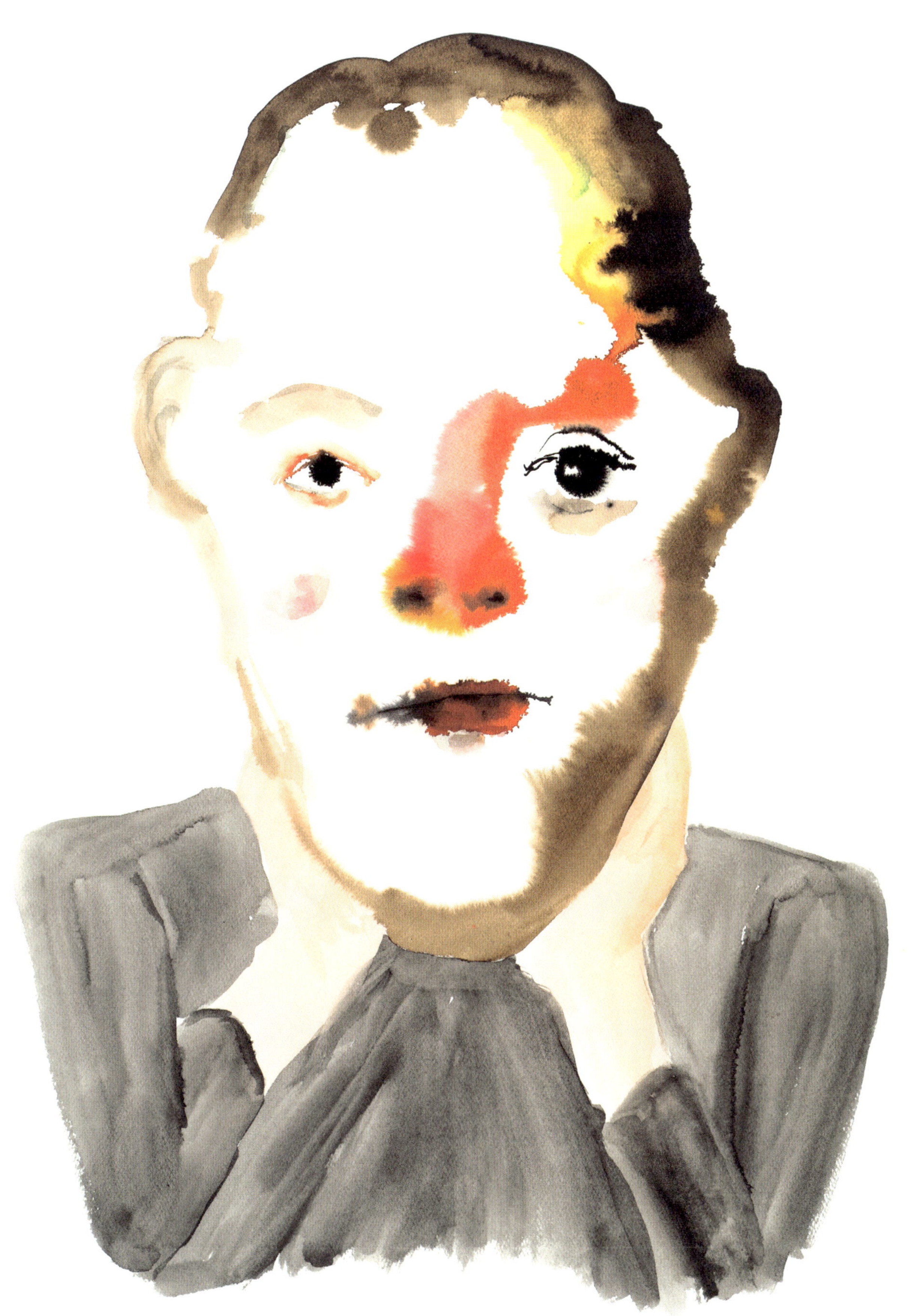

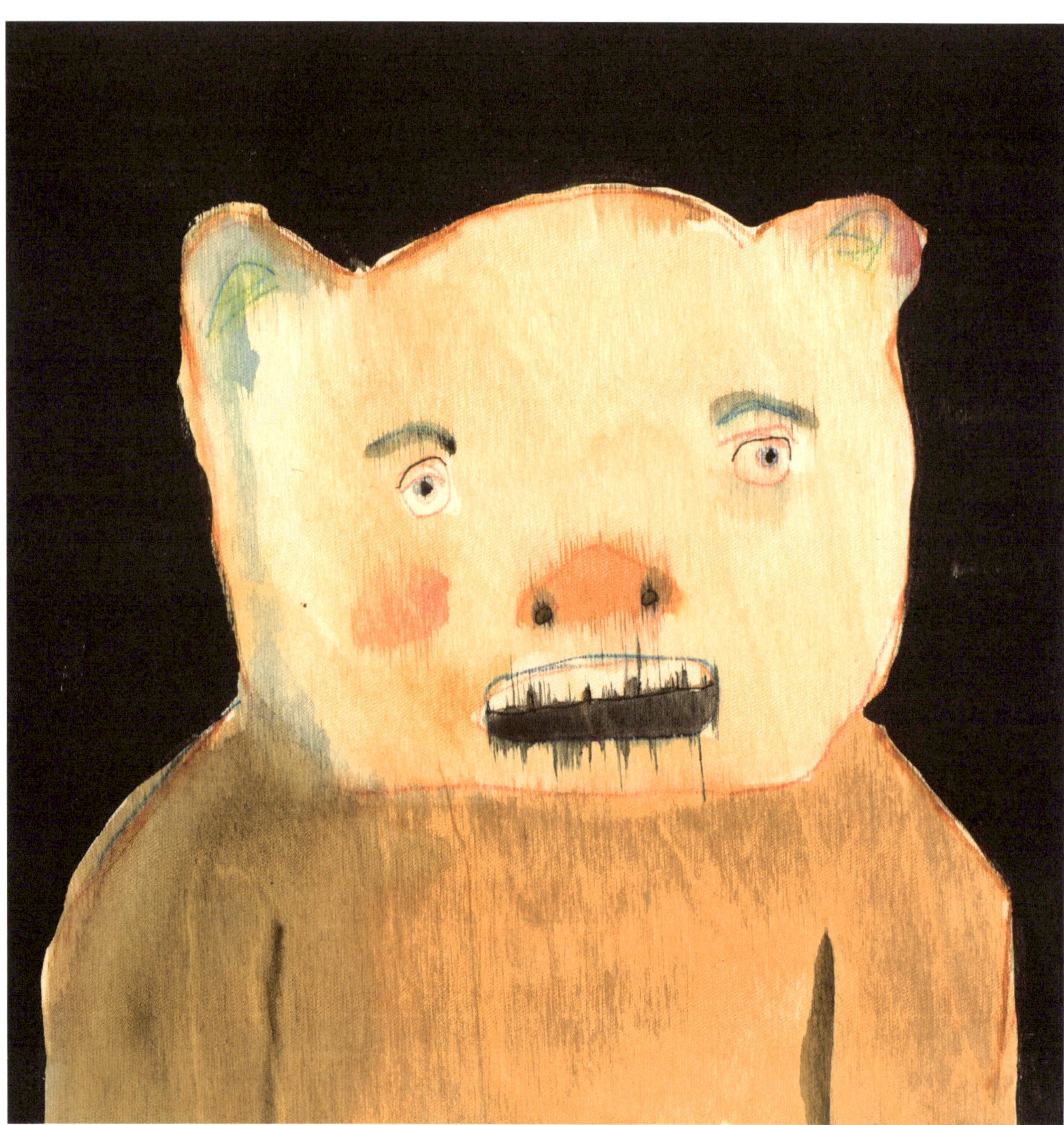

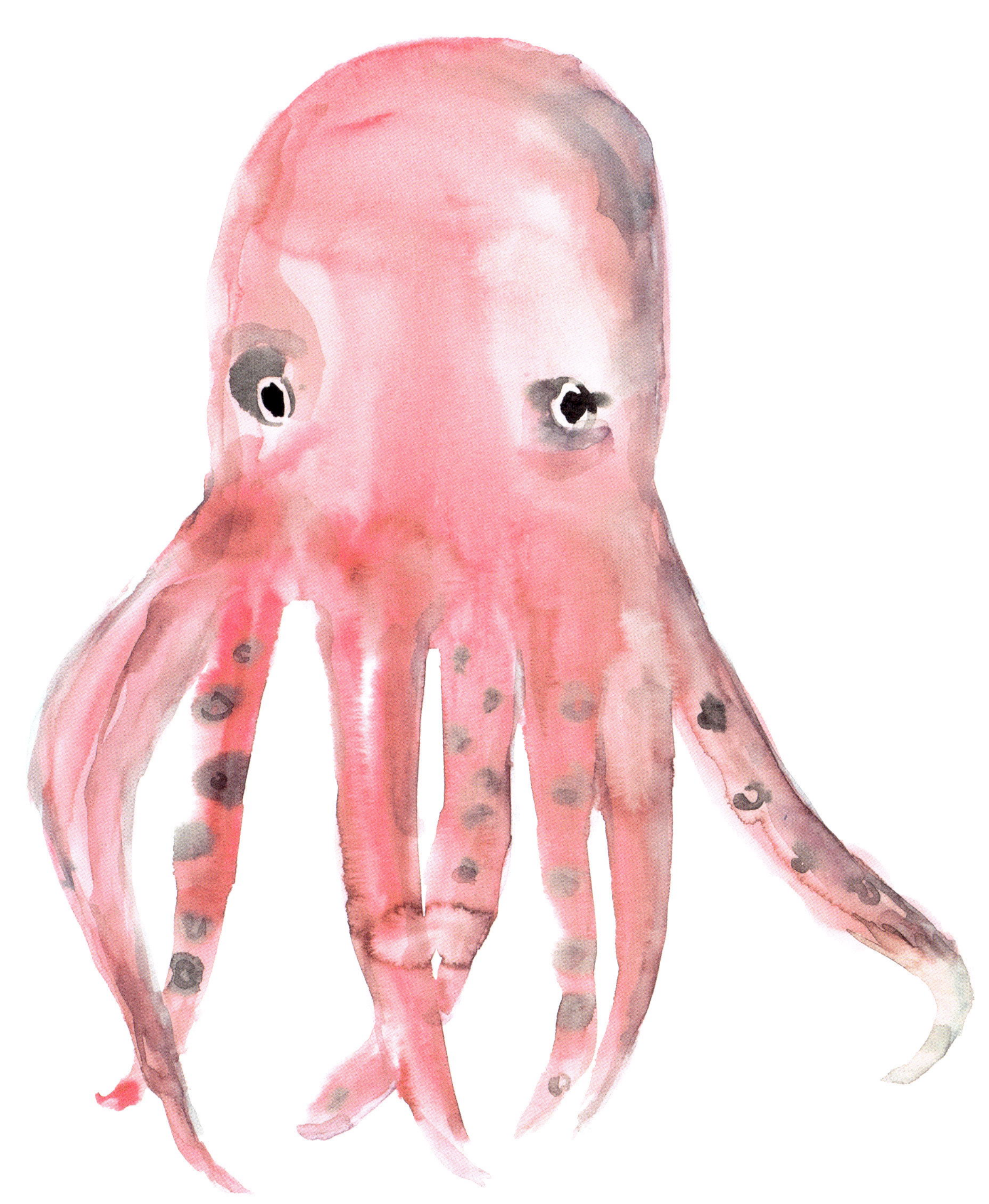

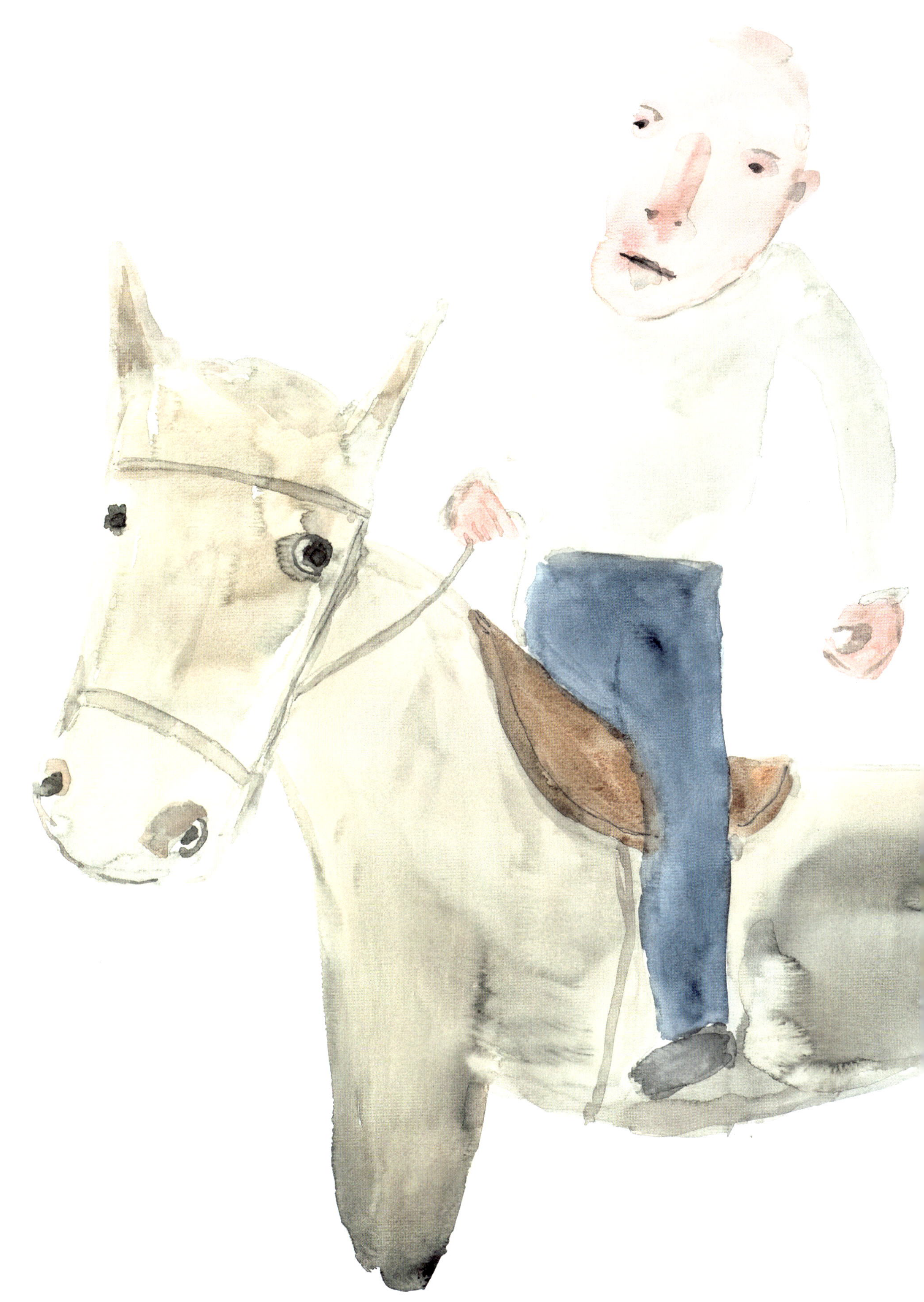

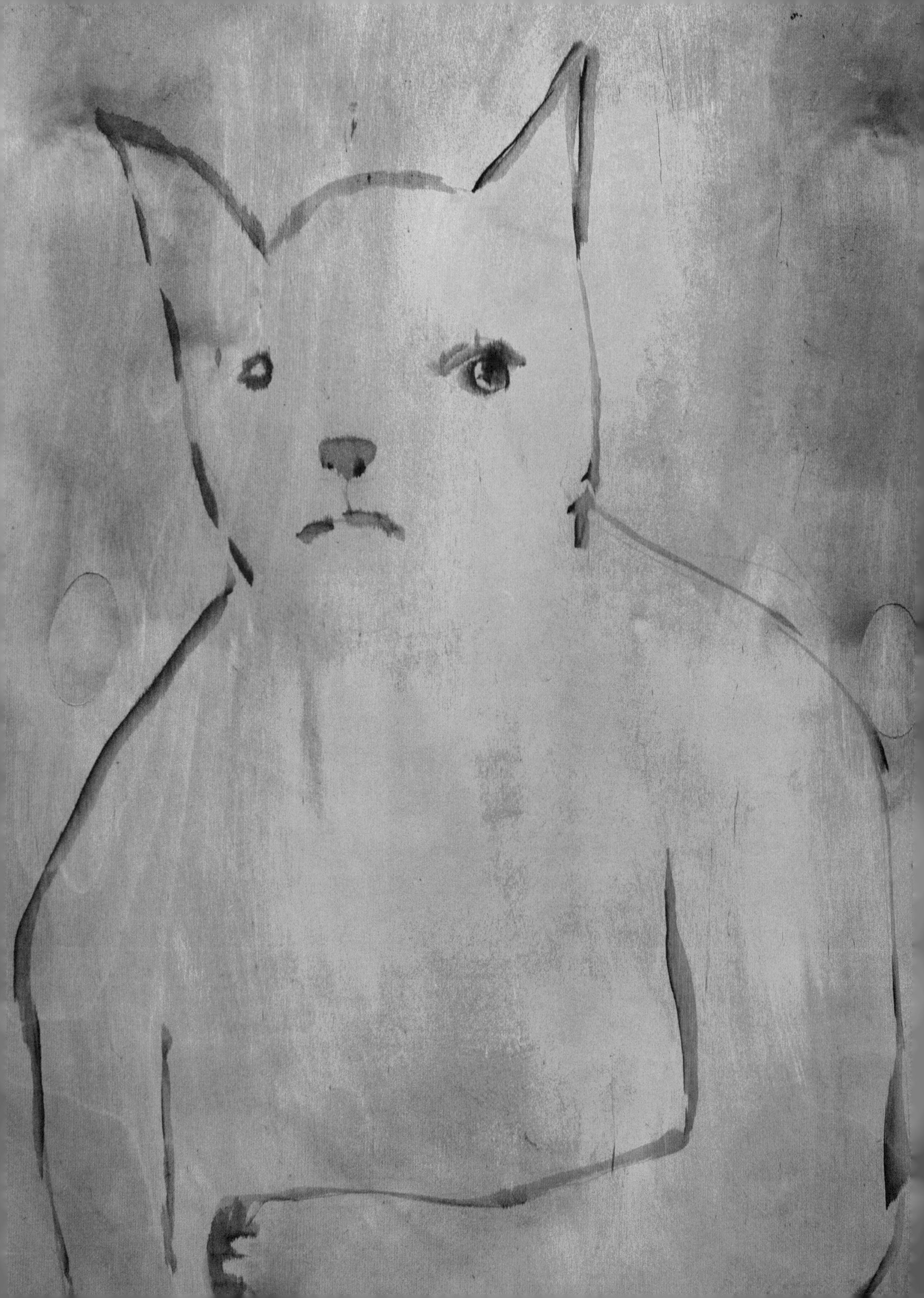

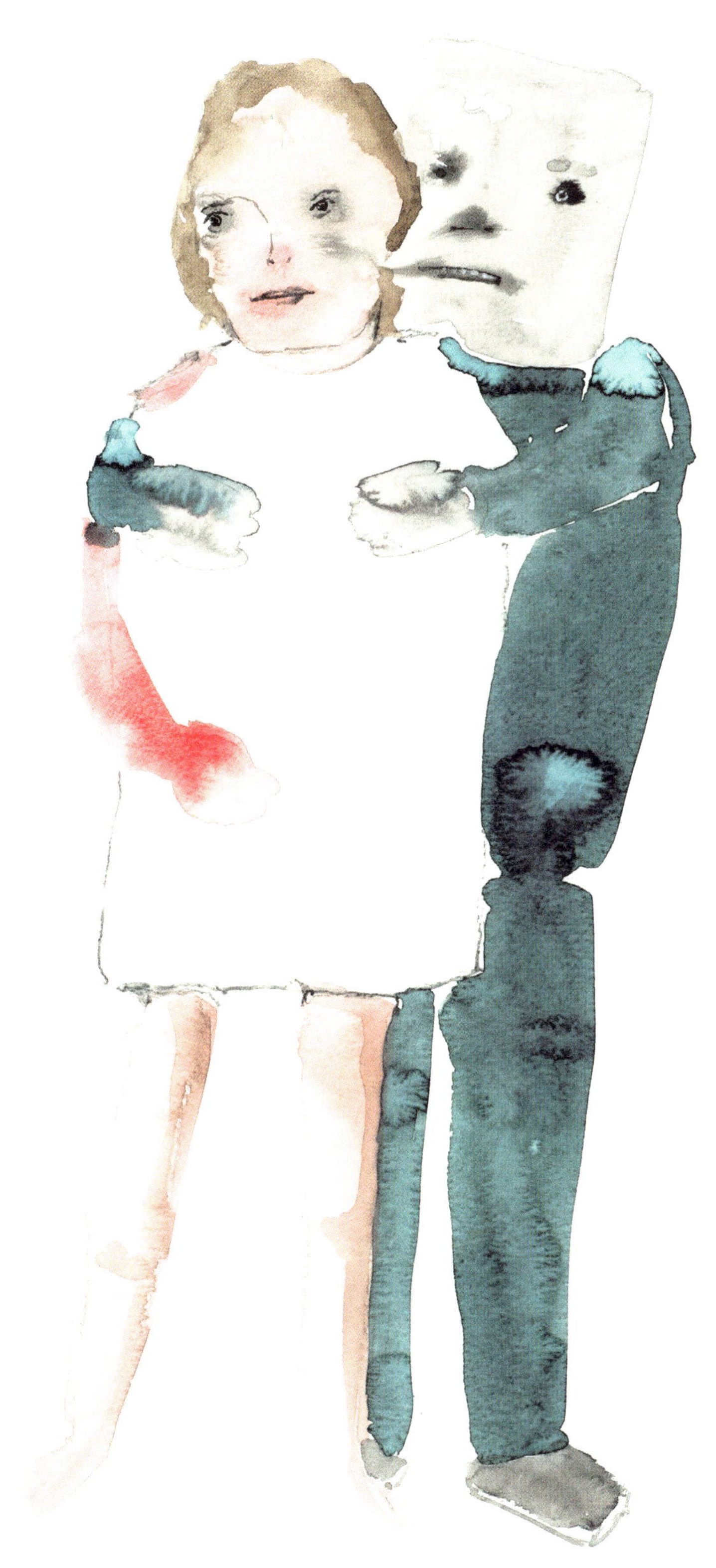

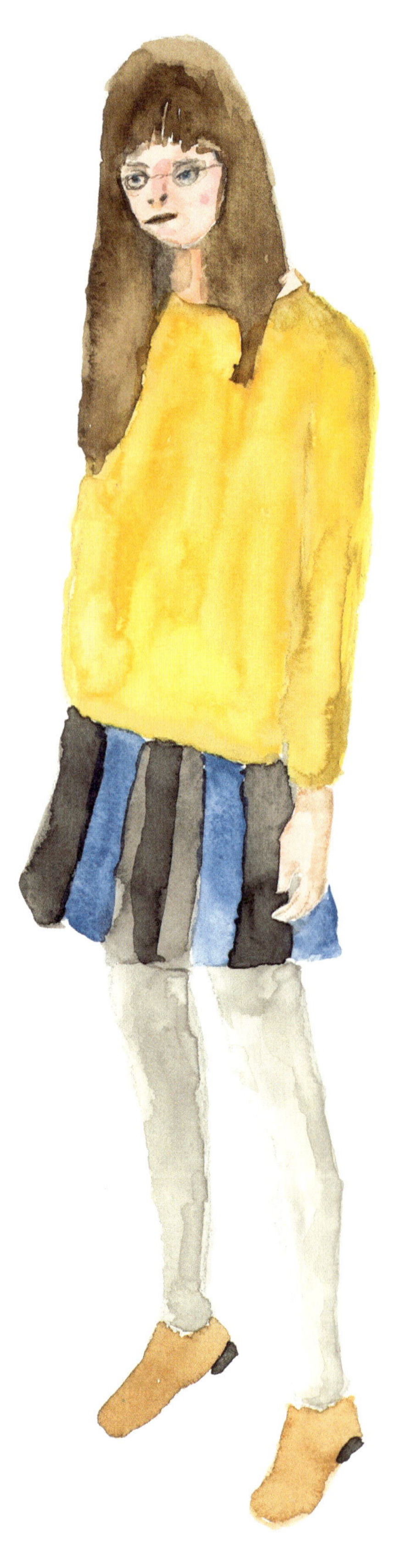

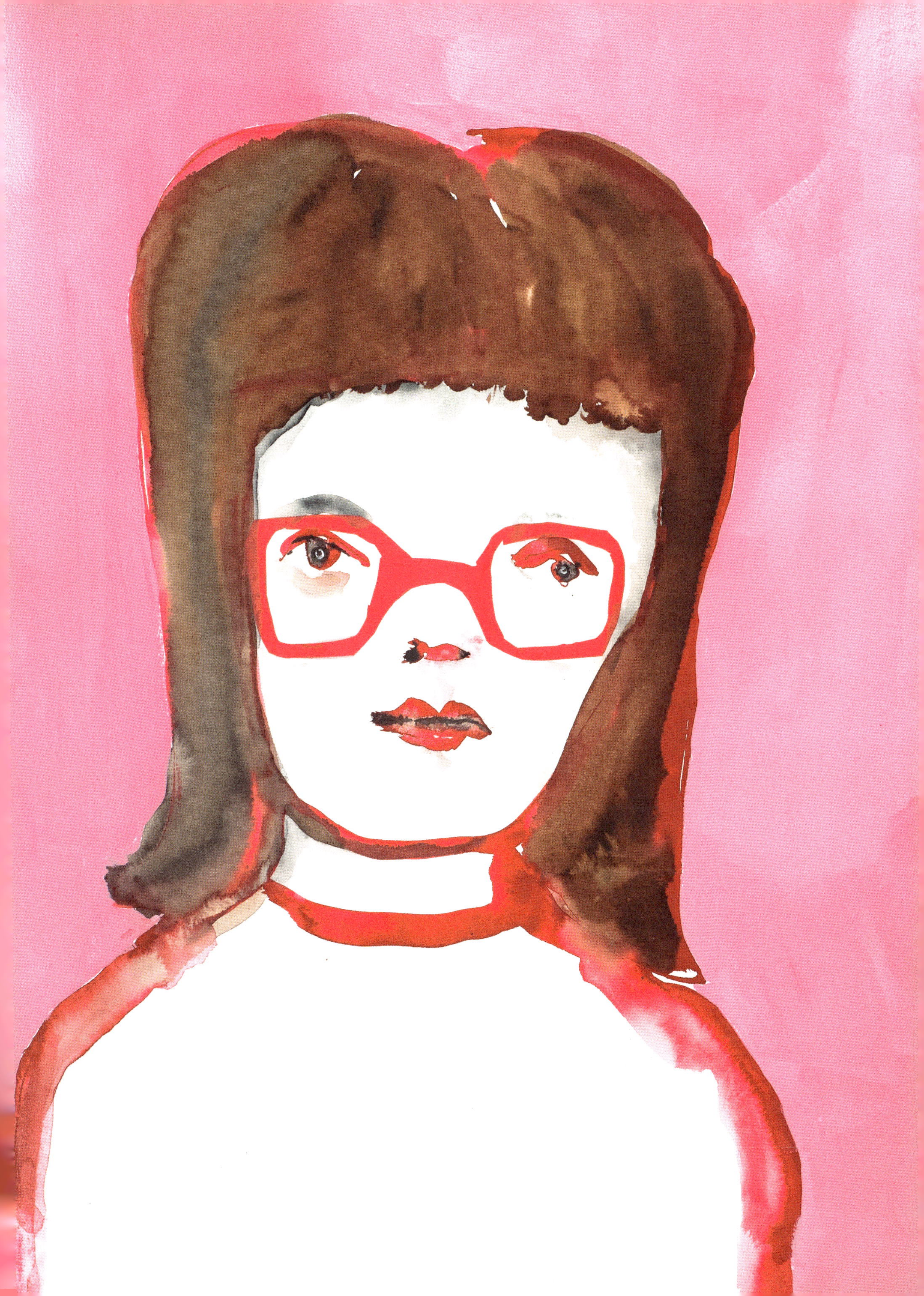

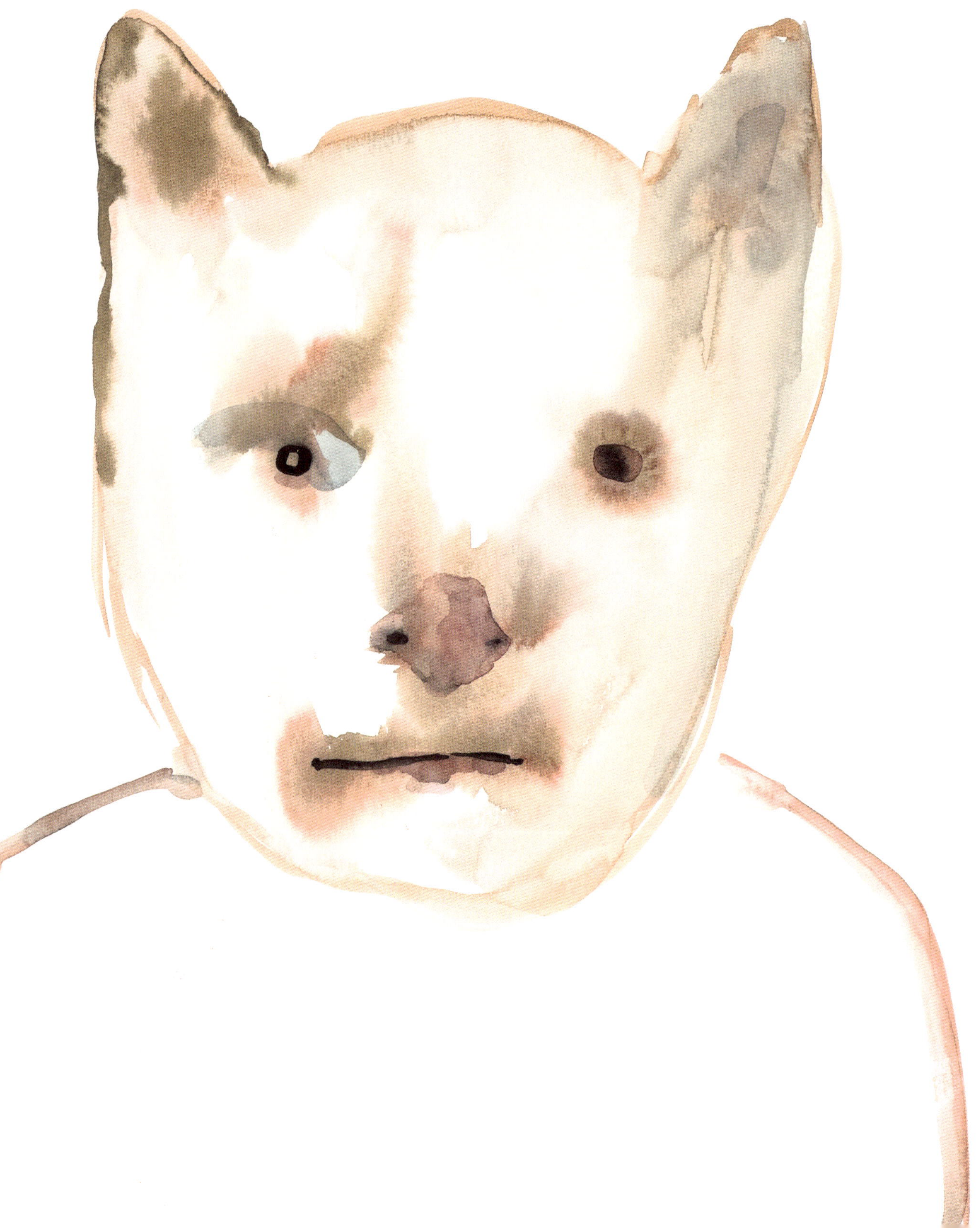

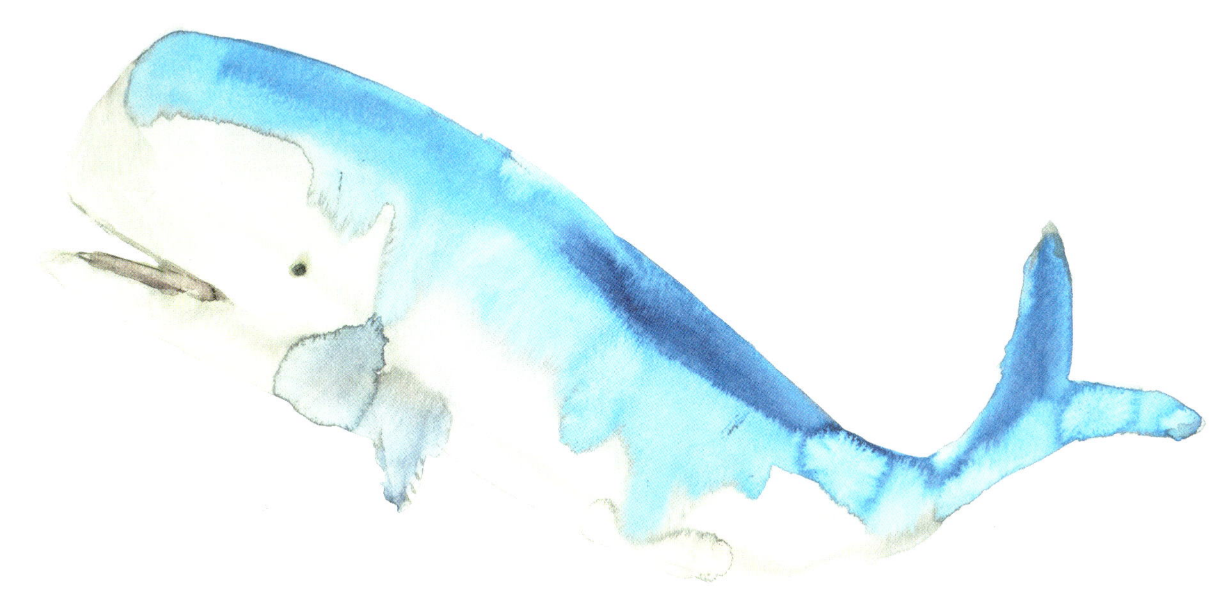

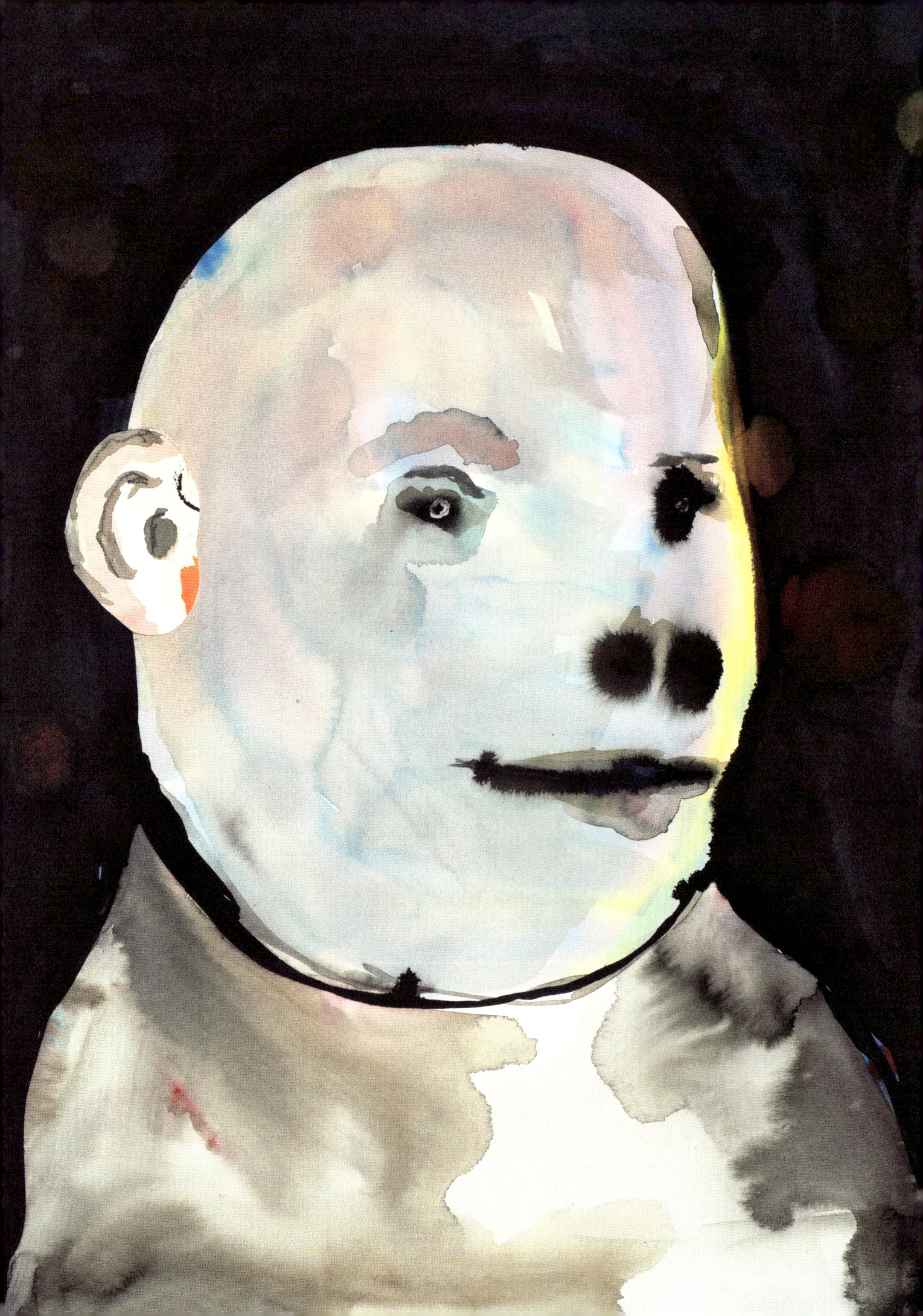

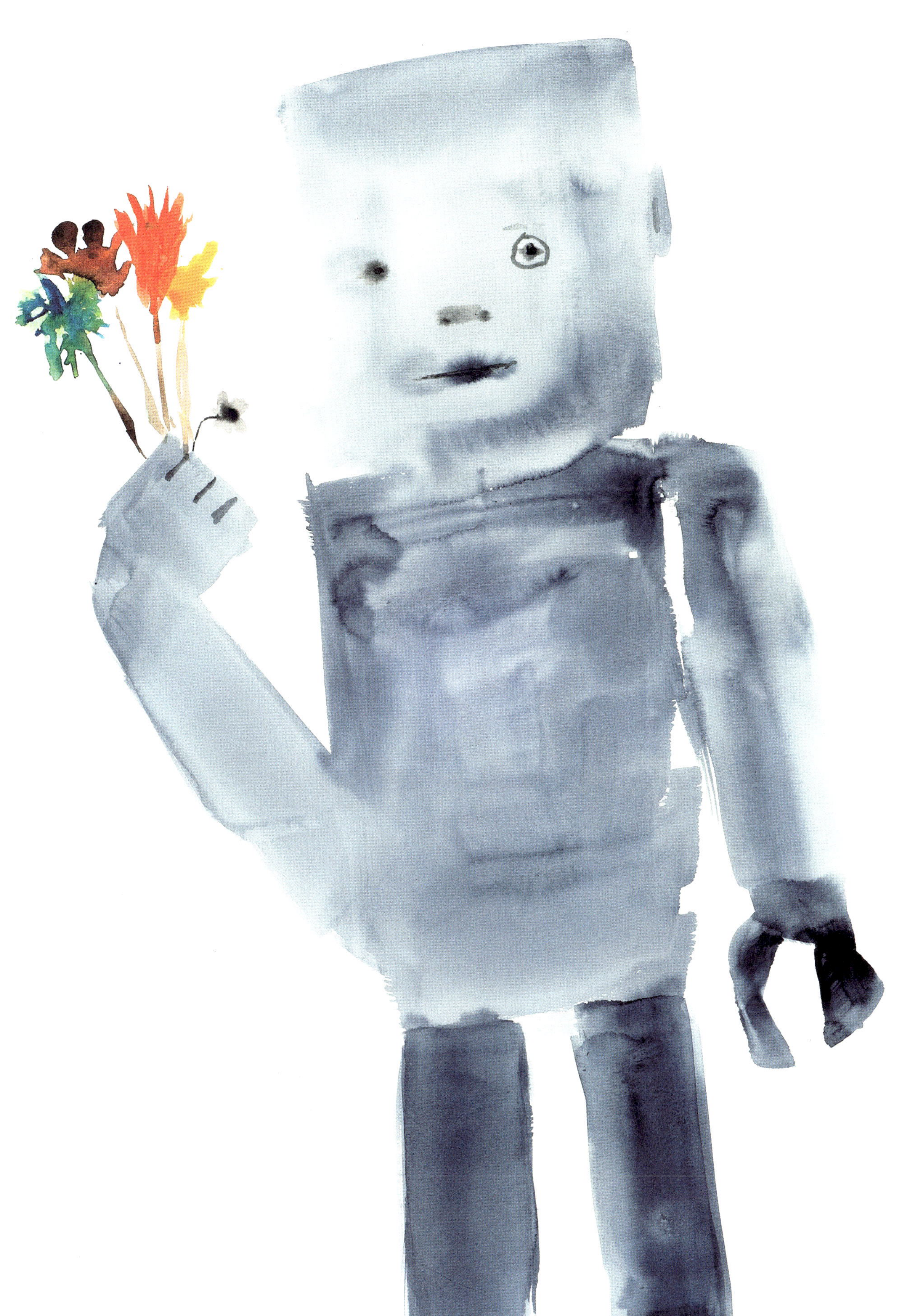

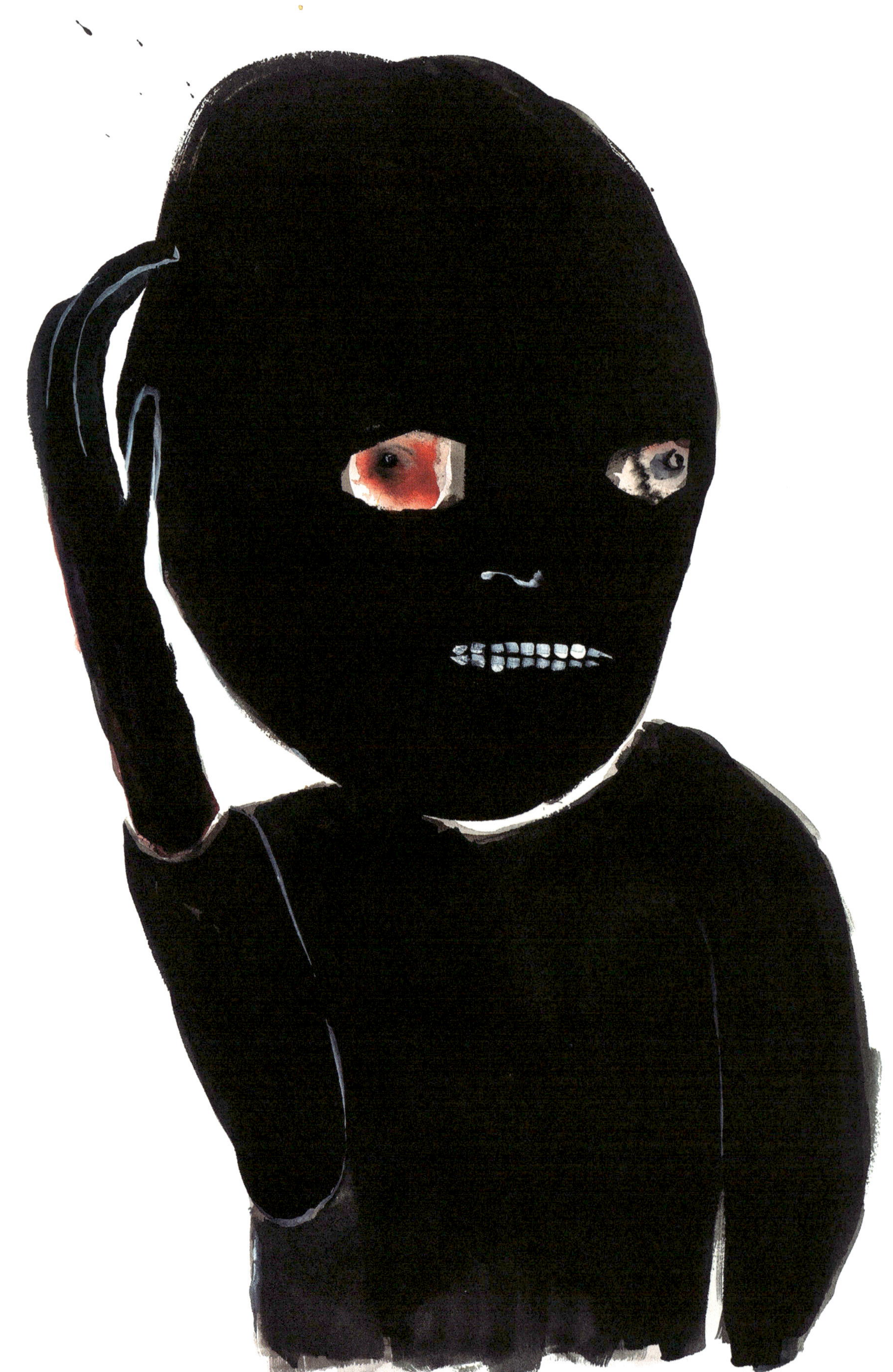

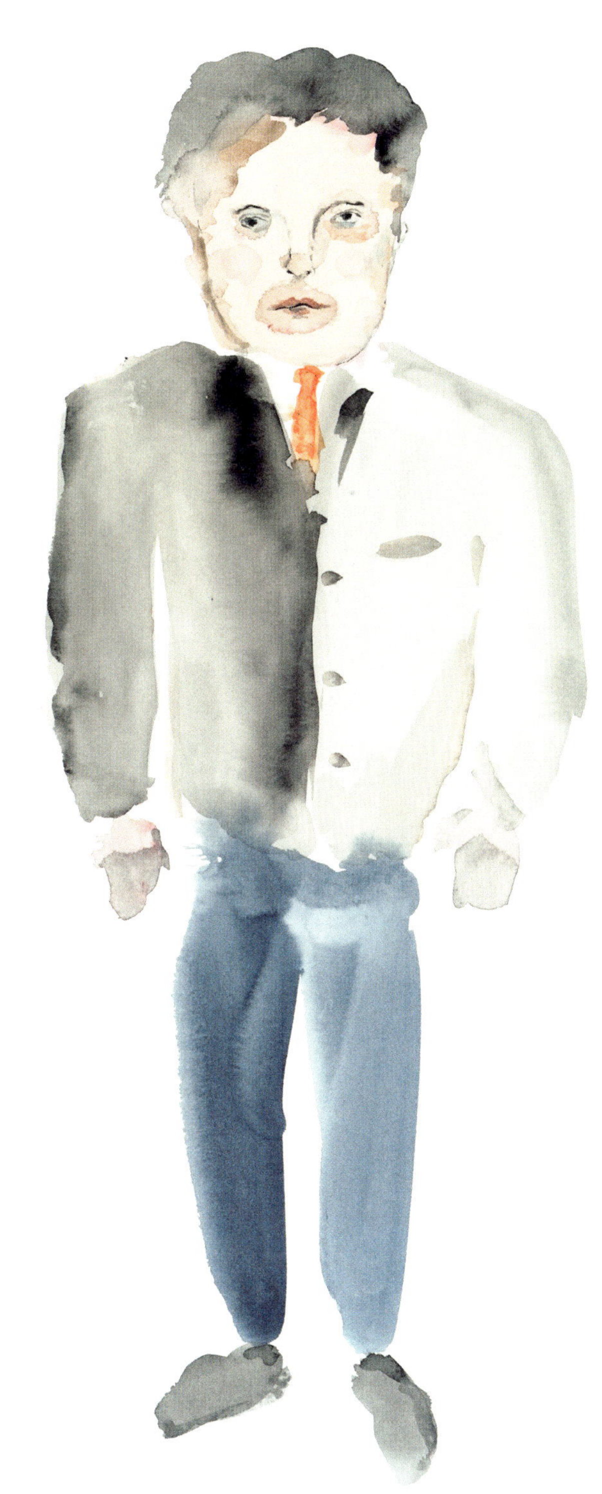

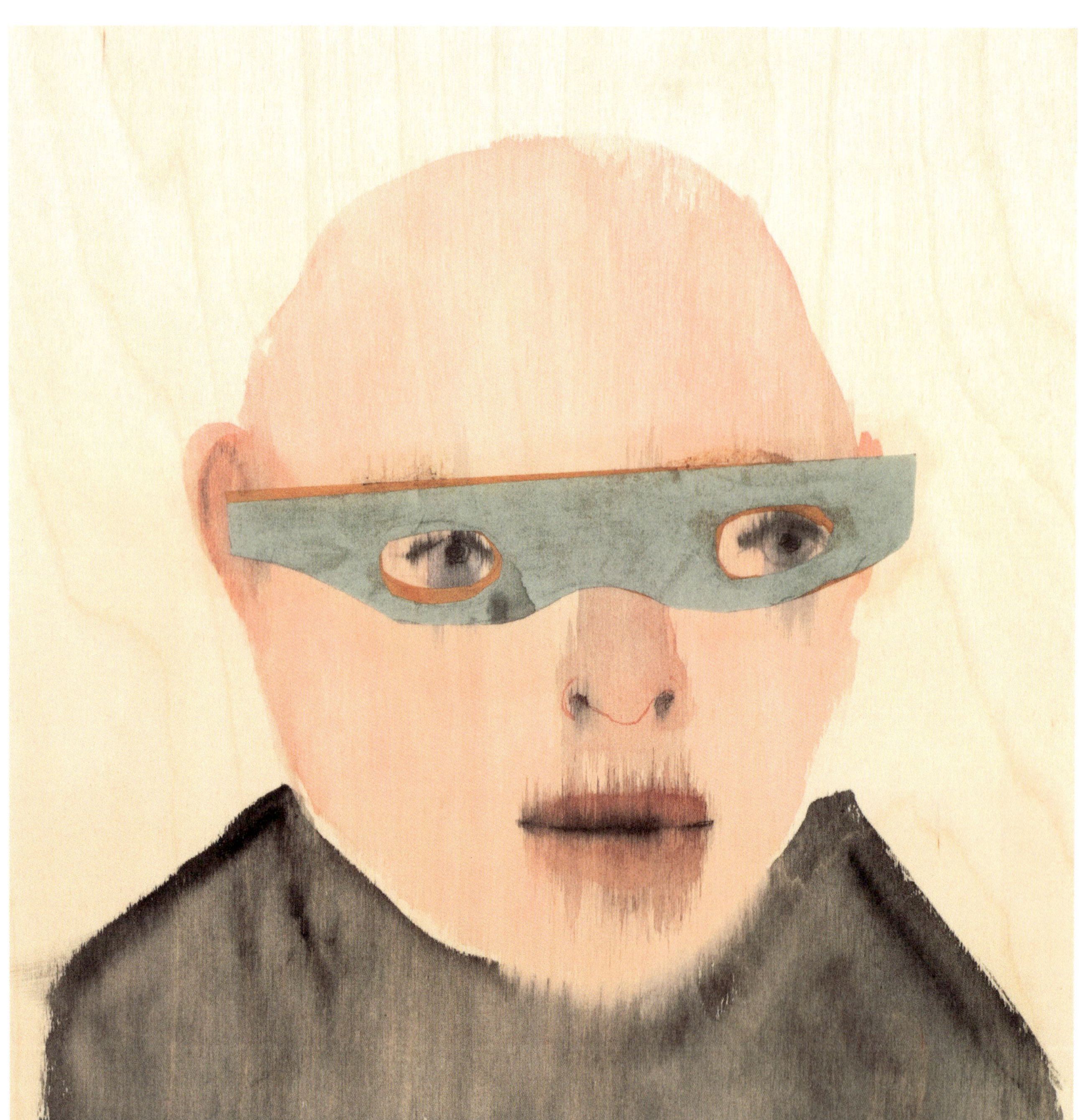

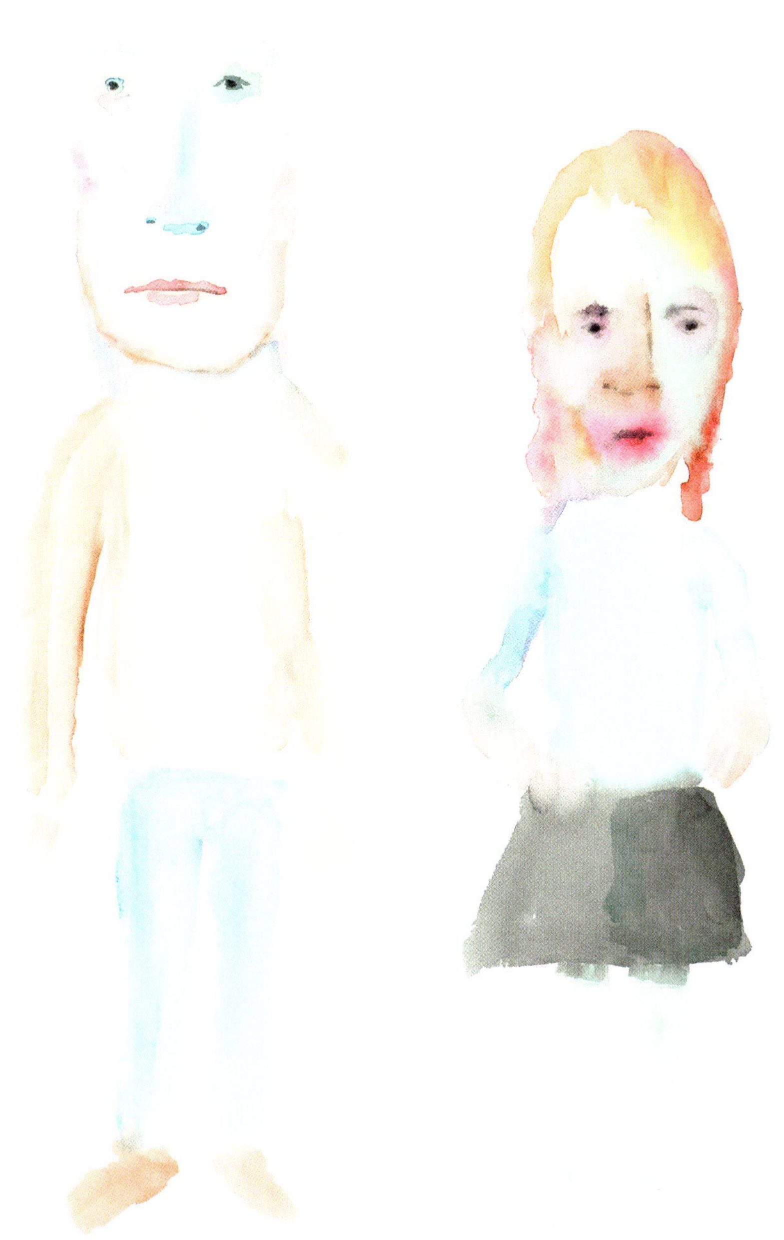

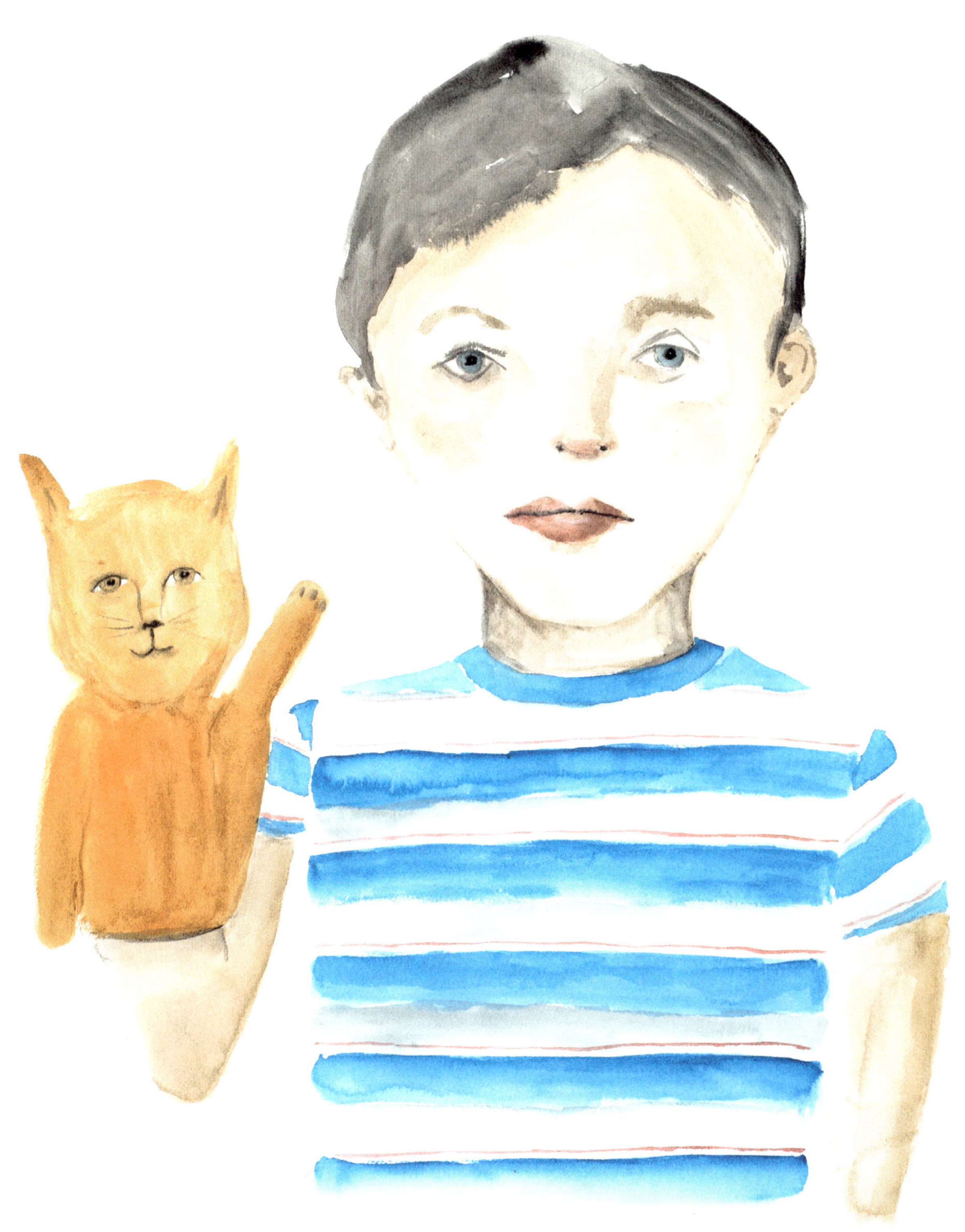

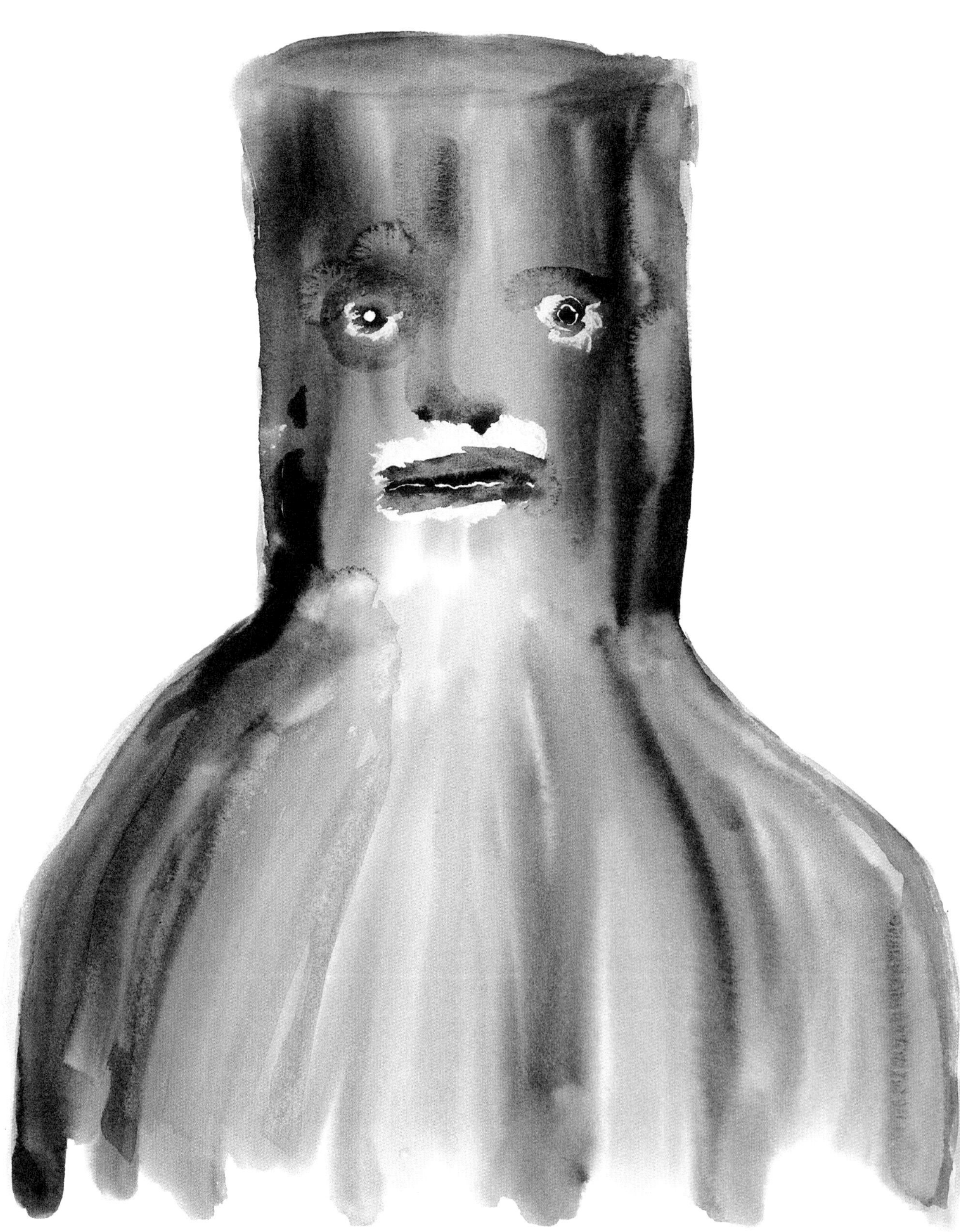

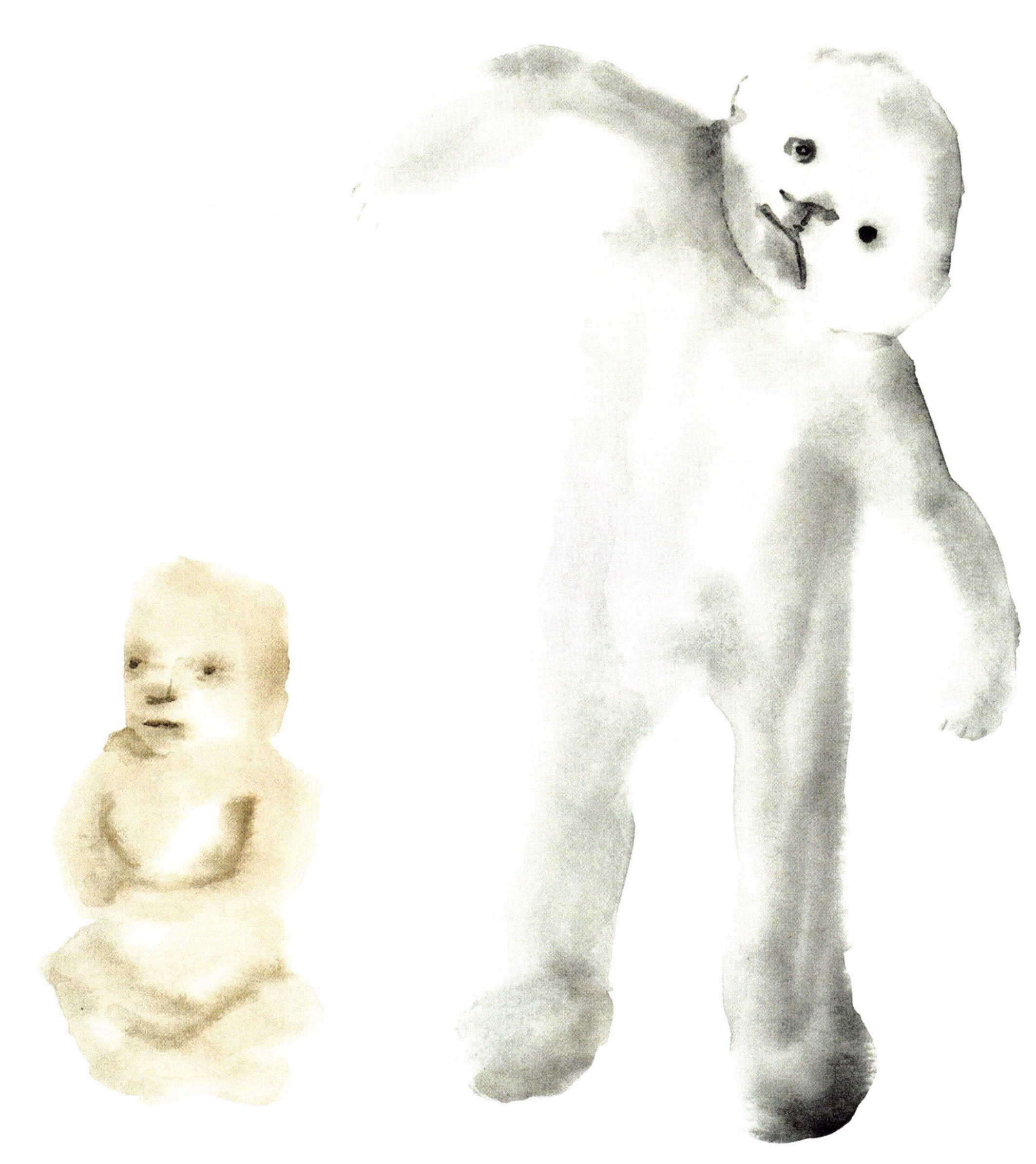

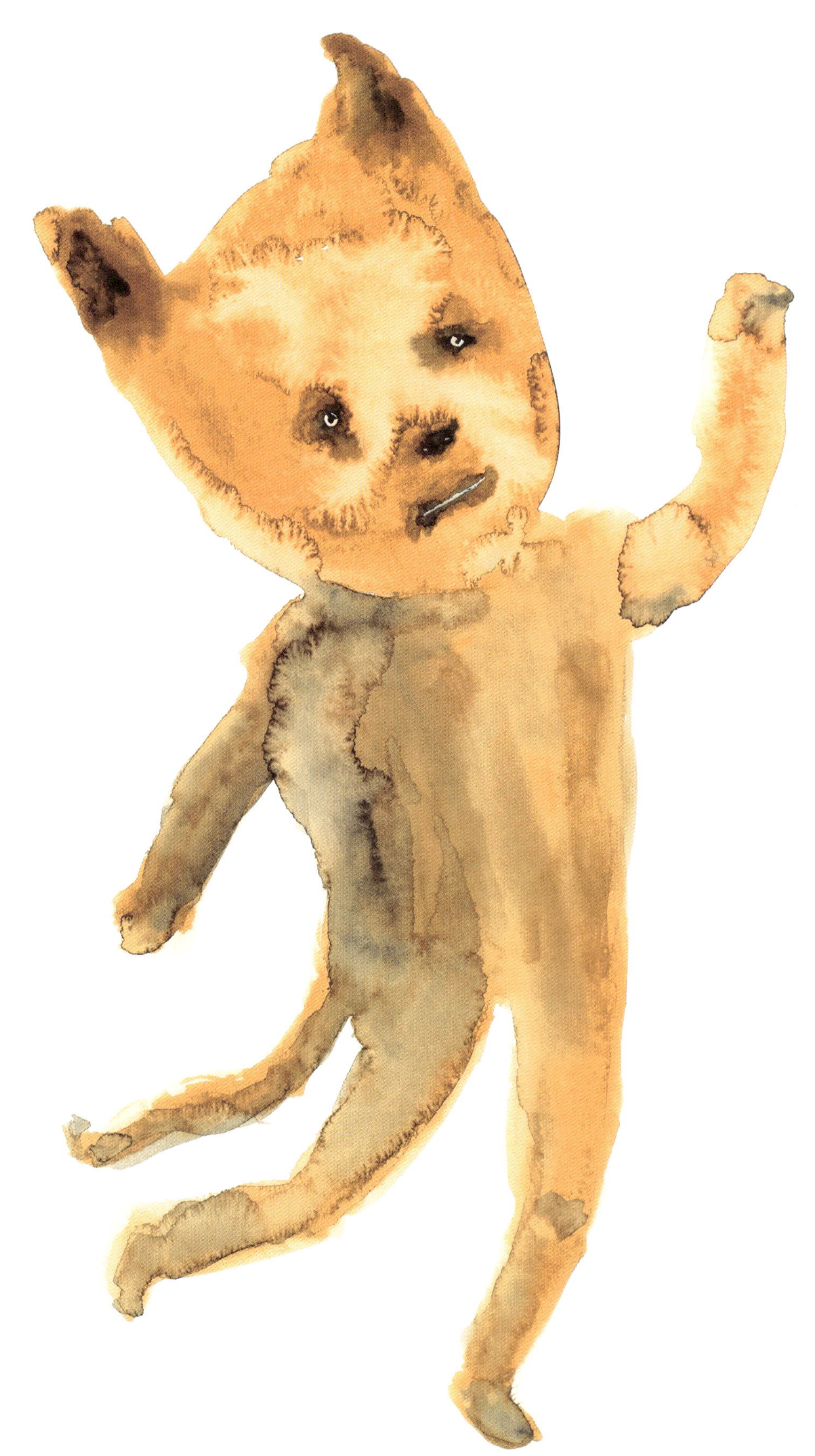

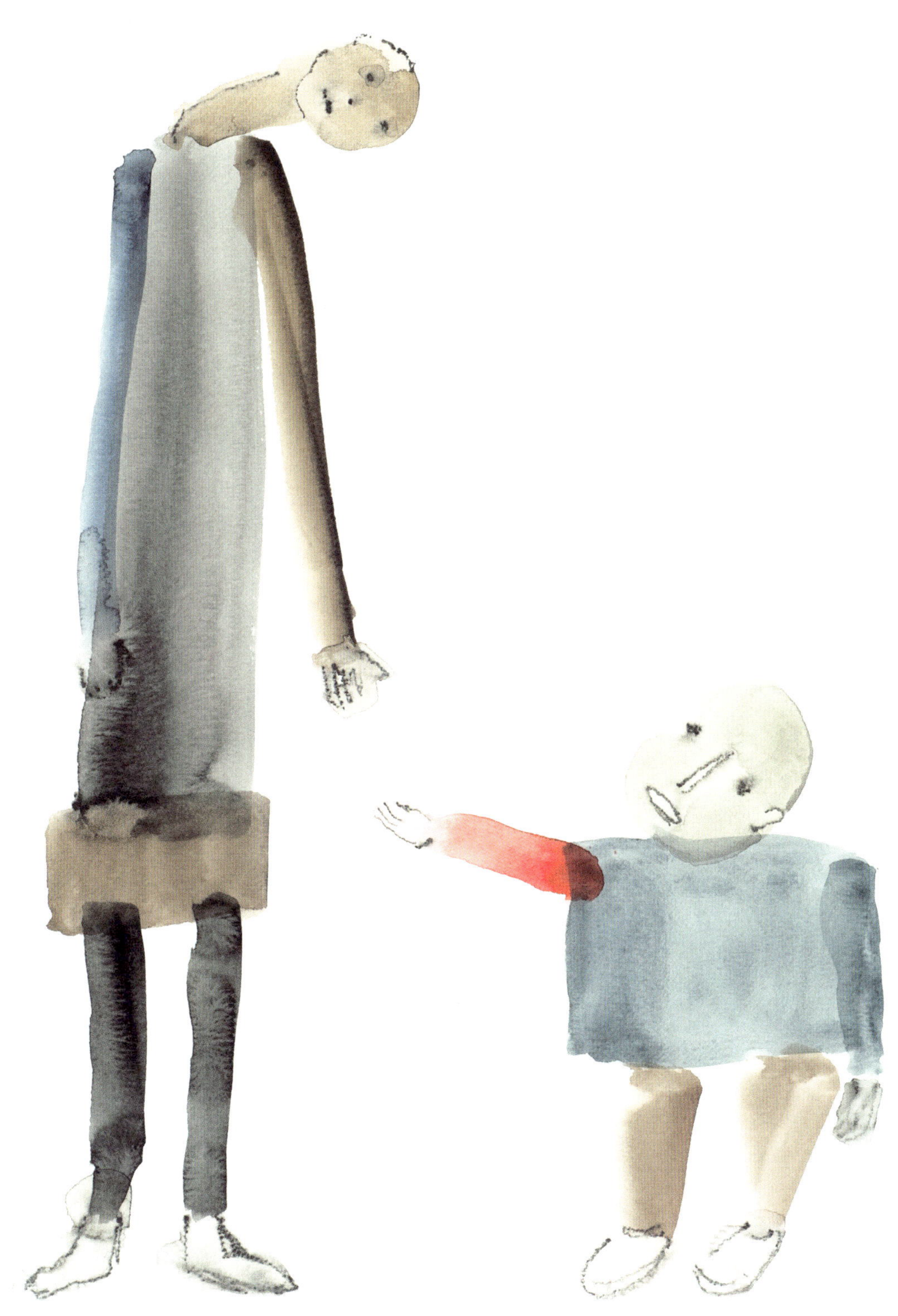

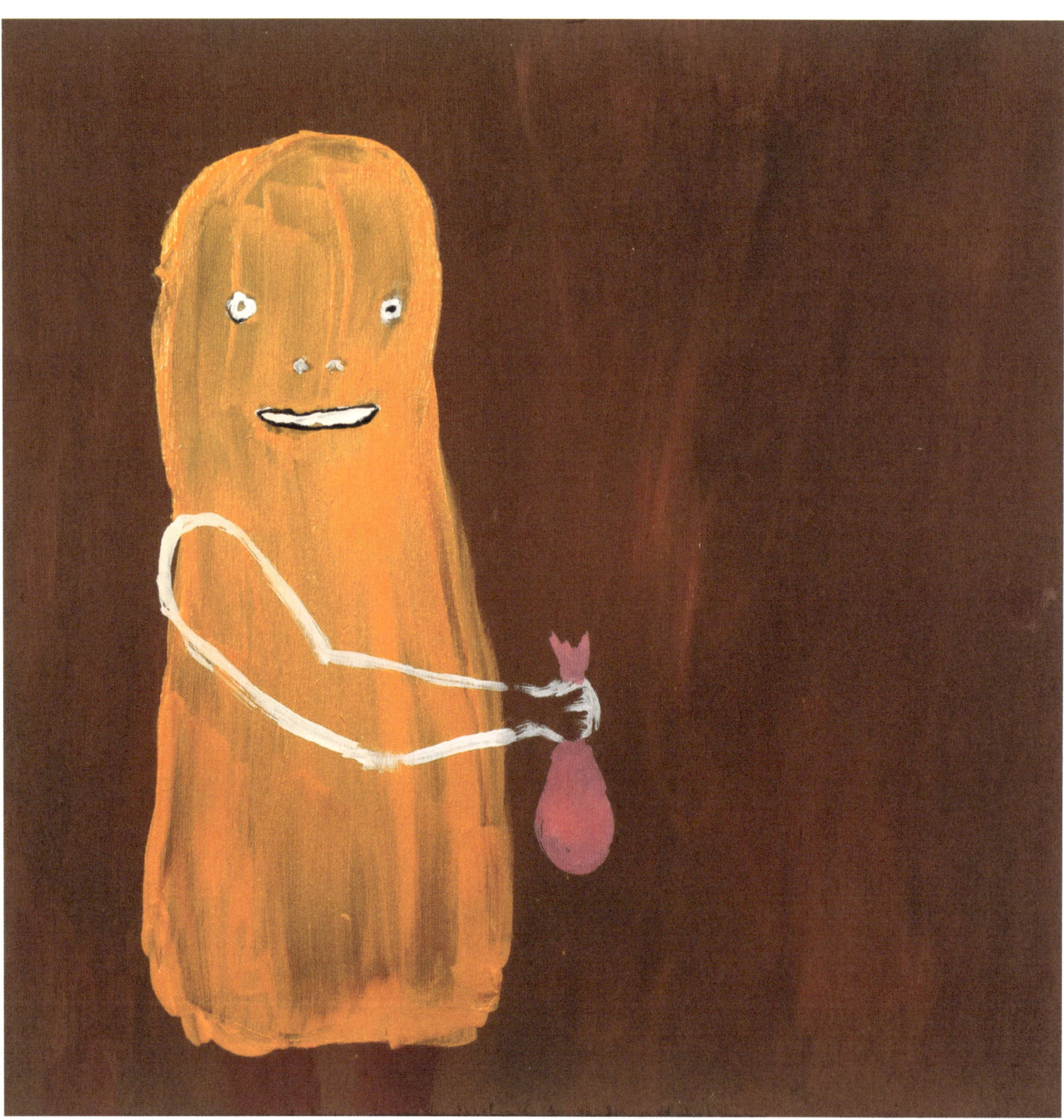

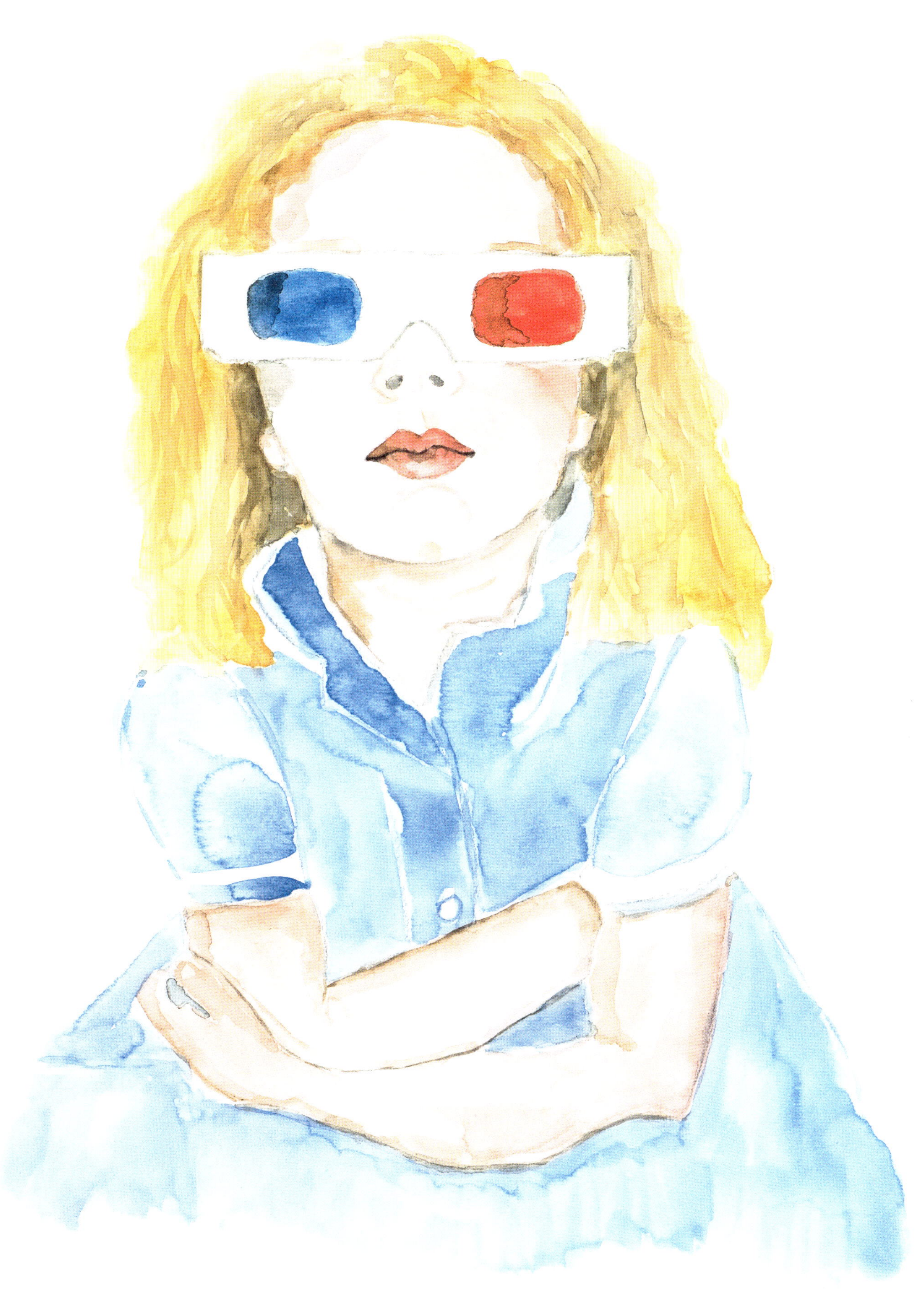

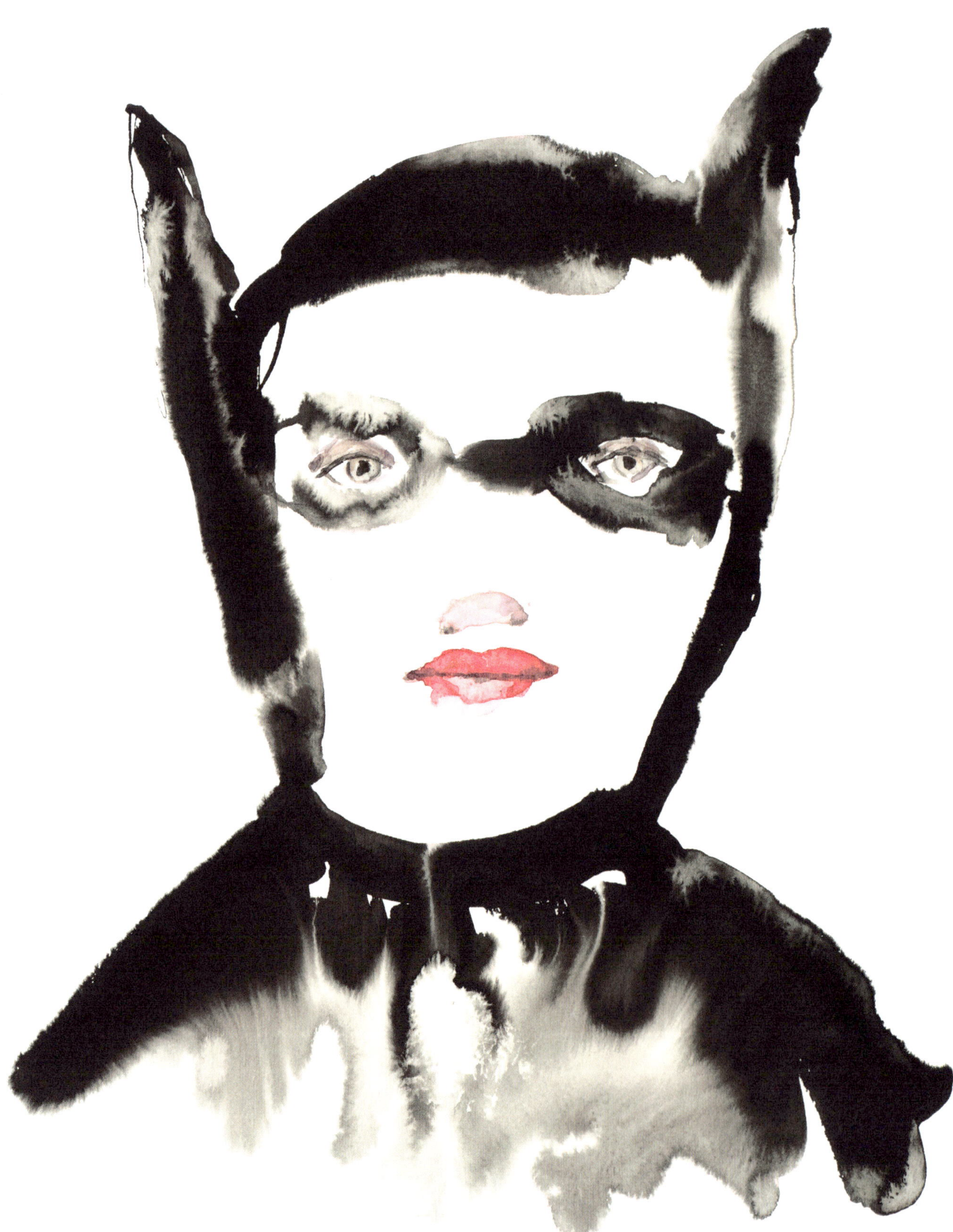

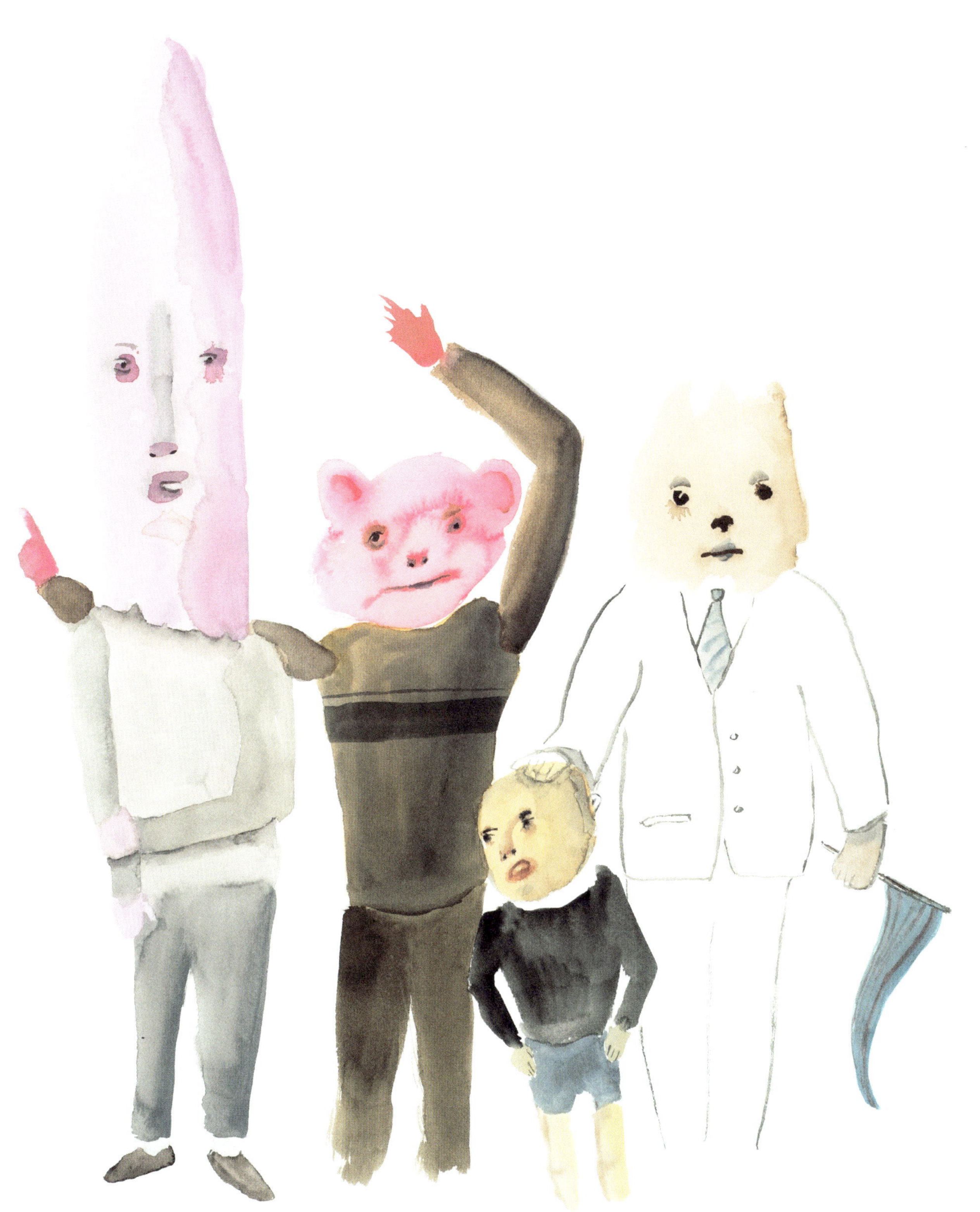

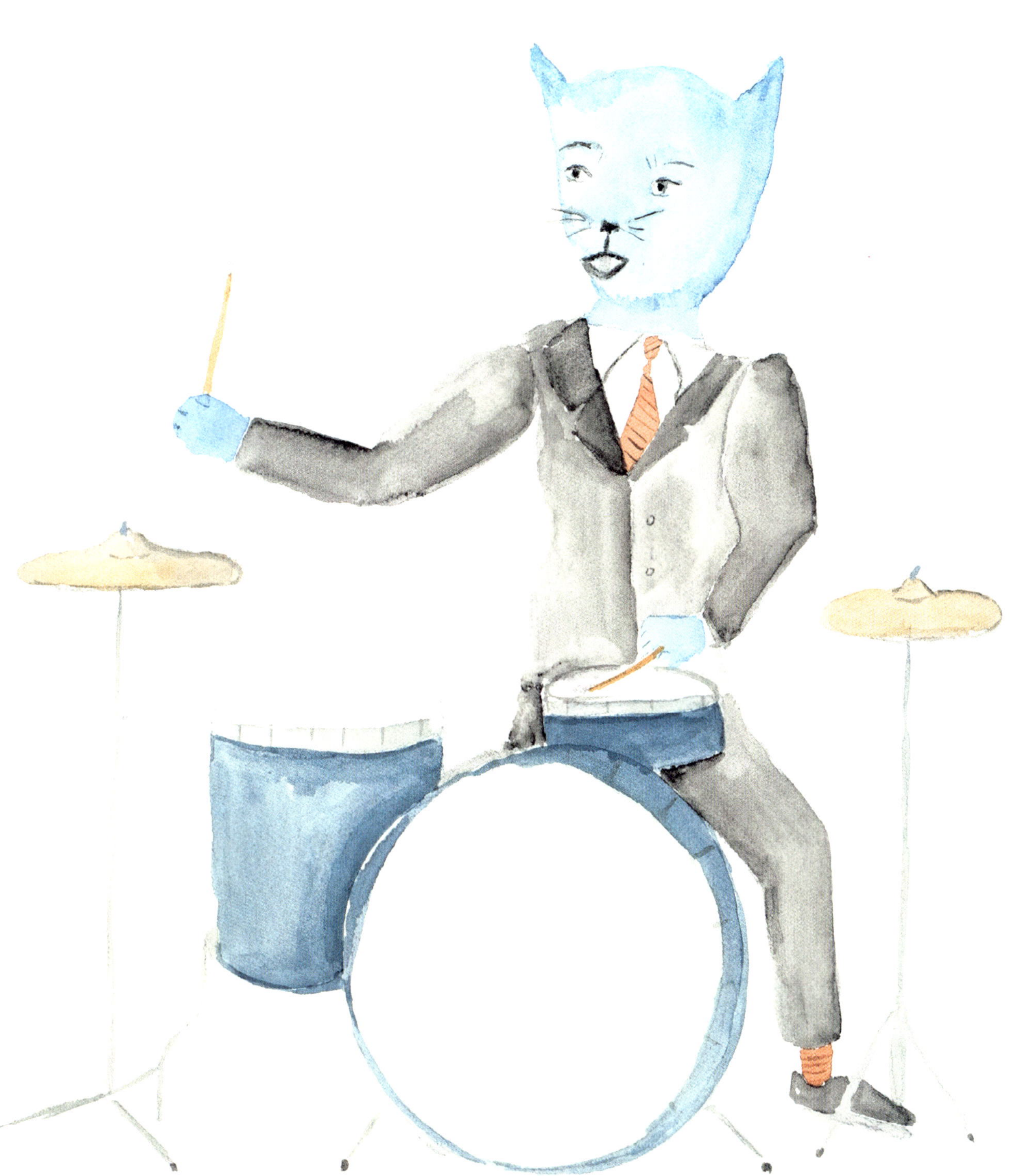

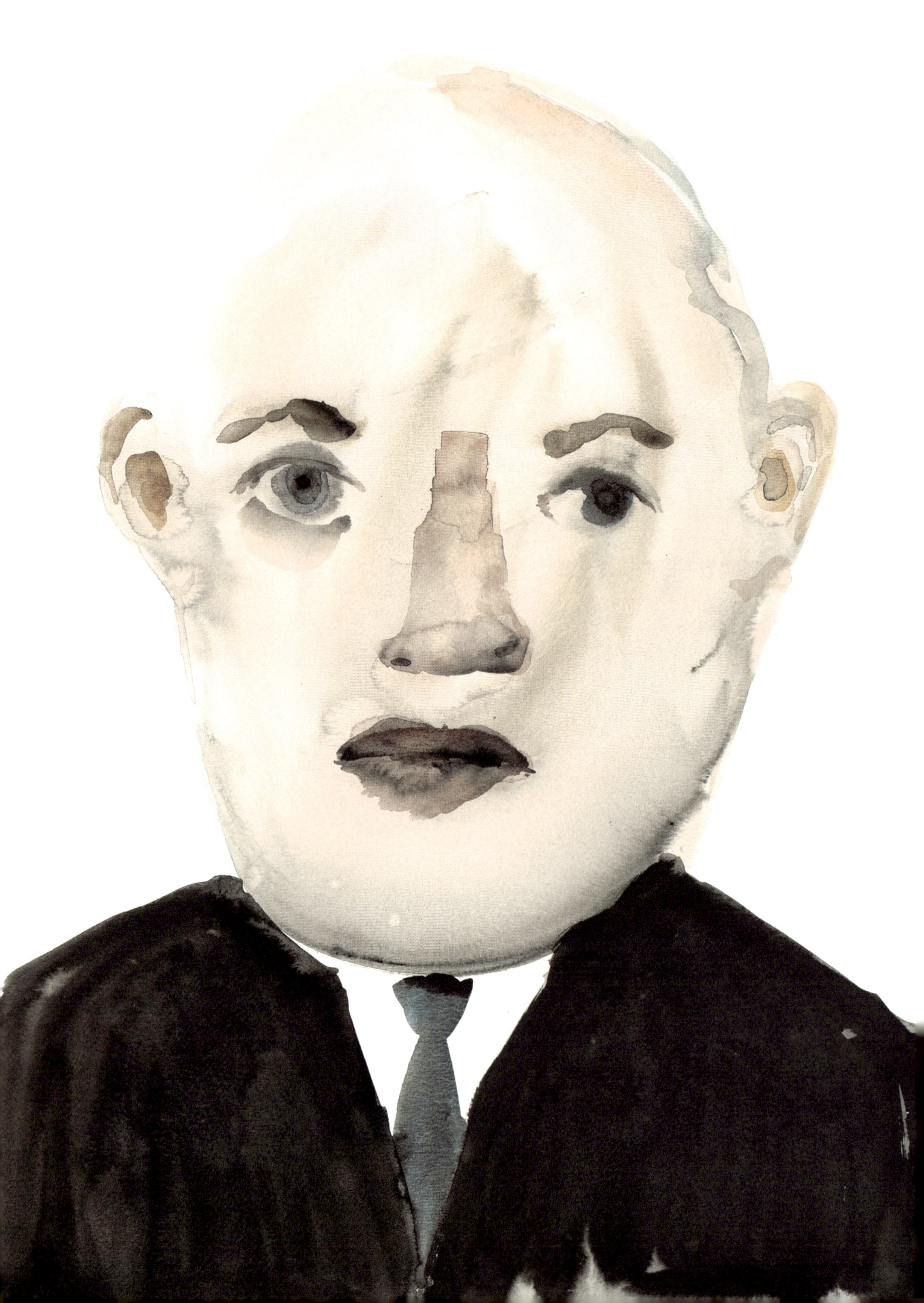

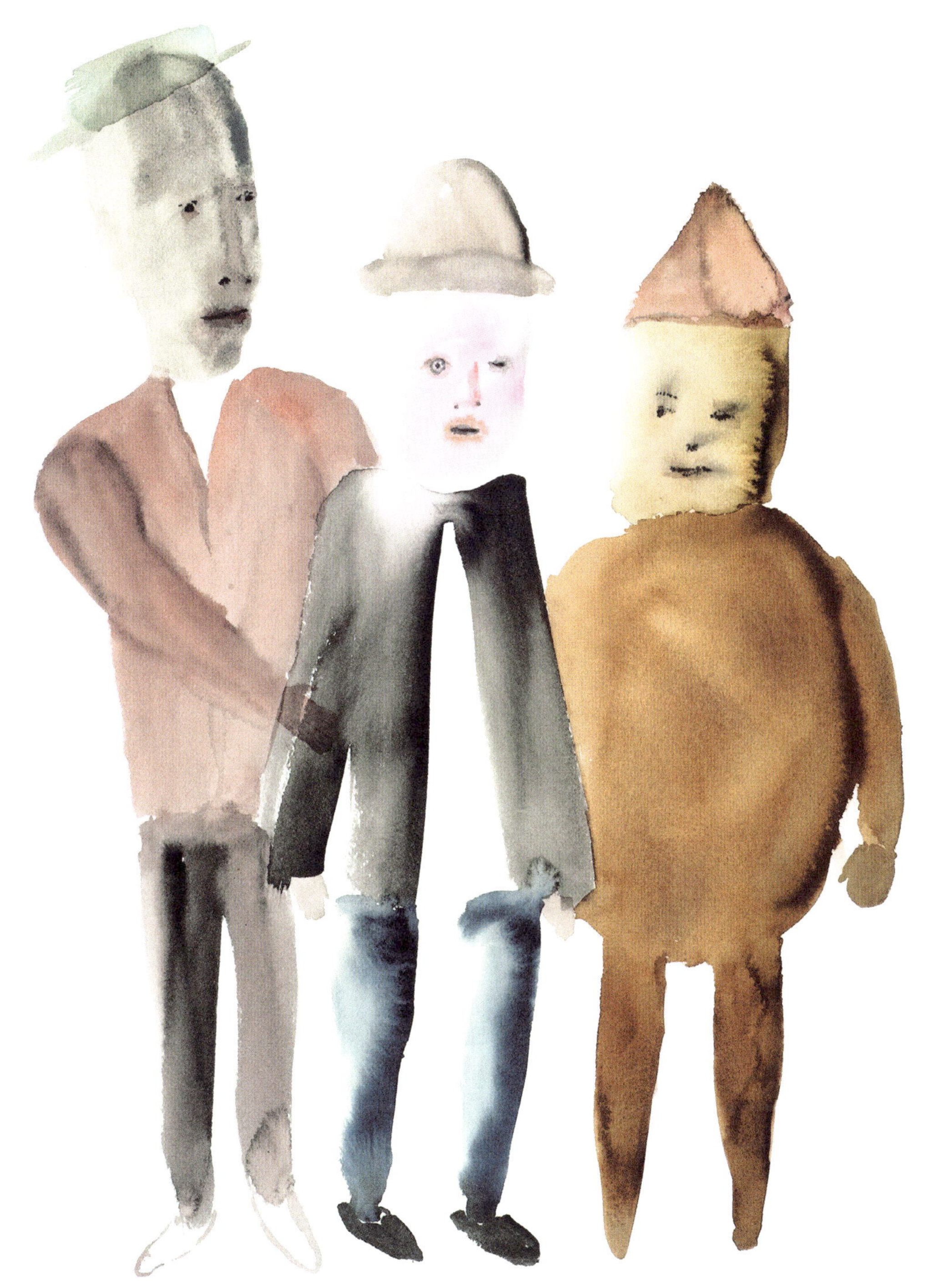

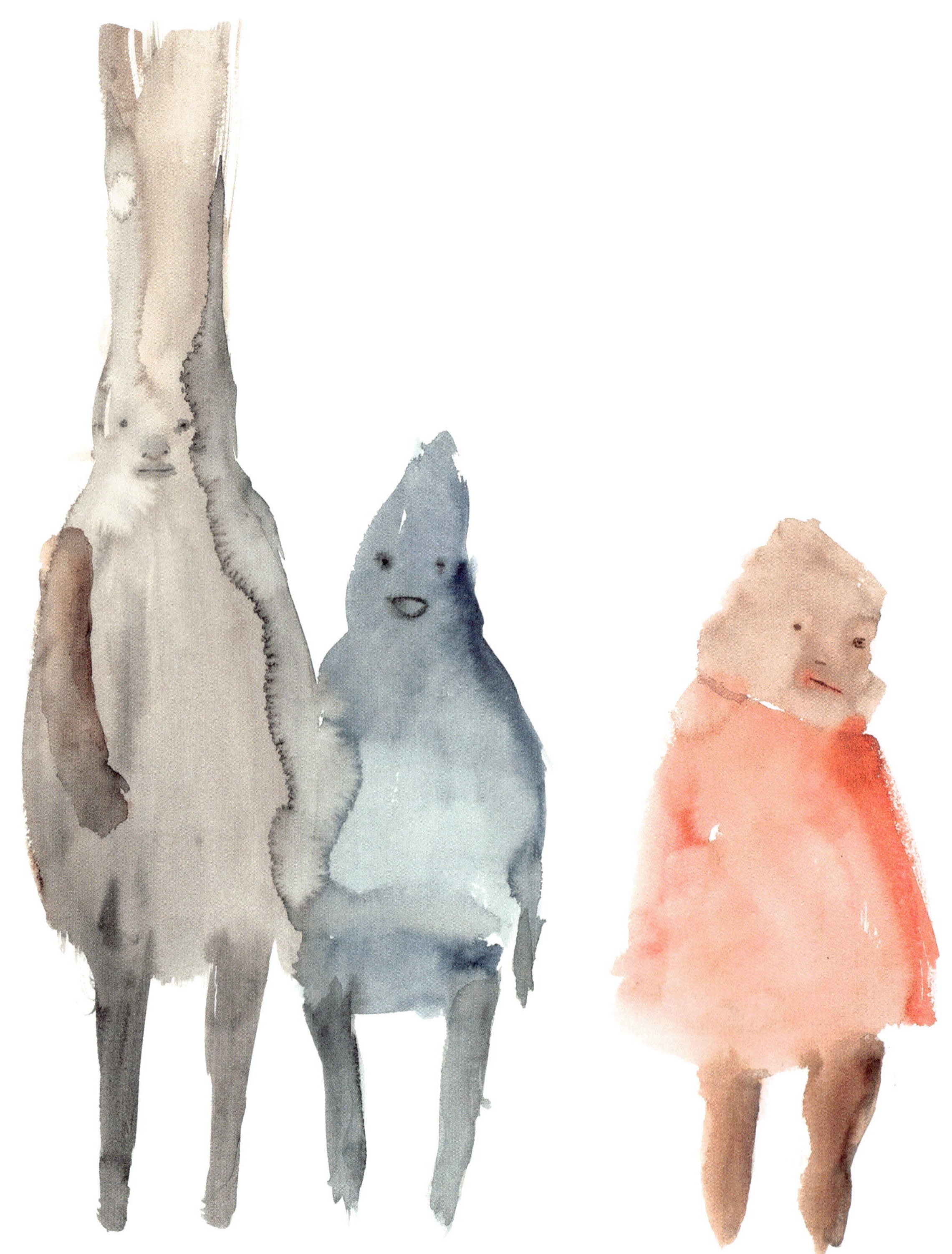

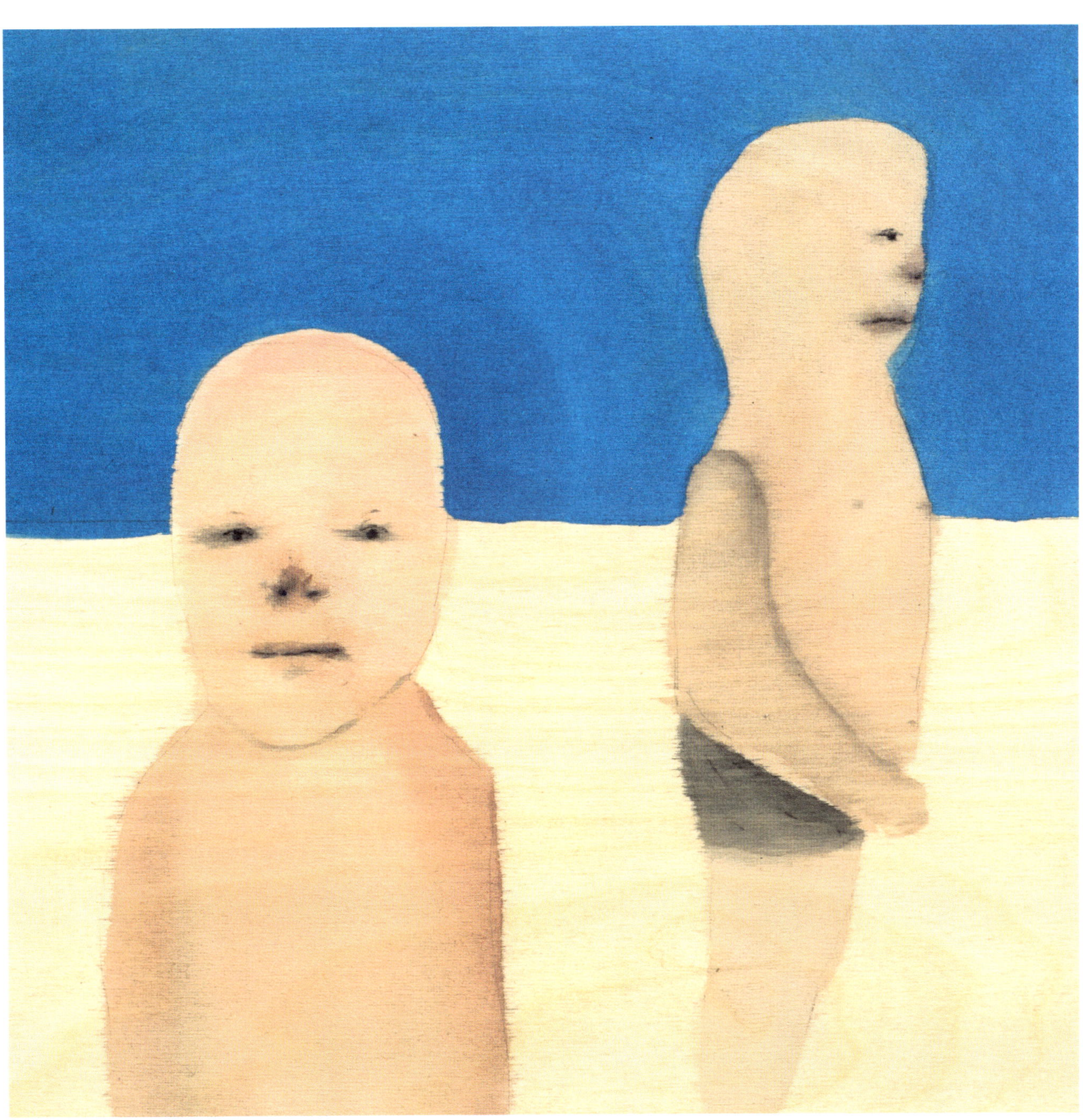

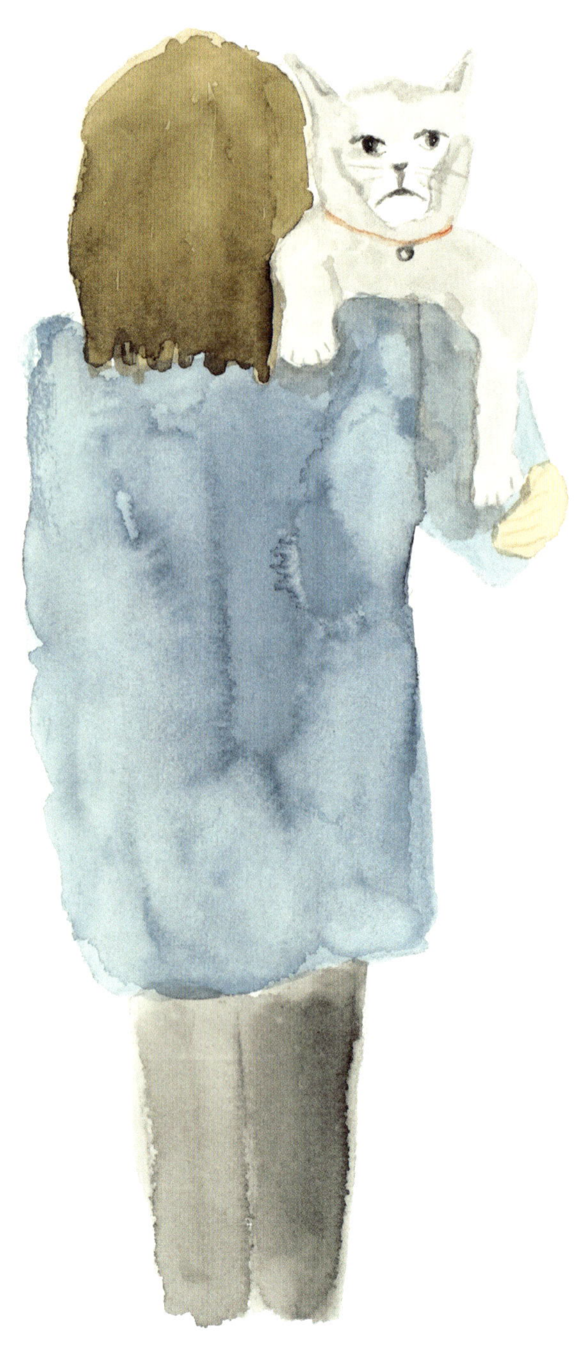

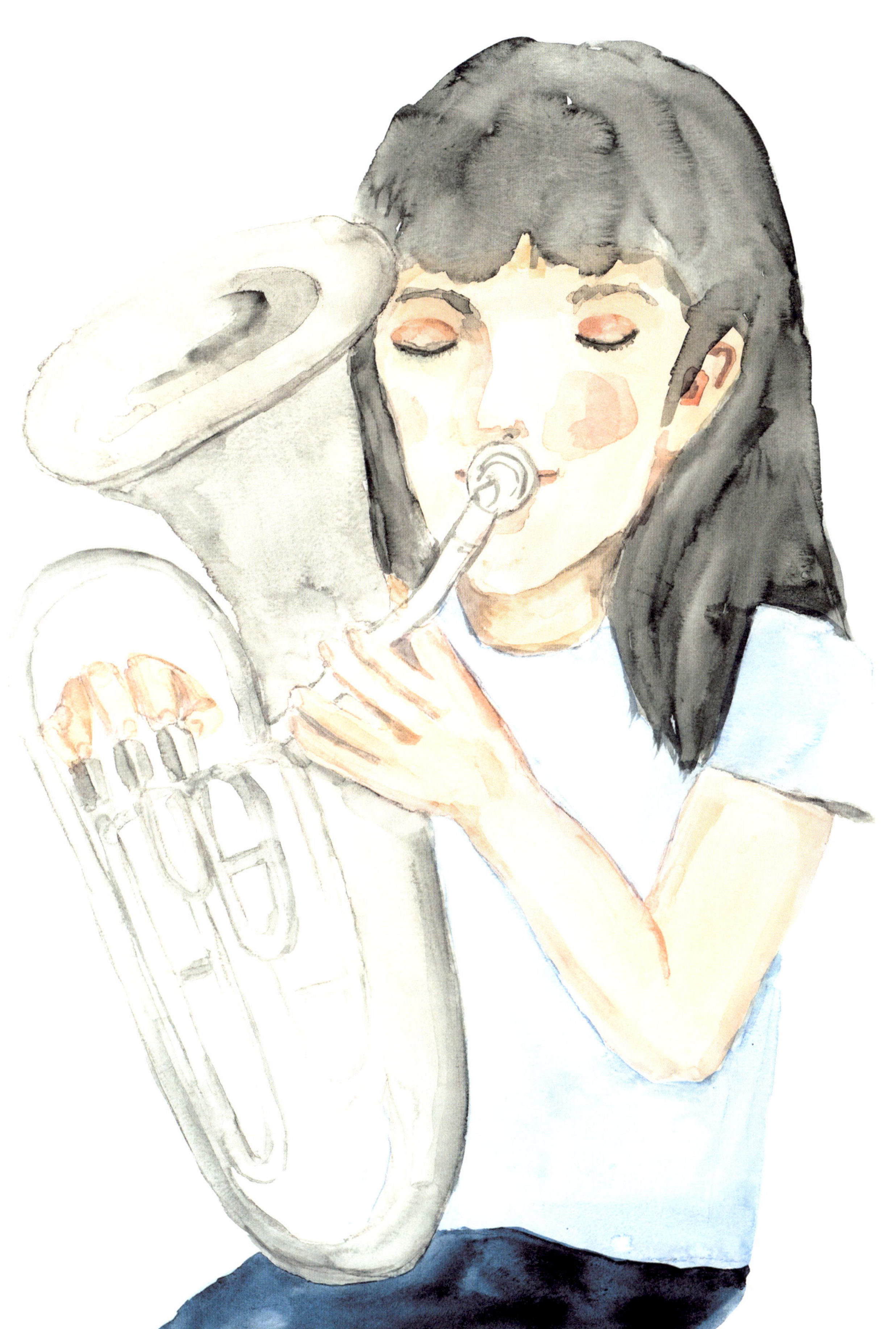

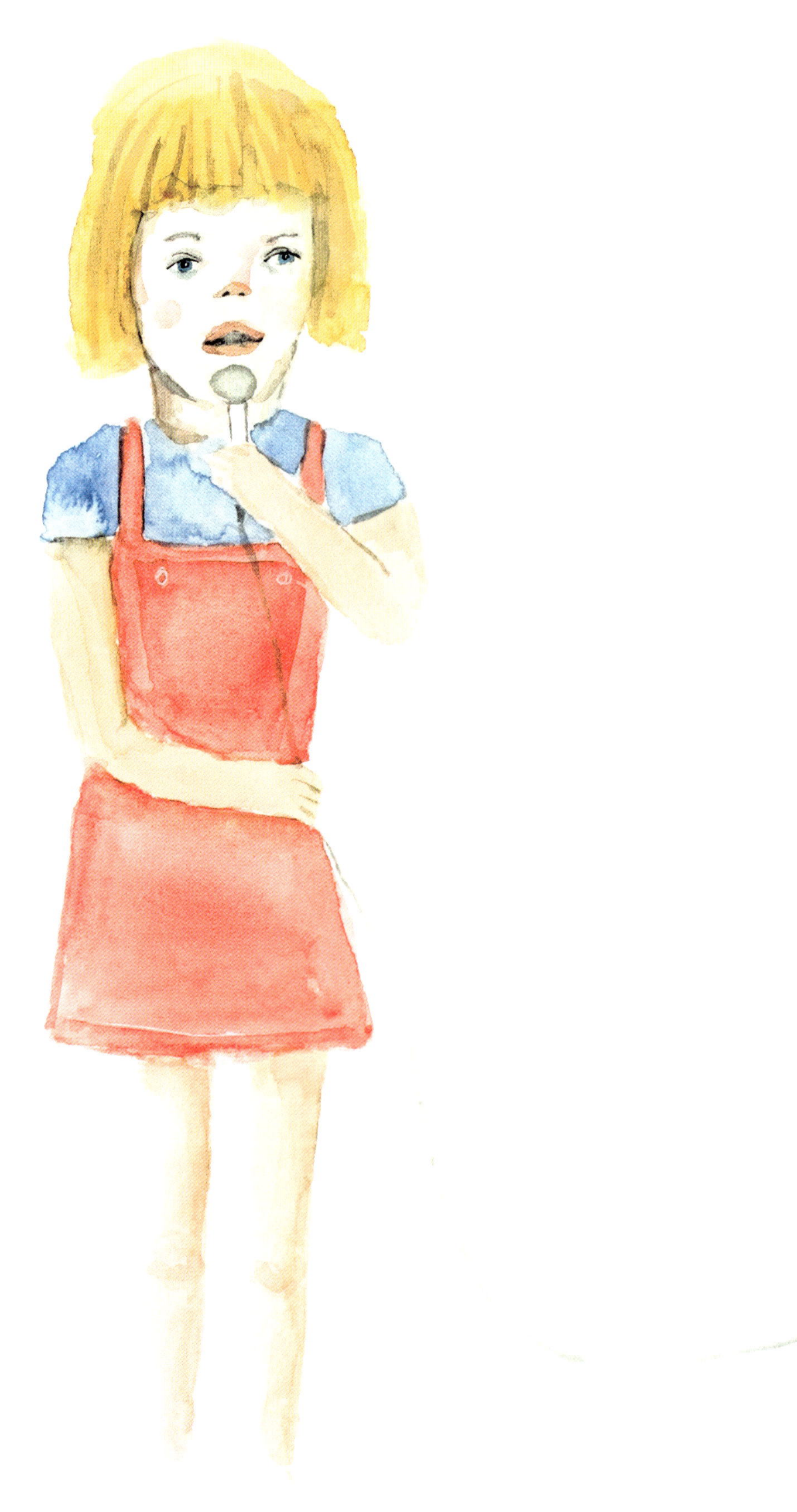

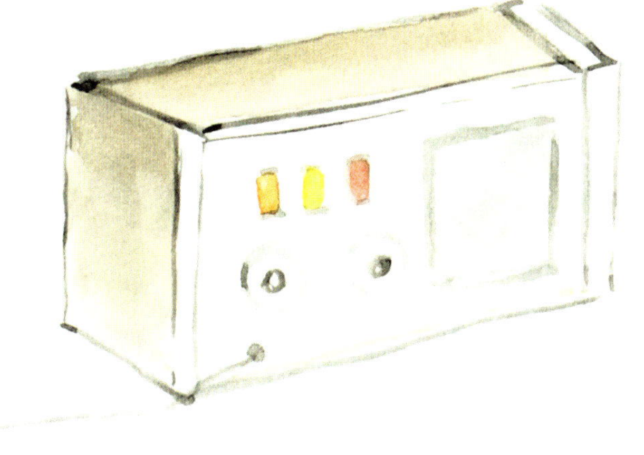

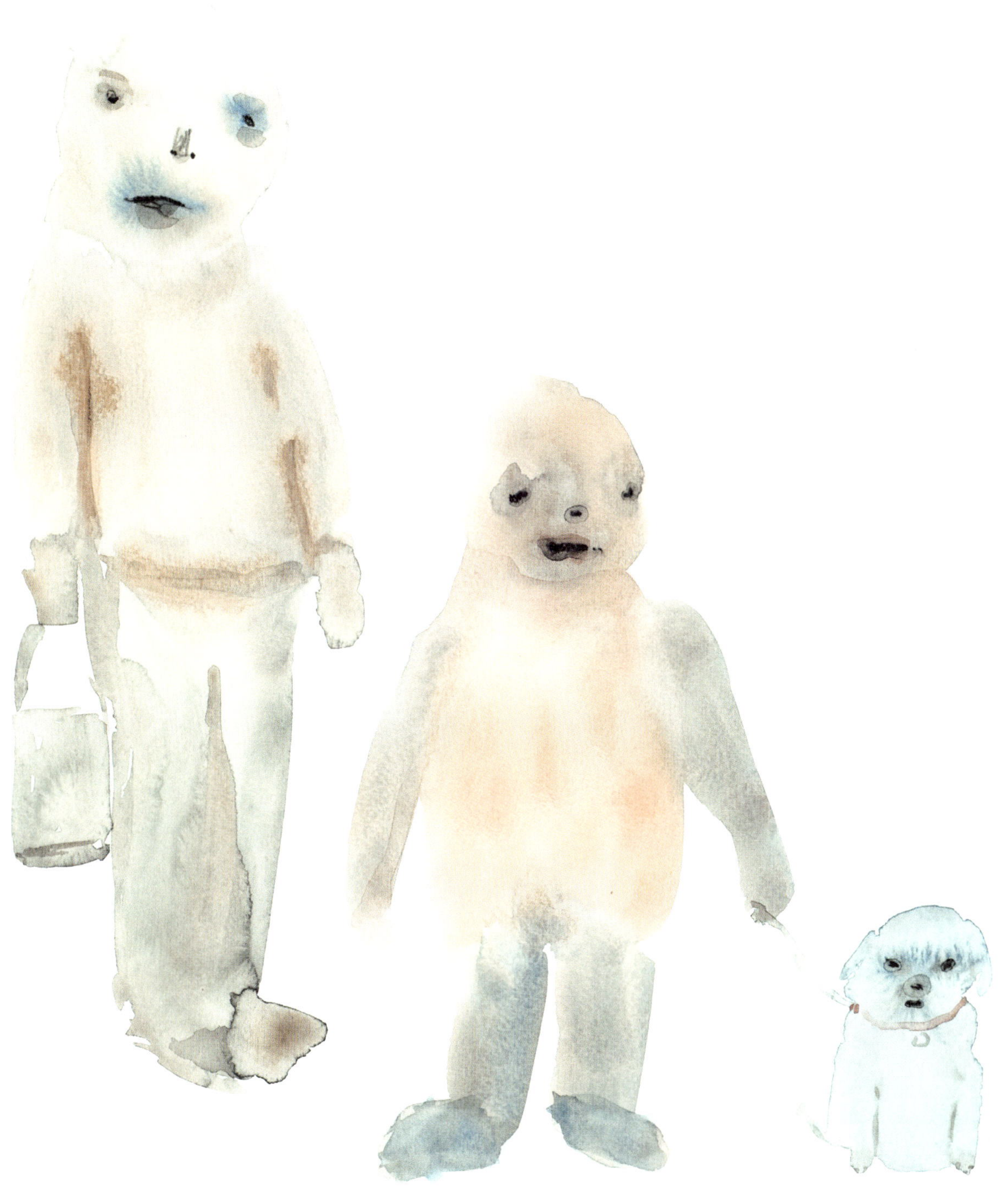

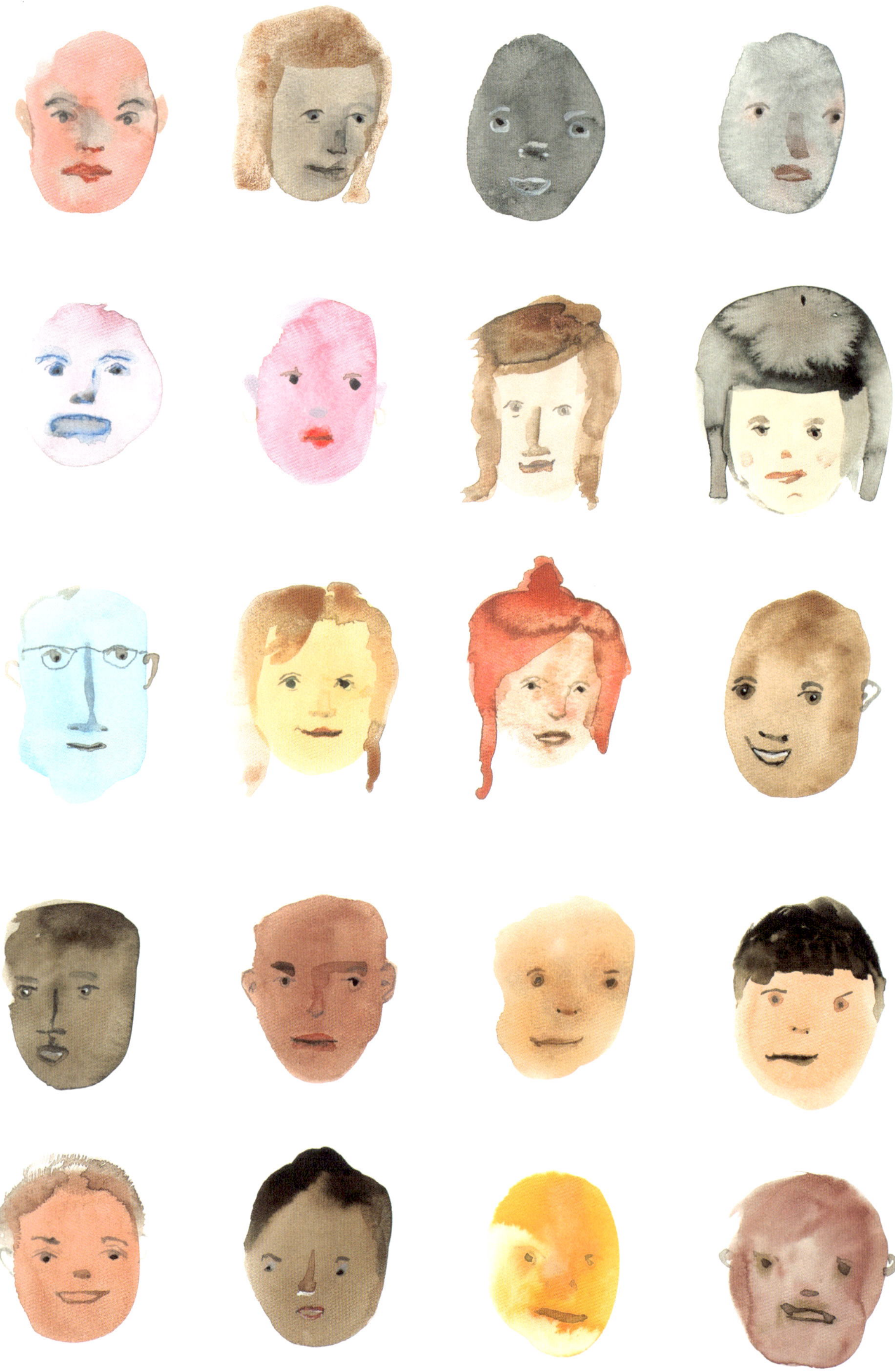

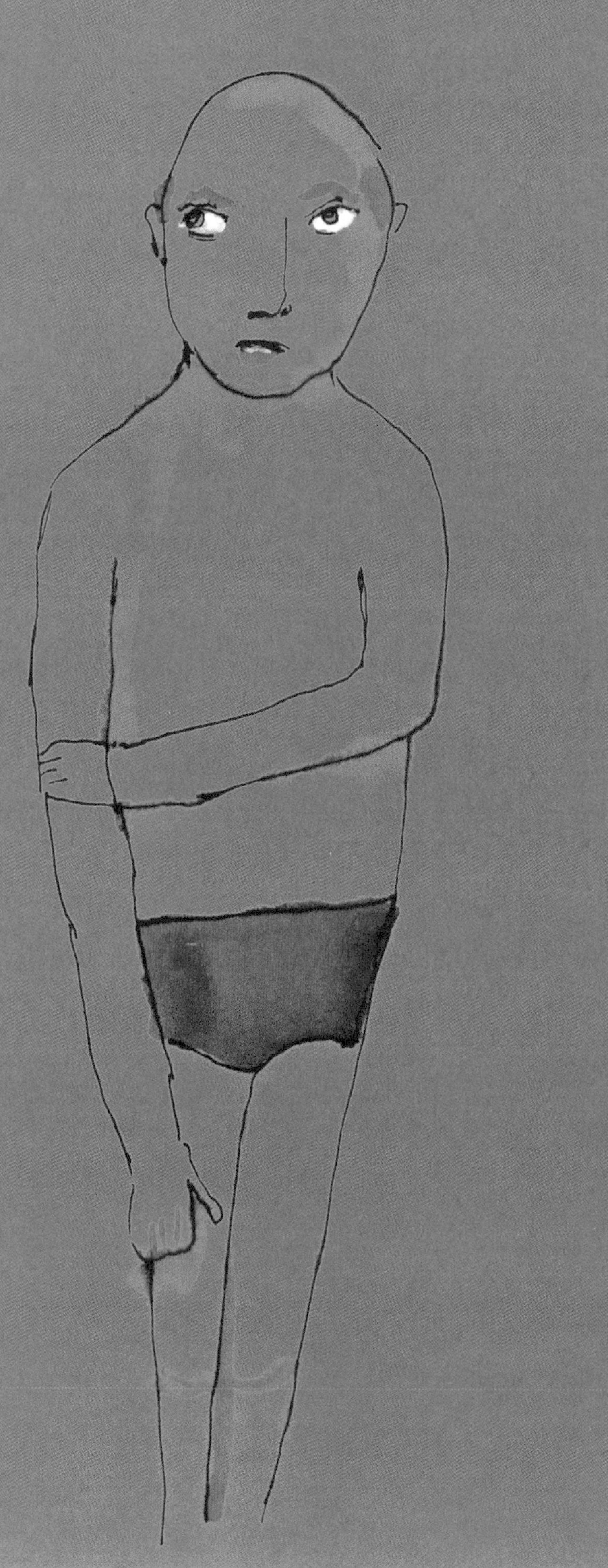

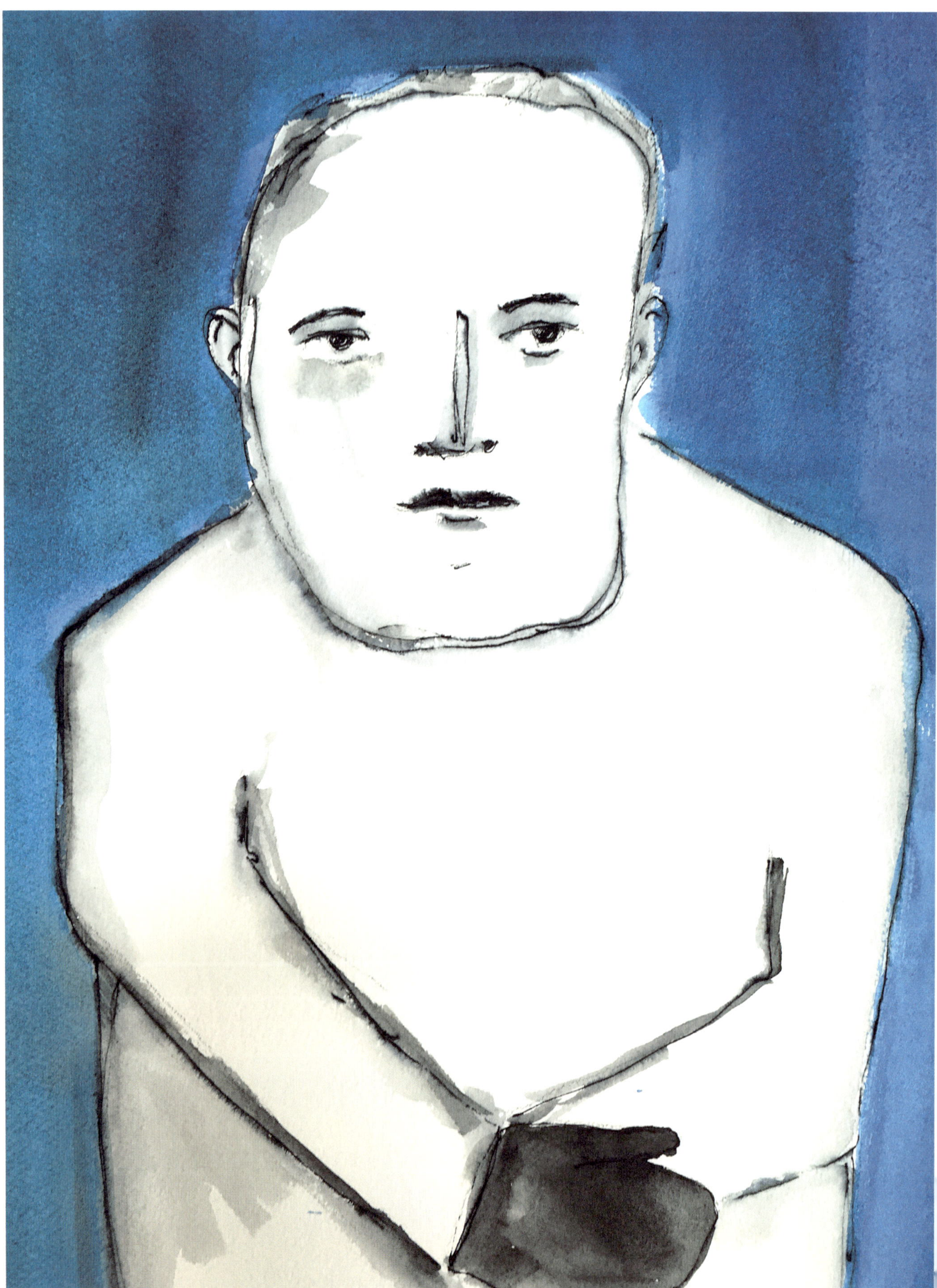

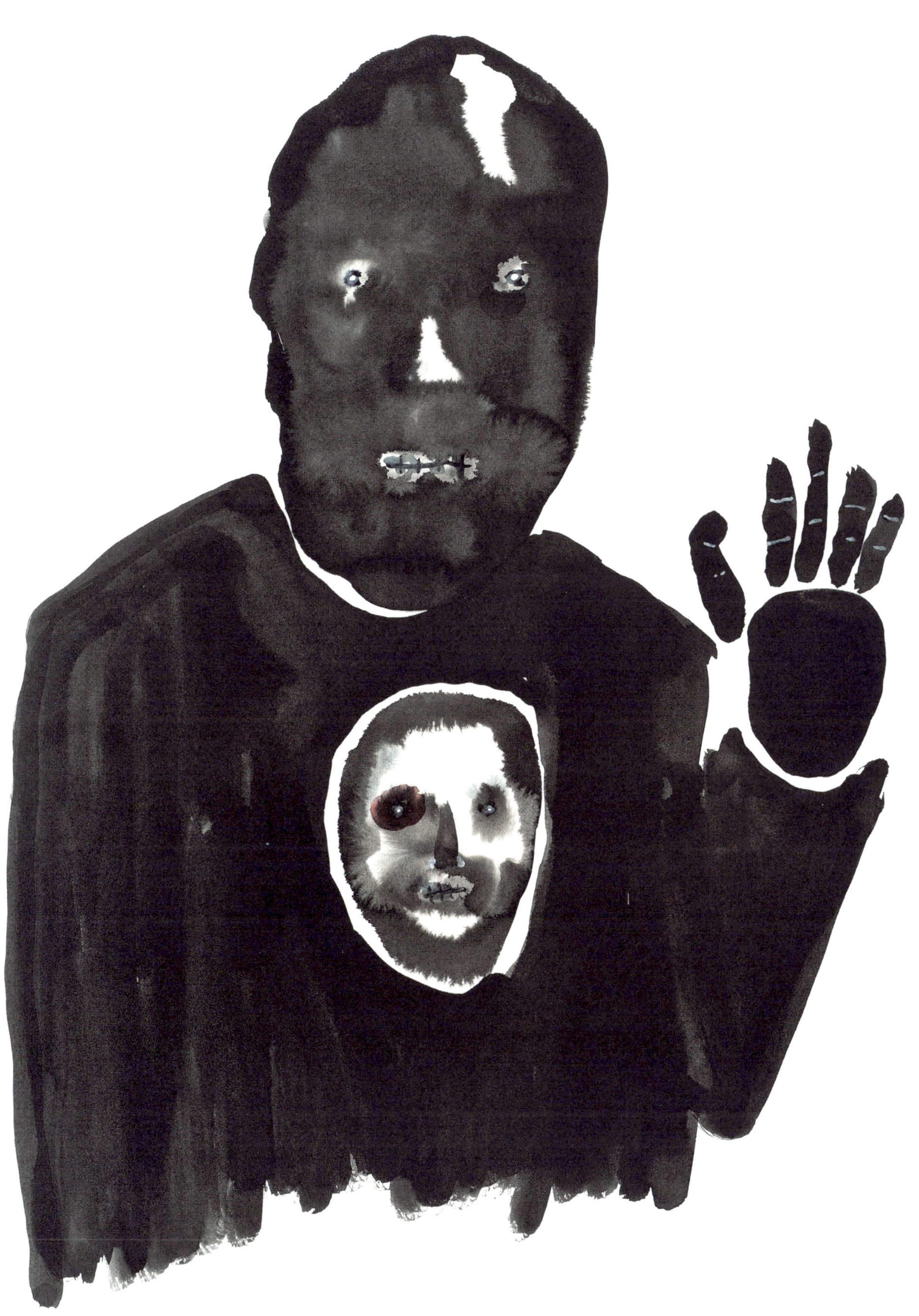

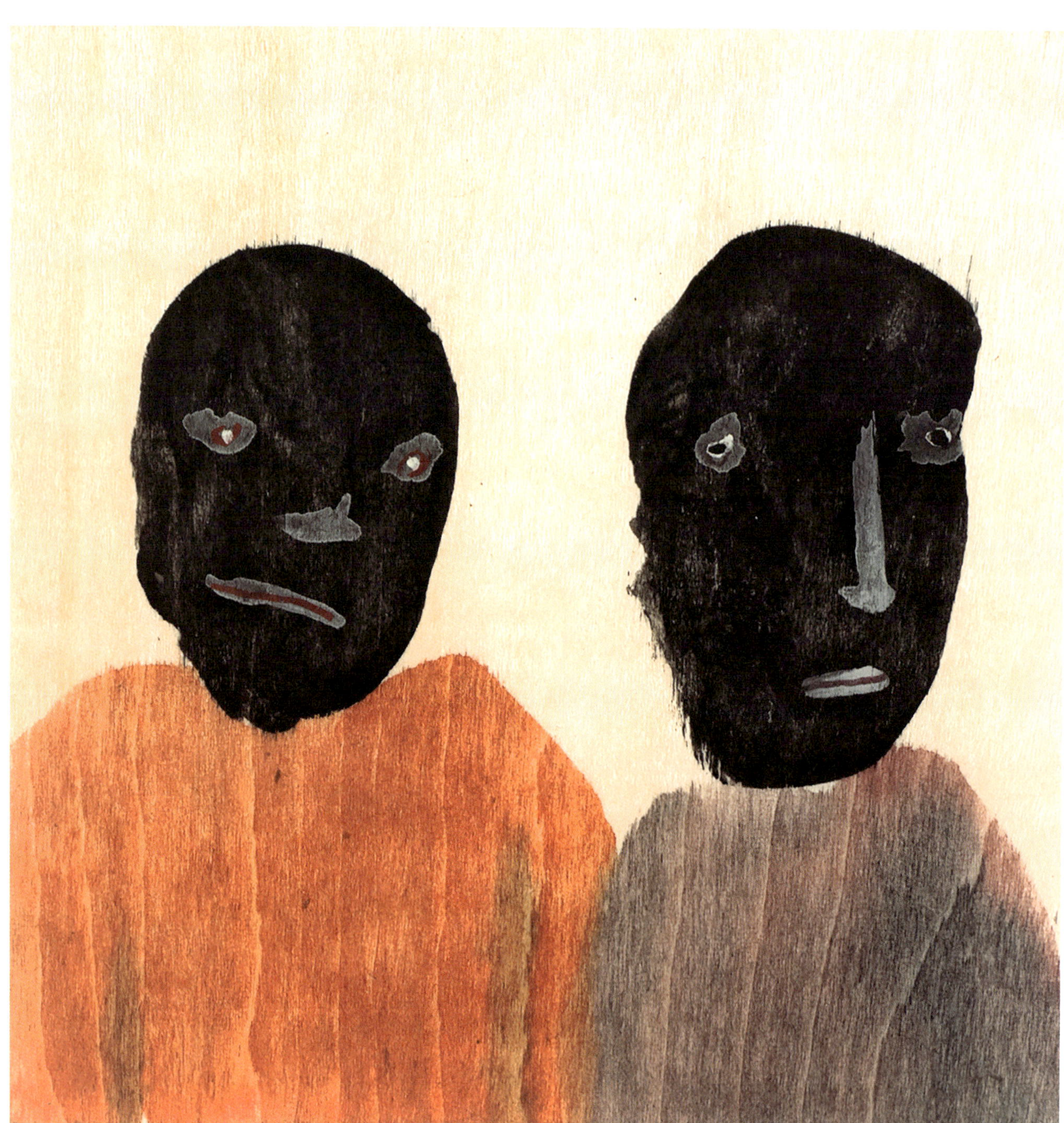

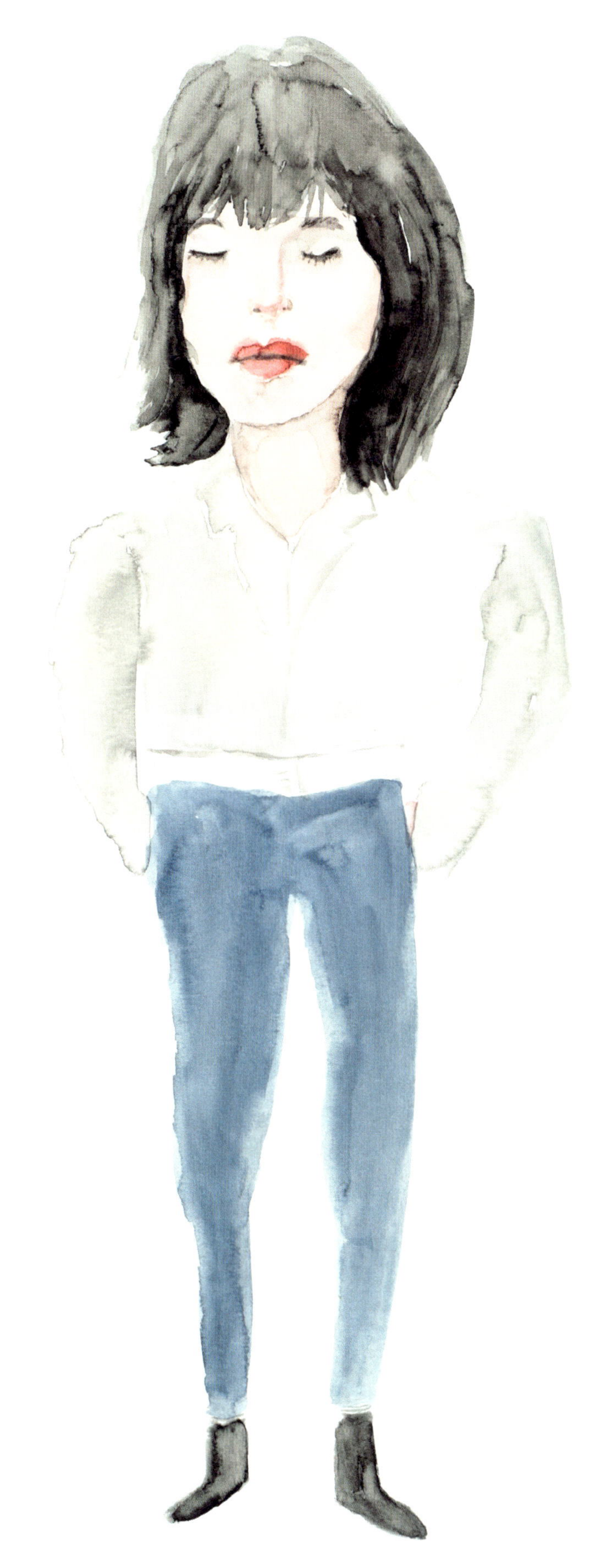

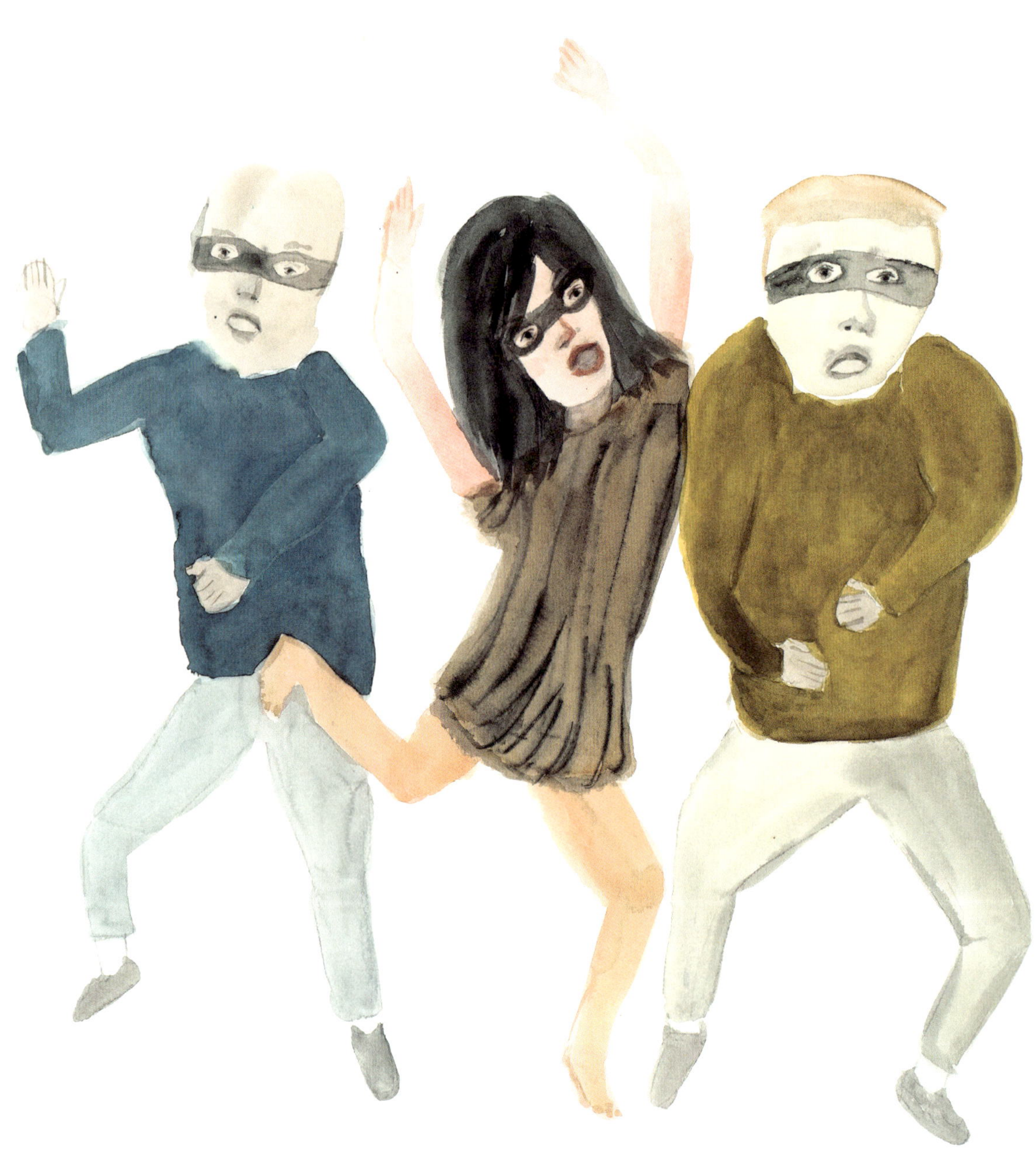

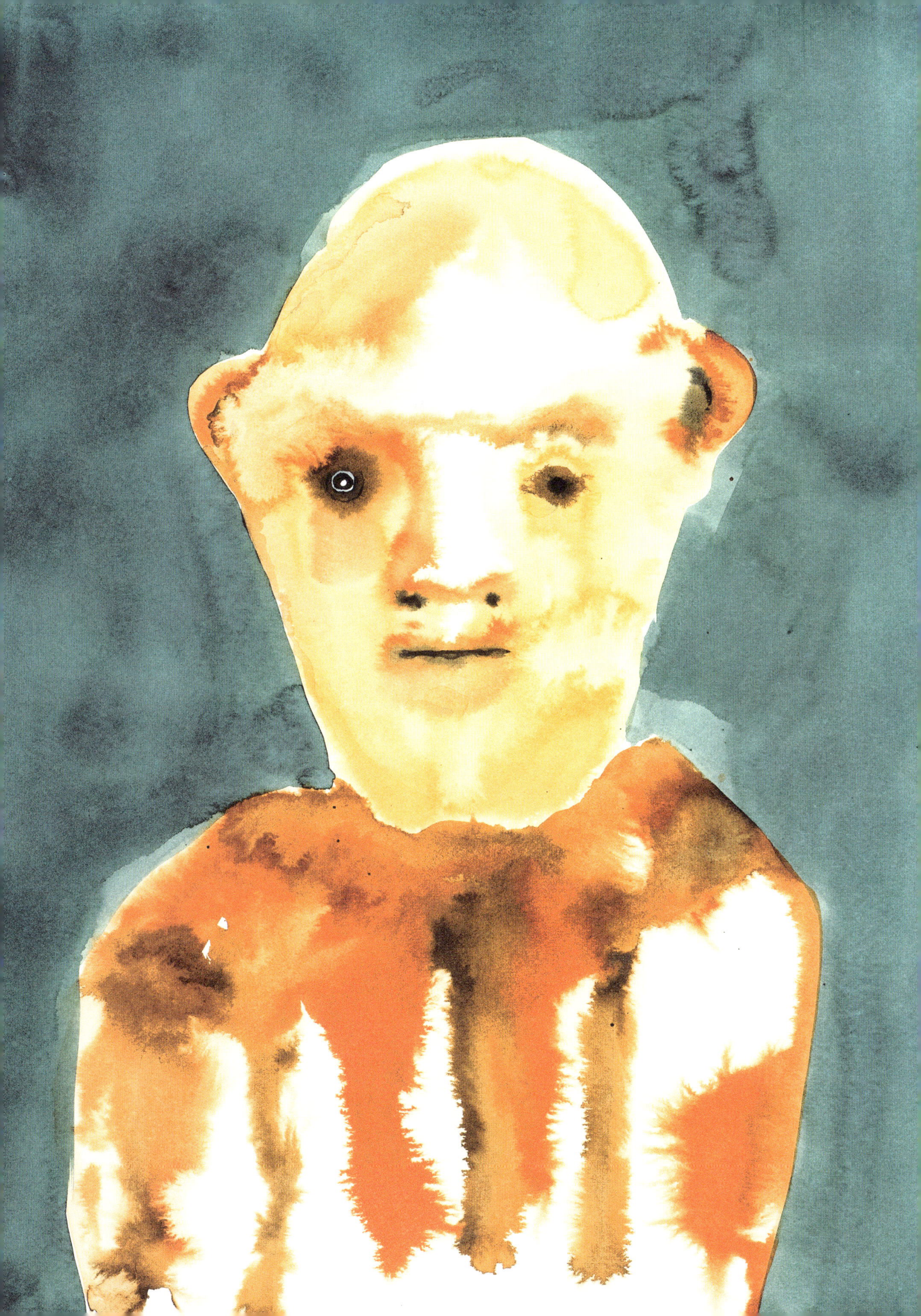

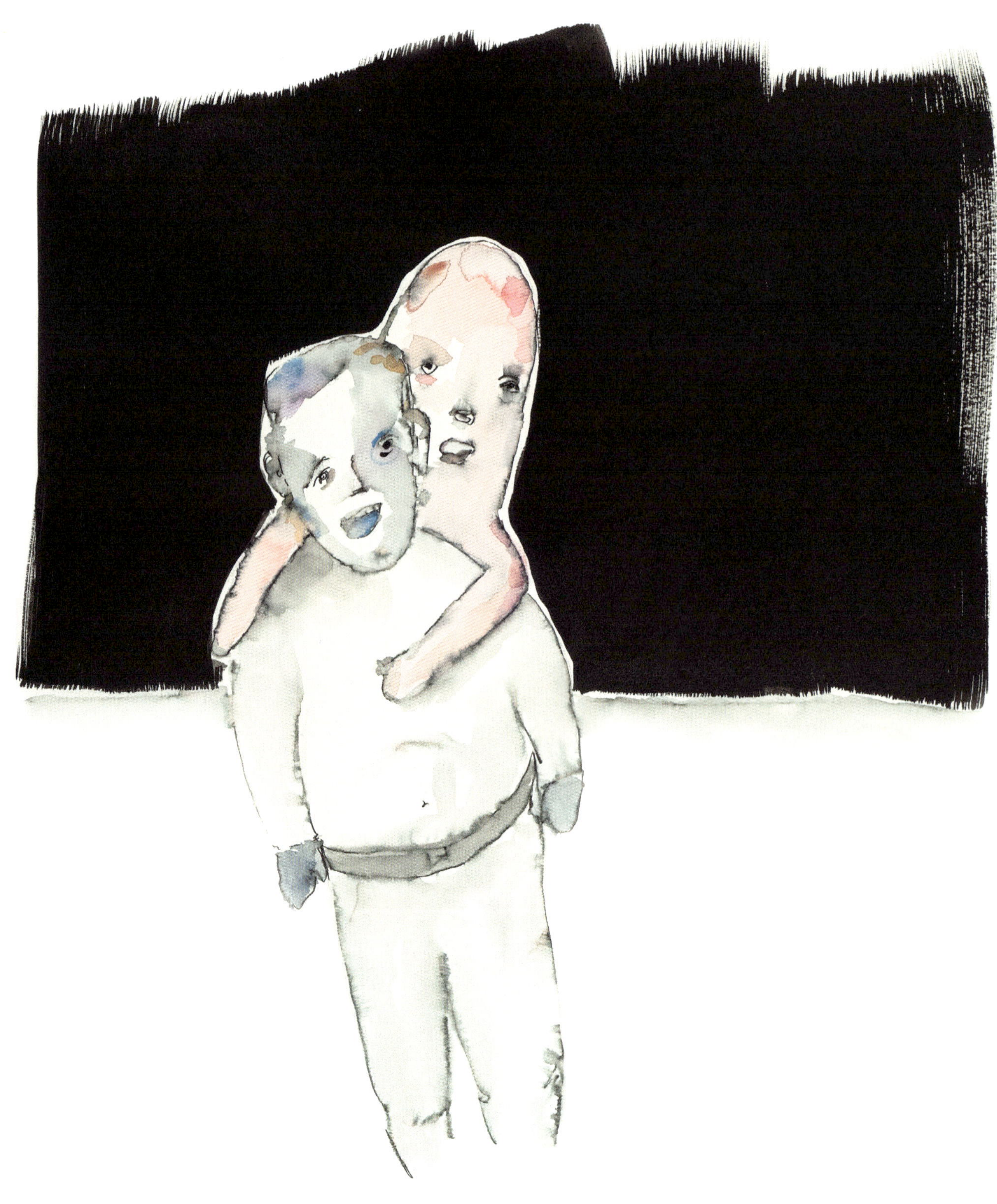

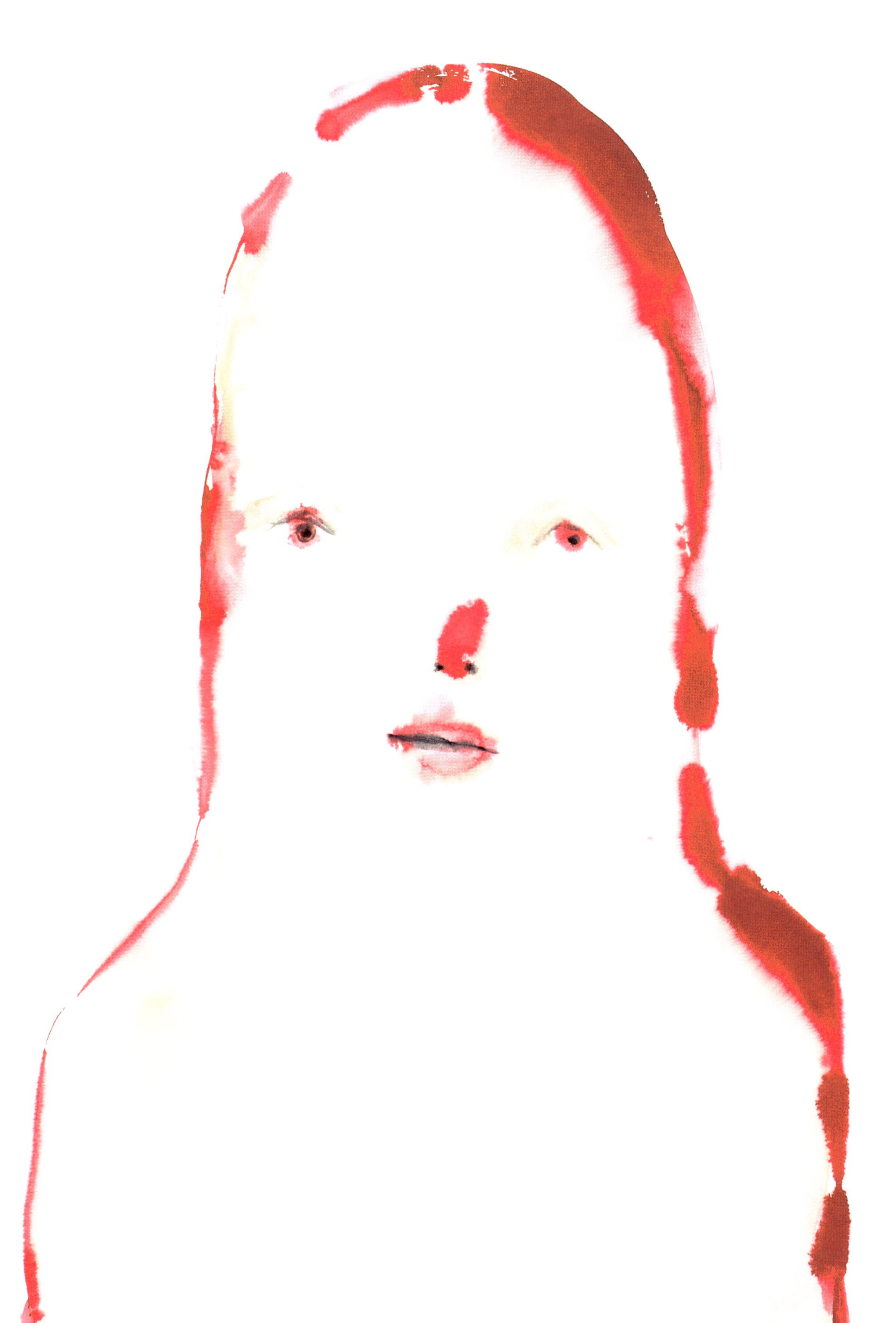

AT THE DROP OF A HAT
JON HUCK

FIRST PRINTING

PRINTED IN ITALY AT GRAFICHE VENEZIANE
DISTRIBUTED BY ARTBOOK/D.A.P.
ISBN 978-0-999-2655-9-8
THEICEPLANT.CC

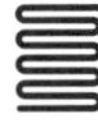

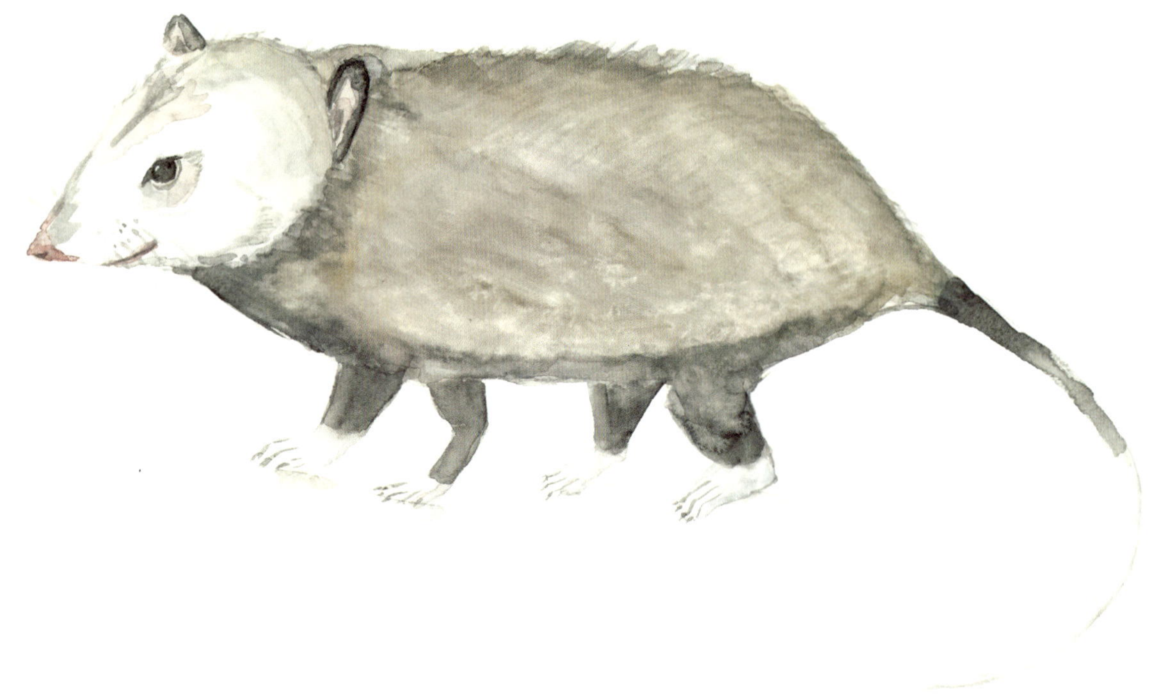